Flying High Over the Cotton Field

The Life and Times of Robert W. (Bill/Bob) Coggin

To Debbie

Bob Coggin

Robert W. Coggin

DEDICATION

**To Mr. C. E. Woolman, founder of Delta,
and to all the great Delta people who worked
with and for me.**

⟶ ACKNOWLEDGMENTS ⟵

For their role in my early years, I must thank my Coggin grandparents, all of my aunts and uncles, especially Uncle Raymond and Aunt Eula Coggin, my aunt Gloria Pate, and my stepmother, Vera Coggin.

A number of people played key roles in my success at Delta, and I would not have enjoyed a successful career without their support.

First, Mr. C. E. Woolman created the Delta culture that influenced my success. Jody Brown, Delta's Atlanta station manager, facilitated my promotion to station agent in Montgomery. Jack Sweigart, Delta's marketing manager in Montgomery, recognized my passion for becoming a Delta sales representative, and Charlie Mashburn, Delta's staff manager of marketing, played a significant role in my securing the Washington sales rep position. Osgood Willis, the district sales manager in Washington, taught me the "tricks of the trade" and to be an excellent airline sales representative.

Ed Preston, Delta regional sales manager, was a great mentor and was always very supportive. Hank Ross, director of advertising and sales promotion, allowed me to influence how Delta's New York advertising funds were spent. Jim Ewing, a manager in Delta's public relations department, created many opportunities for me to influence the media's coverage of Delta's New York marketing activities. Bob Cross, manager of pricing, played a major role in implementing Delta's first version of a revenue management system.

Whit Hawkins, who served as president and chief operating officer, was one of my greatest supporters and played a significant role in my Delta career. Similarly, Tony McKinnon, Delta vice president of sales, was one of my greatest supporters when I fought to change the outdated process being used in the pricing and scheduling areas.

Delta CEO and Chairman Ron Allen was one of my strongest advocates as I rose through the chain of command. Ron also played a key role in supporting my strategy to grow Delta's international network. Art Ford, Delta assistant vice president of long-range planning and chief engineer, helped move my priorities up the chain of command.

Most important of all were Brenda Craig and Carolyn Byrd, two of the great ladies who supported me as my executive assistants.

In addition to the Delta people who made a big difference in my career, there were several non-Delta people who contributed a great deal to my success, and they include my wonderful wife, Millie, who has been so supportive and did a great job raising our son, Jeff, while I was on the road taking care of Delta business. My uncle Tom Richards is the one who first encouraged me and convinced me to apply for a job at Delta.

Glenn Verrill, president of BBDO, Delta's advertising agency, assisted me in leveraging Delta's advertising and in getting significant support from the media, far beyond what my competitors were receiving. And after the Northeast merger, Alamo Rent A Car President Mike Egan directed his staff to develop a number of exclusive car rental deals for Delta passengers that neither Eastern nor National could match.

Also following the Delta-Northeast merger, Creative Travel

Consultants President Warren Binder worked with Alamo and many hotels in South and Central Florida to develop unique vacation packages that Delta's competitors could not match.

Warner Rush, general sales manager of radio station WHN, gave me access to the many promotional assets owned by WHN/Storer Broadcasting, such as arranging for me to use Roy Cohn's yacht to take groups of Delta customers on a cruise up the Hudson and around Manhattan Island.

Finally, I wish to thank the *New York Daily News* sales manager whose name I can't recall, but he arranged for the *Daily News* to print a special edition with a front page announcing that Delta was now flying from New York to Florida and the Bahamas.

Those factors certainly played a role in the success I achieved at Delta, as the Delta culture created by founder C. E. Woolman rewarded those who possessed an over-the-top work ethic. During most of my career at Delta, the company placed a great deal more value on a person's work ethic and dependability than on having a college degree. Most of the Delta employees who started at entry-level jobs and achieved some level of success owe Mr. Woolman a lot of credit for creating Delta's "work ethic and dependability" culture.

In the section where I am promoted to executive vice president of marketing and technology, readers may ask, "How did Bob go from the Delta ramp to being one of Delta's four top executives?" There's no simple answer to that question, but there were seven major contributors to my success:

- The Delta culture created by Mr. Woolman that rewarded those who outperformed their peers.
- My experiences during the first nineteen years of my life.
- The work ethic my dad instilled in me.
- The level of creativity that I inherited from my mother.

- The great people that I worked for at Delta and the great people who worked for me.
- The non-Delta people who supported me and also played a major role in my successful career at Delta.
- The incredible experience I gained while serving as Delta's senior sales and marketing person in New York for over eleven years.

The stories I share in this book are all based on my recollection of my personal experiences, my relationships with family and friends, my career at Delta Air Lines, and my career after Delta. I was motivated to write the story of my life for several reasons:

- First, I wanted to let the world know that much of what I have accomplished over the last eighty-plus years has been done with God's guidance and his blessings.
- Hopefully, those who read about my life's experience will understand that it's possible to move beyond a humble beginning with the right work ethic and a focus on goals and objectives. I should acknowledge that today, it is much more difficult to improve one's life without the appropriate college degree than it was when I began my career at Delta.
- I would like for my heirs—including my son, Jeff, grandson, Robby, and those who come after them—to clearly understand the circumstances of my growing up, how much good fortune has come our way, and the favorable impact these circumstances have had on our collective lives. I also want them to clearly understand that any material things they enjoy as a result of what I might leave behind are not of my creation alone but were achieved in partnership with God.
- I'm also hopeful that individuals and organizations that follow human interest stories similar to mine might enjoy

reading my life's story.

In addition to being very thankful for all the opportunities that God and others have made available to me during my lifetime, I'm also thankful for:

- A wonderful and loving family, especially my wife, Millie.
- Parents who loved me even though they were dealing with their own demons and challenges as I grew up.
- A stepmother, Vera, who helped provide a home for my brother, Gary, and me during some of the difficult times in our lives. Most of all, she loved my son, Jeff, and grandson, Robby, like they were her own flesh and blood.
- A wonderful extended family, including my brothers, caring grandparents, and aunts and uncles who really loved me and helped both Gary and me through the challenges we faced during our early years.
- A forty-two-year career with Delta Air Lines, which was a blessing beyond description. Almost everything I have today, including Millie, came about as a result of my career at Delta. During my time there, Delta was one of the greatest companies in America, if not the world, in terms of caring about its people and giving them the opportunity to grow regardless of any consideration beyond their ability, a strong work ethic, and a willingness to face and address new challenges.
- The lasting friendships developed with my Delta colleagues and the non-Delta people I worked with plus the many people I worked with after Delta.
- The many rewarding opportunities I've had since retiring from Delta to work with other great organizations and companies such as the Nassau Paradise Island Promotion Board, Priceline, Accenture, and Travelport.

One of the most important blessings that God has bestowed upon me is the recognition that we should willingly and thankfully give back to God and those in need a part of what God has provided to us.

⟪⟫ TABLE OF CONTENTS ⟪⟫

The Coggin family today includes, from left, my wife, Millie; me; my daughter-in-law, Cindy Coggin; my grandson, Robby Coggin; and my son, Jeff Coggin.

My life experiences would make a great country music song except that I never served any time in Folsom Prison or threw my mama from a train. My life does, however, contain many other life experiences that are the basis for country music songs.

When my longtime friend and Delta colleague John White knew that God was about to call him home, he wrote a beautiful farewell piece in which he said his life had been "Like Riding on a Magic Carpet." I cannot think of a better way to describe my life, even though the carpet did hit a few bumps along the way, especially early on. When I reflect on the last eighty-plus years, I can only say, "What a Wonderful Life" I have enjoyed on that "Magic Carpet." I have to give most of the credit for the positive developments during my life, both personally and professionally, to the many opportunities God created for me and to the mistakes he kept me from making. How else could a person who grew up in a cotton mill village and on a one-horse farm have achieved the kind of life I have enjoyed the last sixty-plus years?

I also have to thank my wonderful wife, Millie, for all the love and support she has given me during our fifty-five-plus years together. In addition to a wonderful marriage, my life has also included an incredible forty-two years with Delta Air Lines, where I was given many opportunities to advance my career.

After Delta, I enjoyed a great nine-year career at Travelport, a global travel technology and distribution company.

Much of the credit for my financial success goes to Jay Walker, founder of Priceline, and Frank Del Rio, founder of Oceania Cruises. Both of these gentlemen provided me with great opportunities to benefit from the success of their companies, allowing me to provide very comfortable lives for my entire family and to reach out to many people and organizations that needed financial support.

My life story could also qualify as "rags to riches," a description for people who achieved success in spite of humble beginnings. Most of my adult life would have to be described as "riches," not just in financial terms but more in keeping with how blessed I have been with a wonderful wife, son, daughter-in-law, grandson, my nephew Mitch Coggin, and many other wonderful supporting members of the Coggin and Richards families. I have also been blessed with many great friends, both professionally and personally. Later I will identify some specific people who played a role in my success. Most of all, I am thankful that God has guided me in sharing with others a portion of what he has allowed me to acquire during my lifetime. I hope he will inspire me to do even more in the days ahead.

I frequently ask myself, "Why me, God?" He obviously provided me with the determination early in life to look beyond working in a cotton mill or on a broken-down old one-horse farm. The determination to improve my life certainly motivated me to make the most of every opportunity I encountered. People that I respect have told me that my strong work ethic and a high level of reliability have contributed to my success.

*In the earliest photo I have of myself, I am five years old
and living in Whitesburg at the time.*

CHAPTER ONE

The Early Years

I was born to Evelyn Richards Coggin and Roy Lee Coggin on September 25, 1936, in Sargent, Georgia, a cotton mill village about thirty-five miles southwest of Atlanta and about five miles west of Newnan, the county seat of Coweta County. I was not born in a hospital but in one of the Sargent mill village "shotgun houses." I'm not sure of the street name or number back then, but today it is 21 Tigner Street, and the house is still there.

My mother was one of nine surviving children born to Hattie Lassiter Richards and John Perry Richards. They lost two children at birth, and their oldest son, Wilmer, died of a ruptured appendix when he was in his early thirties. I was given my middle name, "Wilmer," in honor of Uncle Wilmer Richards, whom I never met, as he died before I was born.

My dad, Roy Lee Coggin, was one of six children born to Orange M. Coggin and Lou Ella Storey Coggin. The family included four sons and two daughters, and my dad was the oldest of the six children. My dad grew up on a typical Georgia farm during the Great Depression. Because of the Depression, my grandfather struggled to buy basic items such as clothing. In his teens, my dad began working in the Sargent cotton mill to help support the family.

My dad truly believed that if a story was worth telling, it was worth embellishing. Consequently, he had a reputation for adding content and color to his stories.

The Coggin brothers enjoy a moment together outside the old family homeplace.

In this Coggin family photo are, from left, my father, Roy Lee Coggin; Uncle Asa and Aunt Sarah Ruth with my brothers Roy Lee, at front, and Gary, at back; Grandmama Coggin; and me.

My dad was also an avid hunter who used his hunting skills to kill and sell game to some of the "rich folks" in Newnan. My dad apparently sold his shotgun to a cousin, and Uncle Raymond bought it back and about twenty years ago gave it to me. I will pass the gun along to my son, Jeff, and grandson, Robby.

I don't remember much about my early years, from birth to age three or four, but I have either been told about events or remember enough to piece together a few things. When I was still a baby, my mom dropped me off at Mama Richards's house and left me in the care of my teenage aunts, Gloria and Betty. After dinner, everyone apparently moved to the living room, and Mama Richards asked Aunt Gloria to stoke up the fire. Gloria poured a generous amount of kerosene on the smoldering remains in the fireplace, which caused the fire to blaze up the chimney, sending burning soot and tar shooting up through the top of the chimney and catching the roof on fire. Before they realized what was happening, the roof was fully engulfed in flames.

Before the fire started, my aunt Gloria had handed me to a little black boy to hold while she stoked the fire. This little boy was like part of the family, as he was always at the house to do odd jobs. Daddy Richards had been to Carrollton on business and arrived home shortly after fire had engulfed the house. When he didn't see me, he immediately wanted to know where I was. This was the first time anyone realized none of them had gotten me out of the house, causing a panic as they imagined I had perished during the fire. About that time, the little black boy came up holding me in his arms and told them that when the house started burning, he had tossed me out the window to his mother, who was standing just outside. I wish I knew his name, but no one ever shared that with me, and there is no one left to ask.

Between the ages of two and seven, I grew up in a very unstable environment, as my parents had many marital problems during that time, plus they moved at least six times. My parents finally decided to get a divorce when I was about seven years old. For the next several months, my mother, my younger brother, Gary, and I lived with or near my mother's family, including my Richards grandparents.

A few months after my parents divorced, my mother got a job at the Bell Bomber plant in Marietta, and my dad had gone back to work for the Central of Georgia Railroad. In light of these developments, my dad arranged for Gary and me to live with my Coggin grandparents. Since I had failed the second grade the year before, they enrolled me in the second grade at Welcome School. We lived with our Coggin grandparents during that entire school year, and I was promoted to the third grade. The time we spent with the Coggin grandparents was probably the most stable environment I had experienced since I was born.

I do have some good memories of those early years, including the time I spent with my Richards grandparents; my first grade teacher, Ms. Lillie Hilly; and the birth of my brother, Gary.

My great-grandmother Storey and my uncle Asa, who was still in high school, also lived with my Coggin grandparents.

Uncle Asa and I rode the bus to school. Unfortunately, the county wouldn't run the school bus to my grandparents' house to pick up only two students, so we walked more than a mile to Bo Storey Road/Mt. Carmel Road, where we caught the bus, and on a few occasions, Mama Coggin walked with us. One day, she was waiting for us to get off the school bus, something that had never happened before. A neighbor had seen a mad dog in that area that afternoon, and Mama was afraid we might be attacked by the mad dog, so she came to meet us with a hoe in her hand to make sure we weren't harmed by the mad dog.

Doing my homework was another interesting experience, as the Rural Electrification Administration (REA) had not yet gotten that far out in the country with electricity. Consequently, I used to sit by the fire and do my homework by the light of a kerosene lamp.

Unlike the Richards family, who were accustomed to making a pretty good living, the Coggins were just hardworking country people who eked out a living by farming and selling a few cows and hogs. In spite of their hardships, they fed and clothed Gary and me and sent me to school. Still, this was probably the most stable time of my early life, and I have many great memories of living with Mama and Papa.

One of these great memories is of the "Rolling Store" operated by Mr. Chambers, which was certainly a unique experience. I can still see Mr. Chambers pulling up in the yard in his Rolling Store on Thursday afternoons. The Rolling Store was a big room built on the frame of a large truck and was probably eight feet wide by twenty to twenty-five feet long. He stocked a lot of grocery items including sugar, meal, flour, canned meats, and vegetables. The day before he was scheduled to visit, Mama would let me go look for eggs, and she would let me swap those eggs for candy and an RC Cola. Mr. Chambers was a very religious person and might have been one of the preachers at his church. If a farmer didn't have the money to buy what they needed, he would let them trade eggs, chickens, butter, and other farm products for the merchandise.

You can't tell stories about the country during those days without talking about the Ice Man. The Coggins had a big old wooden icebox on the back porch that would hold a very large block of ice. The ice was stored in the top compartment of the

icebox, with the milk and other food stored in a big compartment below the ice. The Ice Man came by about once a week,
and it was always a big event when he brought more ice for
the icebox. Millie and I bought one of those old iceboxes about
twenty-five years ago and still have it.

The other important person was the rural mailman. It was
a thrill to go to the mailbox and wait for mailman Horace Bugg
to deliver the mail. My great-grandmother Storey would get
real excited about the mail when she received her "old age"
pension check. It always amazed me that Mr. Bugg could deliver the mail regardless of the conditions of those dirt roads.

Another great memory is of Mama using what she called
"whitewash" to cover the stone around the fireplace. This
whitewash was more or less blue clay that we dug up on the
road banks. We took a bucket and a small shovel, went up the
road about a half mile, and filled the bucket with the whitewash clay. She took the clay home and mixed it with a little
water to create the whitewash. After it was the right consisten-
cy, she took a rag and rubbed the whitewash over all the stone
around the fireplace.

Going to church with Mama and Papa is also vividly en-
graved on my mind. They belonged to the Mount Carmel Methodist Church. We had to travel on about four miles of a muddy
dirt road from their house to the church. We rode to church
in the mule-drawn wagon, which always made the trip more
interesting. We didn't go every Sunday, but we did go most
nights during revival week. I actually joined the church during
revival week. My second cousin and frequent playmate Lee Roy
Storey also joined the church that night.

Singing was always a big thing in a country church, and one
of my relatives, Alvin Storey, sang beautifully. I always tried to

sit as close to him as possible so I could sing like him. Unfortunately, I could never carry a tune, so sitting close to Alvin never did much to improve my singing.

On many Saturday nights in the wintertime, my Storey cousins and some of the other younger cousins would visit us, and we sat around the fireplace and roasted marshmallows or popped popcorn. We had lots of fun enjoying the simple things of life.

Gary and I didn't see much of either of our parents during our time with our Coggin grandparents, but we saw a lot of Uncle Raymond and Aunt Eula, who often checked on us and Mama and Papa. At that time, Uncle Raymond and Aunt Eula didn't have any children, and they became substitute parents for us. They included me in many of their activities such as fishing and hunting. When Uncle Raymond took me hunting, he let me take a gun, an old single-shot .22 rifle, but I'm not sure he ever actually put a bullet in the chamber. One time, he fussed at me for holding the gun by the barrel and dragging it behind me while we were walking through the woods.

While I was living with the Coggins, Uncle Asa was just a teenager, and he also helped take care of us. Asa liked to read, and he took a big shipping crate and made himself a nice bookcase and storage locker. He saved enough money to buy a big old battery-powered radio, and his favorite program was the *Grand Ole Opry*. When they came home from the field at dinner (lunchtime) every day, Papa listened to WSB to hear the agriculture, crop, and livestock reports.

When we went to live with the Coggins, it was made clear to me that I was expected to earn my keep and work in the fields the same as everyone else. In addition to things like chopping and picking cotton, I had other chores around the house. It was my job to bring in the "stovewood" for the kitchen stove. They had a big wooden box behind the stove, and I stacked it full of wood every evening when we came home from the field.

I also had to bring in the firewood for the fireplace. I stacked it in one corner of the front porch, thankful I could reach the porch from the ground and didn't have to go up the steps. It was also my job to keep the reservoir in the kitchen stove full of water.

The stove—or "range," as it was called—had a big water tank along the side, and the water in the tank was heated anytime a meal was being cooked. From time to time, I also had to churn the milk to make butter and buttermilk. I was glad to have that job early on, but after a while it got boring, and I hated it.

I did chores around the barn, like helping shell the corn used to feed the chickens and putting feed in the stalls for the mules. One of my favorite chores was shucking the corn we took to the gristmill to be ground into cornmeal. I didn't really like shucking the corn so much, it was just that when we finished with the shucking, we took the corn to the gristmill, and I knew I might have an opportunity to get another RC Cola and maybe a MoonPie.

The number one chore I hated was "pulling fodder." The leaves on a cornstalk are called "fodder," and after the corn has been harvested and the leaves turn brown, they're pulled off the cornstalk and tied into bundles, then stored in the barn loft for feed during the winter months.

The other job I hated was putting hay and fodder in the barn loft, as I was deathly afraid of snakes, and when you put fresh hay or fodder in the barn loft, you had to pull all the old hay to the front so it could be used first. Snakes got in the barn and lived in the hay while they tried to catch mice and sometimes steal an egg or two. When you started pulling all the old hay and fodder to the front, the snakes went wild, running all over the barn loft. Mostly they were rat or chicken snakes, and they were completely harmless. I didn't care if it was a rat snake or rattlesnake, I didn't want to be in the barn loft with either of them. One time, I was so scared that I jumped out the loft door, but luckily I landed in a hay wagon.

The Coggins grew a lot of cotton, or I should say as much cotton as two men and two mules could grow, because growing cotton required a lot of hard work. As the cotton plant matured and started creating "bolls," you had to put poison on the bolls so the boll weevils wouldn't kill the bolls. We took care of the boll weevils by mixing a big tub of sorghum syrup with arsenic, a powerful poison that is highly restricted today. We put a big rag on the end of a stick and dipped the rag into the poisonous mixture, then brushed it on the cotton bolls. It was tedious work, and you had to be careful not to get any on yourself, as the arsenic was deadly.

The Coggins didn't have a car, so if we went to town or to the gristmill to grind corn or to the cotton gin, we always went in the mule and wagon. It was so much fun to make a trip into town. I would ride for a while, then get down and run alongside the wagon for a while. The trip was always lots more fun when my first cousin Thomas Hall was with us.

I also enjoyed taking a wagonload of watermelons to town to sell. Most of the time, we went to Sargent and rode around the streets of the mill village, and people would come out and buy a couple of watermelons. I liked doing that because it was better than working in the fields, chopping or picking cotton. The other thing I liked about taking a load of watermelons to town was that when Papa sold a few watermelons, he had a

*Roy Lee and I stand before our family's pickup truck
while Dad pets some of our dogs.*

little money in his pocket, and he always bought something for
me—a shirt, overalls, or a pair of shoes.

Taking a load of cotton to the cotton gin was the best. Not

only did it take all day, but we also got to go all the way to Newnan. Mr. Millard Farmer, who owned the gin, was always good to any children who came along. I usually left the gin with a pocket full of lollipops.

Farming was a lot like taking your money to Las Vegas, as so many factors were involved, like having too much or too little rain, and insects like boll weevils also had a big impact on what a farmer produced.

The Coggins had lots of hunting dogs, and they did a lot of hunting. The game they killed served as food on the table, usually at a time when other choices were slim. My grandmother Coggin could cook any kind of game you brought into the kitchen.

Foxhunting was the other sport the adults enjoyed. Good foxhounds were fairly expensive, so we didn't have any, but Sheriff Lamar Potts was an avid foxhunter and had a pack of great dogs. He and my grandfather were good friends, and Mr. Lamar would occasionally come out to my grandfather's after dark and take the dogs to some high ground in the woods and turn them loose. It wouldn't be long before you heard some of the most "soulful" barking imaginable, the signal that the dogs were on the trail of a fox. Everyone involved in the foxhunt sat around a fire, drank a little whiskey, and listened to the dogs chasing the fox.

After my parents turned us over to the Coggins and my mother moved to Marietta, Georgia, and secured that job at the Bell Bomber plant where they were building B-29 bombers, she met a lady from Montana. This woman was also working at the plant, and they shared an apartment. After I finished the second grade, my mother moved us to Marietta to live with her. The area where she lived was like a housing project with tons of kids, and this wasn't always a pleasant experience.

We didn't live in Marietta long before the lady from Montana decided to go back to Montana, and she convinced Mother to go with her. Mother wanted Gary and me to go with her, so she went on ahead to find a place for us to live and hopefully find herself a job. She had arranged for my aunt Gloria to escort us to Missoula after Mother had gotten settled. "Settled" is probably a gross overstatement.

⟋⟋ CHAPTER TWO ⟍⟍

Moving Across the Country

W hat an experience! We rode the train from Atlanta to Missoula with a layover in Chicago. The entire trip took us three or four days, and when we got on the train in Atlanta, it was full of soldiers in uniform who were headed to the West Coast and the Pacific. No seats were available on the train, but some of the soldiers gave us their seats so we could sit together. This was my first experience of seeing people drinking a lot, as most of the soldiers were well on their way to being intoxicated after we had been on the train a few hours. The rest of the trip to Missoula was boring except for the beautiful scenery as we traveled through the Rocky Mountains. I looked out the window and saw the cars behind us winding around the mountain. This was also my first experience of going through a tunnel, and it scared me when we were in the dark so long.

A few days after we arrived in Missoula, Mother landed a job as a cook on a ranch about ten miles outside of downtown Missoula. In return for cooking for the family and ranch hands, she received room and board plus a small salary. I'm not sure she informed the family who owned the ranch that she had two young children, but something went wrong not long after we moved in, and that job didn't last long. We moved to a hotel in Missoula, and a few days later, Mom landed a job as a waitress in a restaurant and bar outside of downtown. We rented a small house on the hill overlooking the restaurant. While working there, she met a fellow named Sam Blackburn, and they got married. This must have taken place in the summertime, as I don't recall ever going to school in Montana.

Mother and Sam hadn't been married too long before we moved to Spokane, Washington, where Sam's family lived. For a couple of reasons, the drive from Missoula to Spokane was an experience I will never forget. On the positive side, the ride through Idaho to Spokane was an incredible experience. I had never seen such beautiful trees and lakes. The one I remember most was Lake Courtland Lane. I also saw lots of elk and moose when we went through a state park, and I had never seen anything like this in my life.

After arriving in Spokane, we rented an apartment in a big complex and had nice neighbors. At a junkyard a couple of miles from the apartment complex, the military stored aircraft that had been used in World War II. The junkyard was restricted, and only authorized personnel were allowed to go in. One of my little buddies and I decided we would go to the junkyard after school to slip in and sit in the plane's cockpit and pretend we were shooting Japanese soldiers. We did this on several occasions, and one day they caught us and kicked us out.

We lived in Spokane long enough for me to start the third grade, and I have a clear memory of a nice two- to three-story red brick building that housed the school. Going to this school was my first experience with the *Weekly Reader*. I loved that little paper, as we spent a lot of time studying it. While we lived in Spokane, I also had my first experience of listening to radio shows like *Captain Midnight*, which were famous at the time.

My mother and Blackburn split, and she decided to take Gary

and me back to Georgia. That resulted in another long, boring train trip. Not long after we returned to Georgia, my mother went back to Spokane and married a guy named Ray, and he was around for a while.

Before going to Spokane the second time, Mother had arranged for us to live with my dad and stepmother, Vera. This is an interesting chapter of my story, as it opened up a whole new set of challenges. When my dad courted and married Vera, he was still working for the Central of Georgia Railroad. After marrying Vera, he decided to leave the railroad and go back to work in the Sargent cotton mill, where he had worked as a teenager and where he was working when I was born. I'm sure the job change was related to the fact that the railroad job kept him away from home so much.

In Appendix 1, I share additional information about growing up in Sargent. Appendix 2 includes additional information on the Coggin family, and Appendix 3 includes additional information on the Richards family.

Living with Dad and Vera was interesting, as my dad had neglected to tell Vera about Gary and me prior to their marriage. She might have known we existed before we went back to Georgia, but I'm not sure she had anticipated that we would move in with them in that three-room mill village shotgun house. About a year after we went to live with them, my half brother, Roy Lee, was born. And when he was about two years old, my stepsister, Darlene—Vera's daughter from a previous marriage, who had been living with her father's parents—came to live with us. So now we had six people living in that three-room house. For a while Vera was not too happy about Gary and me being there, but over time, she adjusted to our living with them.

When we moved to Sargent, I finished third grade at Sargent

This photo from the early 1900s shows my father's classmates from the Handy community. I believe that the branches hanging over the schoolhouse served as something of an awning to help shade the building.

School and was promoted to the fourth grade, even though I had missed a few weeks of third grade during the move back to Georgia. My third grade teacher was Ms. Mary Elliot, a big, tall, red-headed lady with a bit of a temper, and I was often in trouble. We had to walk to school, which was at least a couple of miles. On many weekends, Gary and I visited Mama and Papa Coggin, and we frequently walked from Sargent to their home in Handy, four or five miles away.

President Roosevelt died while we were living in Sargent. When it was announced on the radio, I was standing in the backyard, and one of the neighborhood ladies came running out of her house with the news. People ran out of their houses crying about his death and asking, "What will happen to us now?"

My dad's brother Robert and his wife, Margie, and their two

children lived next door. Unfortunately, Uncle Robert died in his sleep at a very young age from a cerebral hemorrhage. It was a sad situation, as he and Aunt Margie and the entire Coggin family were so close. Relatives came from as far away as South Carolina for his funeral, and in the 1940s, that was a long way to travel for a funeral. I vividly recall how all the family gathered at our house before and after his funeral. Uncle Robert's death devastated Mama and Papa, and it took a long time for my dad to get over the loss as well.

A couple of years later, my grandfather Coggin died from something they called "heart dropsy," though I'm sure they have a much better-sounding medical term for it today. Most people who knew him would tell you he actually worked himself to death. He was only in his mid-sixties, but the poor man never knew anything but hard work. His death was another tragic event, as he was so special to all of us, and I still have a mental picture of him working in the cornfield or plowing cotton. He was a short little man, very thin with gray hair and usually a bit of a five-o'clock shadow, as he didn't shave every day.

We had been in Georgia less than a year when my mother decided she wanted us to go back to Spokane with her and her new husband, Ray. So at the end of the school year, off we went to Spokane, and this time on a bus. Poor Aunt Gloria had to escort us west again.

The second time around in Spokane was not much better than the first with the exception that Ray had a nice family in Spokane, and we visited them frequently. Since Mother didn't have many skills, the best she could do was get another job as a waitress in a big restaurant next door to a large commercial stockyard. Although I was only about nine, they let me work as a busboy, but I don't think I ever saw any of that money.

The apartment we rented was next door to the restaurant but a pretty long ways from the school where I began the fourth grade. If I didn't have to work in the restaurant or do homework, I went down to the stockyard to see the animals. I made some good friends there, especially a couple of young guys who worked at the stockyard. I wanted to adopt an animal as a pet, but that never happened. I remember my school very well, as the teachers and some of the students kidded me about my Southern accent. I don't think they had ever encountered anyone from the South before. I also remember how far I had to walk to the school from our home. Not long after I started that school, Mother decided to move us back to Georgia.

CHAPTER THREE

Georgia
On My Mind

The move back to Georgia was the same old routine, and as soon as we settled in with Dad and Vera, I started fourth grade at the Sargent School. Ms. Grace Davis was my teacher, and she was a very sweet and caring person who really focused on helping her students get an education.

When we came back to live with Daddy and Vera the second time, Vera was very accepting of us and actually grew to love us as though we were her children. This was a stable time in our lives, as I actually attended school in Sargent from fourth through seventh grade.

The Sargent mill operated a company store that was housed in a large red brick building and carried groceries, clothing, and many hardware items. One of the best features of the company store was that an employee and their family could charge items, the price of which would be deducted from their next pay envelope. Those of us who had to walk by the store on the way home from school were tempted to stop by and charge a Coke or some candy. Because of the low wages and relatively large families, many who worked in the mill occasionally owed the company more than they were paid for that week's work, so their pay envelope was empty and had a balance due posted on the front. My dad occasionally had a "balance due" pay envelope, and when he did, he went through all of the charges with a fine-tooth comb, as all of the purchases were listed on the pay envelope. That was always a tense time at our house, because we knew that my dad would find out about the "dope," which is what we called soft drinks back then, and candy we had charged to his account. He would sit us all down and try to make us tell him who had charged what. I don't recall getting a spanking over that issue, but I'm sure we did.

When we first moved back to Sargent, I was the center of attention at school. Everyone including the teachers wanted to hear about my experiences while traveling out west and living in Spokane and Montana. Being somewhat of a chip off the old block, I took advantage of their interest in what I had done to become as popular as I could, especially with the girls. I do recall a few of the boys getting a little irritated with me. Unfortunately, the mystique of my travel wore off pretty quickly, and I went back to being just another cotton mill kid.

Until about 1949-50, houses in Sargent didn't have indoor plumbing, so the water for drinking, washing clothes, and other needs was supplied by a water line that had been installed along the street. About every fourth house had a water faucet in the front yard. We were one of the lucky families and had a water faucet in our yard. Not too long after Gary and I moved back to Sargent, the owners of Sargent decided to put toilets and running water in all the mill village houses, and to add a bathroom, they had to build a room on the side of the house.

We loved to go out to Mama and Papa's, but the trip was an adventure in the wintertime, as the roads between Sargent and Handy were awful. Several miles of those roads weren't paved and had big, deep ruts and mudholes. We got stuck in one of those mudholes on more than one occasion but always managed to get out. In a worst-case situation, we got someone to hitch up a mule to the car and pull us out. My dad drove old cars, including a 1937 Ford and, later, a 1938 Chevrolet. They were frequently broken down, but there was usually someone around who could fix them.

The owners of the cotton mills at Sargent and Arnco were pretty generous in letting the employees use the open land between the housing area and the creek for livestock and chickens. They also fenced an area so the employees had a place to keep their milk cows. We were lucky and had a big open lot across the street in front of our house and a big backyard, where my dad kept his laying hens. He also kept several hogs in some pens he had built closer to the creek, and he supplemented his income by selling hogs and eggs.

We were one of the few families in Sargent that actually raised, killed, and sold hogs. My dad used his old green '38 Chevrolet to haul everything, including pigs and chickens that we bought from farmers. I was always embarrassed that my dad would load up the back seat and trunk of the old car with hogs. Helping Dad take care of chickens and hogs created a good bit of work for Gary and me. We also had to gather the eggs every day. Seemed like the chickens were always getting out of the pen, and we stayed busy catching the chickens that got out and repairing the holes in the fence made by dogs or varmints trying to catch the chickens.

Sargent had a baseball team and a great baseball park that was right in front of our house. The ballpark was a major playground for all the kids, especially those of us who lived on that side of town. Almost without exception, several of us would gather there to play every day during the summer and frequently after school.

Back in those days, Newnan had a baseball team, the Newnan Browns, who played in the Georgia-Alabama Class D league. The Browns played at Pickett Field, and my dad enjoyed going to the Browns games, so we got to see a lot of baseball games. On a few occasions, we even drove to Carrollton or Griffin to see the Browns play.

About two years after we returned from Montana, Grandfather Richards died, and like Grandfather Coggin, he also had a heart problem. He was in the hospital for several days before he passed away. The day he died, I was walking down the street toward the mill when one of my dad's friends stopped his car and told me I needed to go back home, as my grandfather Richards had just died. I don't recall going to the funeral, but I know from experience that it was a very emotional time for all the family. I have many great memories of the times I was with him, and they will be with me as long as I live.

Our world changed the day my dad announced he had bought the farm right next door to Mama and Uncle Asa. This farm had been in the Storey family for several generations and, at the time he bought the farm, belonged to a Mr. Smith, who bought it in the early forties. The last Storey to own it was Charles Storey, one of Mama Coggin's brothers.

Mr. Smith's oldest son had gotten into some serious trouble with the law, and as was typical in those days, the sheriff, Lamar Potts, told Mr. Smith that he would forget about the problems if he would take his son and move the family back to Alabama. Poor Mr. Smith had just planted the crops for that year when all this happened, so my dad bought a farm with crops already in the ground.

CHAPTER FOUR

Life on the Farm

The farm was somewhere between eighty and a hundred acres, with a pretty nice old house. Two barns stood at the back of the house, with one used primarily to store corn and the other for livestock feed. The second barn was more traditional and had stables on the back side. And of course there was a typical "lot" type fence around the barn.

While Gary and I had some expectation of farm life, we weren't fully prepared for the extent of the change in our situation. It didn't take long for us to understand that when Dad bought that farm, we lost a lot of the freedom we had enjoyed to lounge around, play ball, and fish. We also lost our indoor plumbing. My dad put some pretty heavy demands on us to do a lot of the work around the farm, as he and Vera were still working the second shift at Sargent. My dad was never known for his patience, and with the new responsibility of paying the mortgage on the farm, he was even less patient.

In addition to acquiring a farm with the crops already planted, we also acquired most if not all of the livestock, including a couple of horses. One Saturday morning, I was told to plow the cornfield at the top of the hill behind the tenant house. I had plowed a little behind a mule, but on this occasion, I had to plow one of the horses we had acquired. I caught the horse and put on all the gear, and we went up to the top of the hill, as I was going to plow from the top down, roughly a mile from the house and barn. As we started, she walked all over the corn, and I knew my dad would beat the crap out of me if I let her keep doing that, so I tried to get her to stay straight in the middle of the row of corn. When she started drifting back toward the corn and stepping on it again, I whacked her real hard with the plow line, and she took off toward the barn as if she had been shot from a cannon.

Since my dad continued to work at the Sargent cotton mill, he put in a lot of hours on the farm and at Sargent, so in some ways I have sold my dad short, as the poor man worked all the time. He would come home around 11:30 p.m. after working at the cotton mill and get up the next morning around 6:30 or 7 a.m. and work in the field until time to go to work at Sargent.

When we moved to the country, we could no longer go to the school in Sargent, where we had gone for the past four years. We had to enroll in Welcome School that fall. This is the same school I went to when I was in the second grade and lived with my Coggin grandparents.

We rode the bus to school, and the route had never included a pickup on Coggin Road. My dad's first cousin J. B. Storey was driving the school bus on this route, and he didn't want to drive to our house to pick us up. My dad used his political influence with Sheriff Potts and others to change J. B.'s route and have us picked up at the door.

Living in the country wasn't all bad. We lived so close to Mama, we could visit her often, and she always fed us and looked after us. The Coggins all liked to hunt, and we had a couple of good hunting experiences while living on the Smith farm. That first fall, my dad decided not to gather all the corn and put it in the crib. Instead, we put a fence around a big parcel of cornfields, turned the hogs loose, and let them eat the corn in the field. They scattered a lot of it around, which attracted hundreds of doves. Gary and I hid under some pine trees and blasted away at the doves as they came into the field to get the corn.

My dad never seemed content with what he had, and the Smith farm just wasn't big enough, so he leased some more property on Bud Davis Road, about four miles from our house. That tract consisted of at least thirty or forty acres, and it had not been farmed for years. I guess we could have planted cotton, but my dad decided to plant corn.

This forty acres we were farming—plus a couple of thousand acres west of the land we were leasing—had been owned by the Glover family for generations. Not long after my dad leased this land, the Glovers sold the property to Dupree Manufacturing Company. Dupree had a plant in Atlanta, where they made packing material out of chipped-up pine trees. A number of black families had lived on and farmed the land for the Glover family for generations, and when Dupree bought the land, they let everyone continue to farm it. The most senior of this group was Mr. Arthur Allen, and I believe he was related to most of the younger people who lived there.

Mr. Arthur was a very hardworking man and a good friend of my dad. Arthur either made or bought and resold corn liquor, and on several occasions, especially around the Christmas holidays, I would go with my dad and Uncle Raymond to buy liquor from Mr. Arthur. They were great friends and wonderful people.

I may have made it seem we worked all the time, but we did have some recreation, at least what we called recreation. The Coggins were a hunting and fishing family and never missed an opportunity to do one or both. On the fishing side, there was a big creek up in the woods about three miles from our house. Over the years, the Coggin clan, including my dad and Uncle Asa, had restored an old swimming hole that had been used for a long time. After we moved to the Smith place, Gary, Roy Lee, some of the cousins, and I would go up there to fish and swim. We always had pretty good luck with the fishing.

When we neared the end of our second year at the Smith farm, my dad had an opportunity to lease a large tract of land down on the Chattahoochee from the Duprees. He was able to lease the land for a small amount of money, as the Duprees wanted someone to live on that property and look after it for them. I don't remember the exact acreage, but it was a beautiful piece of farmland and pasture that ran for miles along the Chattahoochee River. In addition to the great farmland and miles of river bottoms, it also had huge tracts of land that were covered by swamps, hilly wooded areas, and many, many acres of pasture. My dad had leased some of the best hunting ground in Georgia, and that was about the only thing about that place that I found attractive.

We had four tenant houses on the property we leased, plus the house we lived in. With the stroke of a pen, we went from being pretend farmers to real farmers with a lot more farmland than the three of us could begin to work. One of my first thoughts was, "Thank the good Lord for those tenant houses," and hopefully before planting time next year, my dad would find some good sharecroppers to help us work that farm. He did. He found four families, including my uncle Earl Hall. I had mixed feelings about what my dad was getting us into due to the impact it might have on my schoolwork.

⌒ CHAPTER FIVE ⌒

My High School Years

I n the fall after we moved to the farm on the river, I began the ninth grade, and my dad was slow to buy us school clothes. I occasionally went to school while wearing overalls, and I was the only ninth grader there in overalls. This added to my embarrassment and concern, as I had already

In 1952, the ninth grade class at Western High School in Welcome, Georgia, included Betty Hall, Gloria Hubbard, Joanne Turner, Leroy Storey, Martha Richardson, Ellen Gordon, Betty Hardegree, Mary Hope Shire, Lunelle Hubbard, Joe Wortham, Elaine Newman, Eldridge Pierce, Bill/Bob Coggin, Sara Morrow, Shirley Rainey, Kenneth Bryant, Bobby Estep, Jimmy Polk, Charles Gordon, Billy Smith, Rebecca Stephens, Bruce Payton, Ivaline Richardson, Lewis Copeland, Hazel Cook, and Elizabeth Jones. Our teacher was James B. Walker.

heard that people were making fun of us for living in that old house down on the river.

We had other school-related issues associated with living on the river, the number one issue being the school bus route. As before, my cousin J. B. Storey didn't want to drive the bus all the way down to our house. He wanted to continue to drop us off at the "old Lyle place" two or three miles from our house, and that was what he did initially. One day, it came up a terrible rainstorm just about the time Gary, Roy Lee, and I were about to get off the bus. J. B. said to me, "I would take you on home, but you know how it is," and he made us get off the bus and walk home in the rain. When my dad got home from Sargent that night and I told him what had happened, he was furious. He got up the next morning and went directly to the office of the county school superintendent, Mr. Smith, and raised hell. I think he also went to see one of the county commissioners. Within days, J. B. was driving us right up to the front door. Not long after he had to start driving us to the door, I told him, "J. B., we would walk home today, but you know how it is." When I told my dad what I had said to J. B., I thought he was going to kiss me, which would certainly have been out of character for him.

Another issue related to school and living on the river was the fact that I loved to play baseball, and I could already see that it would be impossible to stay after school for baseball games, as there would be no way for me to get home. The list of reasons for me to hate that place went on and on.

While I was unhappy with many aspects of living on the river, I was intrigued by our neighbor, Mr. Bud Davis. Mr. Bud was about ninety years old when we moved down there, and his daughter was Ms. Grace Davis, who was previously my fourth grade teacher at Sargent School. I think Ms. Grace had passed away by the time

My grandfather, great-grandfather, and great-uncle are on the ferry as they take a load of cotton to the cotton gin.

During a season of drought, my grandfather and his brothers had to plow the sand of the river bottom in order to be able to get the ferry across and transport cotton to the local cotton gin.

we moved down on the river.

Mr. Davis's son, Mr. Jim Davis, was a very nice older man who would do anything he could to help you. I occasionally stopped by to visit with Mr. Bud, and he would tell me stories about what used to go on down on the river years and years ago.

Also on the bright side, I discovered a lot about my Coggin ancestors after we moved to the river. My great-grandfather Coggin's family had moved from South Carolina sometime in the late 1800s and settled in an area a mile or so east of the Chattahoochee, where they lived and farmed. On one of my many hunting trips with my dad and Uncle Raymond, they took me by the remains of the old house the Coggins lived in many years ago. In addition to farming, my Coggin ancestors operated a ferry across the Chattahoochee called the Bowen Ferry. The road to the ferry ran right by our house. I have some great pictures of my grandfather Coggin and his family hauling cotton across the river on the ferry. I also have pictures of them in the river, plowing out the river bottom during a drought in order to get the ferry across. My dad and I actually found one of the ferry cables wrapped around a big old oak tree.

By the time we started planting the next year, we had families in all three houses on the farm and a family in the house on Bud Davis Road. My dad still worked a full shift at Sargent and a half day on the farm.

Unfortunately, by the end of the second year, my dad had managed to alienate Uncle Earl, got into a big fight with sharecropper Bud Ward, and ran one of the other tenants off, so we had only one tenant and the local black folks helping us with the farm when we planted during the third year.

From the time Gary and I got off the school bus until we went to bed at night, we had our hands full doing the chores, which included feeding all the livestock, getting water from the well for Vera to use the next day, cutting firewood, working in the field, and much more. About the time the sharecroppers were leaving, my dad bought a big old Farmall Super C tractor, and that made a big difference in our ability to work all of that land.

After we would "lay by" the crops in late June and early July, we cut pulpwood until it was time to start picking cotton and gather the other crops. To haul the pulpwood to the rail yard, my dad bought a brand-new International truck with a long bed, capable of hauling a large load of wood. While cutting and hauling the pulpwood was hard work, it broke the monotony and gave us a chance to make trips to town when we delivered the pulpwood to the rail yard in Sargent. On these trips, we frequently stopped at Mr. Baxley's store to buy Cokes or candy.

We occasionally stopped at a restaurant, if you wanted to call it that, to have lunch. It was on these occasional stops to eat that I began to realize that white people treated black people very badly, especially when you considered how hard the black people worked and how loyal they were. We always had two to three black folks who helped us deliver the pulpwood, and when we stopped to eat, they couldn't go in the restaurant. They had to go around back and eat on the steps, and I would go out to check on them. I can recall even now how much that bothered me. It was on these occasions that I realized that some white people were disrespectful to black people. It wasn't until I left the farm and joined the Air Force that I observed a more balanced treatment of people regardless of their race.

My dad and I had many disagreements because of his temper and my stubbornness, and after he and Vera left to go to work at Sargent, Gary and I decided we would run away to Whitesburg and stay with Mama Richards. My dad apparently knew we had gone to stay with Mama Richards, and the next morning, he came and got us. My mother found out what had happened, and as soon as school was out, she had us come live with her. By that time, Mother had rented half of a duplex on Dorsey Avenue in East Point. She had some great neighbors, including the Nash family, who lived next door. The Nashes had a son, Wayne, who became my new best friend. He also had a sister named Carlene, whom I fell in love with.

Since school was out, I had to get a job, and my new best friend, Wayne Nash, told me about a program at Russell High School where you could go to school half a day and work half a day. So that summer, I got a job at Woolworth's as a stock clerk, and in the fall, I enrolled in the eleventh grade at Russell and continued to work at the Woolworth store in East Point.

Gary had also moved to East Point and worked at a grocery store on Main Street. I was truly the poor kid in my homeroom class at Russell, but everyone was nice to me. I took Wayne's sister, Carlene, to the Russell High School prom that year. This was the first and only prom I ever attended. The good news is that before the prom, I sold my Model A Ford for enough money to buy a 1939 Ford sedan.

While I was working at Woolworth's, I had spotted the old Model A Ford on a used car lot not far from the store and bought it for a small amount of money. Most of the time, I had to start it with the hand crank, so I finally got tired of that and traded it for the '39 Ford sedan. I thought I was hot stuff with that car. Unfortunately, the Ford was broken down more than it ran.

During this time, I also started going to church with the Nash family, as they were devout members of the Hapeville Church of Christ. I actually joined the church, and like the Nash family, I was there every time the doors opened. I still recall the minister, whose name was David East.

Aunt Gloria, who had escorted us on two of our trips out west, and her husband, Uncle Willis, lived a short distance away in Hapeville, and we saw them often. We also went to Whitesburg to visit the rest of the Richards family, especially when they had a family gathering. Christmas was always a big event, and all of the relatives would come to Whitesburg to be with the Richards family. While Gary and I were living with Daddy and Vera in Sargent, we sometimes rode the train from Sargent to Whitesburg for these family events. The ride cost about sixteen cents per ticket. I think there were two passenger trains per day. Mother usually rode the bus from Atlanta to Whitesburg, and Gary and I went down to the store where the bus stopped and waited for her to get off.

I never did well in school, as I never had any pressure from anyone to do homework or prepare myself for school. Assuming I did well enough to move on to the twelfth grade, I planned to live with Mother and enroll in my senior year at Russell. For some reason, they moved from East Point to a remote community in South Fulton County called Welcome All. I didn't plan to move with them, but I wasn't sure what I would do.

Once again the Nash family came to my rescue, as Wayne's brother, Billy, and his family, who lived in College Park, were aware of my dilemma and invited me to rent their extra bedroom, which I did. They had two little girls, and since the house was small, the living arrangements didn't work out too well, so I started looking for a new place to live. Billy Nash's brother in-law, Charles Hopkins, had also become a good friend. While all this was going on, Charles joined the Air Force, and his mom and dad invited me to come live with them. They were very nice people and treated me like family.

After hearing all the good stories from Charles about his experience in the Air Force, I decided to skip my senior year at Russell High School and enlist. Since I didn't have a high school degree, I decided to get my GED before I tried to enlist. Fortunately, I scored very well on the GED test. I should have known better than to believe all the good things Charles said about the Air Force, as he had only been in basic training three or four weeks when he wrote those letters about what a great time he was having.

An Air Force buddy and myself are outside our barracks during basic training.

CHAPTER SIX

Off to the US Air Force

A fter deciding to join the Air Force, I had the unpleasant task of going to Newnan and telling my dad. It was a trip I hated to make. He was already mad at me for going to live with Mother and wanted Gary and me to live with him and Vera. It wasn't that we meant so much to him but that he wanted us working on the farm. He accused me of letting him down after he had spent so much money raising me, and when I got big enough to work, he said, I ran off and left him. I guess Dad forgot about all those days that Gary and I spent behind a mule and doing other chores between the time he bought the Smith farm and my decision to leave the farm on the river.

When I joined the Air Force, I had that old '39 Ford, and I'm sure I drove it to Newnan and back the day I went to see my dad. I'm not sure what happened to it after that. I think I gave it to Mother.

Having completed all my Air Force paperwork, I was directed to report to a facility for a medical checkup. If I passed, I would be part of the next group headed to Lackland Air Force Base for eleven weeks of basic training. About twenty of us were in that group of enlistees, and we were all accepted that day. After the officials finished all they needed to do with us, they put us on a train that night via New Orleans to San Antonio and Lackland Air

Force Base.

After we left Atlanta, all twenty of us started bragging about how much we drank and all the girls we had been with, and I'm sure some of these guys were telling the truth. Then there were the ones like myself who had hardly ever been out with a girl or drunk much alcohol. At that time, I can only recall having had one beer.

When we arrived in New Orleans, we had a two-hour layover. One of the boys with a little money got off the train, went into town, and bought us a quart of bourbon. I had never had a drink of real whiskey in my life, but I was not about to tell anyone, so I joined in the drinking and got so sick it took me a day to recover.

Since so many Korean War vets were being discharged, the Air Force was aggressively seeking new recruits. I was surprised by the large number of recruits arriving about the same time our train pulled into San Antonio. Teams of Air Force guys were at the train station to meet us and put us on buses to the barracks.

First, they had us go to the depot, where they issued us our uniforms and lots of other stuff such as shaving gear. After we got to our assigned barracks, we met our drill sergeant, and it didn't take him long to get right in our faces about the way we looked, dressed, made our beds, and kept our footlockers. It would be an understatement to say that I had not lived in the neatest or most orderly environment these past few years, so early on, I got a lot of heat about my hygiene and lack of neatness, but I changed my style pretty quickly. Being on the shy side in those days, I found that going to the bathroom and showering with fifty to sixty other guys was something I had to get used to.

From the day I joined the Air Force, all I heard about was how tough it was to pull KP duty. Compared to some of the work I'd done on the farm, it wasn't that bad, plus you ate very well when on KP duty. I have to confess that some of my positive attitude about KP was because I'd met a sergeant from Newnan who worked in the mess hall, and if he was on duty, he made sure I got a nice soft job when on KP duty.

My barracks mates were a mixed breed of people from all walks of life and had different ethnic, racial, and religious backgrounds. Except for the Jewish merchants in Newnan, I had never encountered any real hard-core Jewish people until I met the Jewish boys from New York who were in my barracks during basic training. The one I remember most was Solomon, and that guy could figure out more ways to get out of work than anyone I had ever seen. His last resort was to volunteer to work with a rabbi at the temple.

I made some good friends in the Air Force and stayed in touch with some of them for many years. There were some tough, mean guys who came out of the New York and New Jersey area, but we old country boys gave them a wide berth. There were a few married men in our group who had been unable to find work and had joined the Air Force. Shortly after we arrived at Lackland, I found out from one of the married guys that you could get extra pay and benefits if you had bona fide dependents at home. By that time, Mother was having a hard time getting by, so I decided to try to get her certified as a dependent and was successful. I can't recall how much I sent her each month, but the Air Force matched a certain percentage of what I gave her, and that continued for a long time.

We weren't allowed to go off base for the first five to six weeks. On the Friday before we were to go off base for the first time the next day, they assembled all of the new recruits, and the first sergeant stood on a platform and told us about all of the places that were off limits due to the high risk of getting VD if we encountered any of the women who hung out in those places. The only thing I wanted when we went into town was some ice cream. We had to go back to base before nightfall, as we could not stay in town overnight. The highlight of that day was going to see Judy Garland in the movie *A Star is Born*.

We did a great deal of classroom training and a little combat training, like crawling over barriers, under barbed wire, and scaling walls. My time in basic training was a good experience in learning how to deal with people of other faiths, races, and cultures. Basic training was also a culture shock. Having lived a good part of my life on a farm, most if not all of my encounters with African Americans had been cordial and friendly. Boy, did I encounter a different environment in the Air Force. The majority of the blacks I came in contact with had a huge chip on their shoulder. But now that I look back on it and recall how most white people treated blacks in those days, I can sympathize with the attitude blacks demonstrated in 1954.

I had no idea what kind of job I would be given in the Air Force after basic training but hoped it would be something I could use afterward. I still remember the morning they assembled my group and gave us our orders. I learned that I was part of a group of about sixty people, two busloads, who were being assigned to Altus Air Force Base in Altus, Oklahoma. When they assembled us for the trip to Altus and started handing out orders, I was told that I would be assigned to a communications group and would learn to code and decode classified communications.

That surprised me, as I certainly didn't have any experience that would qualify me for that work. But the bigger surprise came when they told me I would be in charge of the two busloads of airmen and I would have all the meal vouchers to feed the troops as we made that ten-hour trip to Altus. Our only stop was in a small town just south of the Texas-Oklahoma border, where we had lunch. I worked with the owner of the little restaurant to make sure I had given him enough vouchers to cover the cost of the food we'd eaten. I had been instructed to turn over any unused vouchers to the first sergeant of my unit when we arrived at Altus, so as soon as I had settled in my barracks, I went to the administrative area and turned the vouchers over to a staff sergeant who was in charge of administration.

Altus had been an active base during World War II and had been reopened as a Strategic Air Command base around the 1952-53 time frame. It was home base to the Ninety-Sixth Bombardment Wing (B-47s) and a KC-97 refueling unit that supported the Ninety-Sixth Bomb Wing.

I don't know exactly what I'd expected to find when we arrived at Altus, but I was surprised by the flat, barren landscape. The facilities consisted of several large hangars where maintenance was performed on the B-47s and KC-97s, a large operations center, control tower, mess hall, communications center, Officers Club, and NCO Club.

The barracks assignment was related to the area where you worked. For example, everyone in my barracks was assigned to some phase of communications or part of the administrative staff of the unit. My first roommate was a nice, quiet young man from Connecticut. We kidded him a lot about being shy and not having a girlfriend back home. Later I had a great roommate by the name of Rosser who was from Huntsville, Alabama.

Only a couple of the people who traveled with me to Altus from San Antonio were assigned to the communications unit, but I met a number of nice people right away. My first sergeant was a salty old guy from Louisiana, and he didn't waste words when dealing with people. There was also a staff sergeant from Pennsylvania who worked on our communications equipment. He was very nice, and we became good friends.

The communications operation was a twenty-four seven operation, and we were assigned rotating shifts. New guys like myself started out working as telephone operators, mostly on the evening and overnight shift, as they had several ladies who worked as operators in the daytime. In between our phone calls, they expected us to study the material they had given us on coding and decoding classified communications. Working as phone operators, we also managed to arrange dates with a few girls we met over the phone.

Having access to the "chow hall" was another benefit of working the night shift in the communications center. Typically, three to four of us worked the night shift, and we took turns going to the chow hall and getting some SOS, which was chipped beef on toast.

While working the phones at night, I put a lot of time and effort into learning all I could about the classified communications and how to use the equipment. Not too long after arriving at Altus, I secured a top secret clearance and was promoted to airman second class. After the promotion, I became a shift supervisor. There were a few sour grapes, and for a while, I got a lot of flak from some of my peers.

I stayed in touch with the Nash family after I joined the Air Force, especially their daughter, Carlene, whom I had a crush on. Believing that a boy in the service needed a sweetheart back home to correspond with, I started writing her letters soon after I reported to Lackland, and I continued to write her after I was transferred to Altus. She had other interests, and nothing ever came of the relationship. I had enjoyed attending the Hapeville Church of Christ with the Nash family, and because of that relationship, I started attending the Altus Church of Christ shortly after I arrived in town. I met some nice families and was frequently invited to their homes for dinner and other occasions. I ran around with the sons of one of the families I met at church.

Unfortunately, after a while of being a good churchgoing guy, I fell in with a group of fun-loving guys. One of them had a car, so we started driving down to Texas on Saturday nights to go to a drive-in restaurant called Whataburger. We would stay out late, and I felt so bad the next day that I got out of the habit of going to church.

Most of us didn't have a lot of money to spend, but we did go into town pretty often. It was easy to catch a ride to and from town, as the locals would come out to the base in the evening just to give us a ride into town. If we wanted to catch a ride, we would walk up to the front gate and stand on the street, and pretty soon someone would come along and pick us up. We all had a few favorite places where we liked to eat and have a beer, and the people who worked in those restaurants got to know us on a first-name basis. I dated one girl who worked in one of the bars, but that was short-lived when she found out how little money I had.

Somewhere along the way, I bought a radio and a small 45 RPM record player, and I spent a lot of my free time playing good old country music or listening to the radio station in Quanah, Texas.

After being at Altus for six months, I arranged a two-week furlough, got on that Greyhound bus, and took off for Georgia. It was a two-day trip via Oklahoma City and Memphis. My uncle Willis Pate picked me up at the Greyhound station and took me to my mother's. I had planned to hang around a few days and go to Newnan and see what kind of reception I got from my dad, but I wasn't sure what to expect.

As it turned out, other things developed. Little did I know that the family that shared the duplex with Mother had a beautiful redheaded daughter who was about as sexy as anyone I had ever seen, and she was also "frisky." I was kissing her within twenty-four hours of meeting her. A day or two after I arrived, I was supposed to slip over to see the redhead that evening, but she stood me up and went out with someone else. I was so angry I left the house and went to a local bar for a few beers. When I got back to my mom's place and started up the steps, the redhead was sitting on the porch. We had an interesting evening, but I had already made up my mind that I had to go to Newnan the next day, so I gathered a few clothes, hitchhiked to Newnan, and caught a ride out to my dad's farm. The visit was a little more pleasant than I had expected, and I visited for a few days, borrowed his truck, and went to Whitesburg to see Mama Richards. It was nearly time to go back to Altus, so I asked my dad to take me to Newnan so I could catch a Greyhound bus back to East Point.

That last night, I spent a tearful evening with the redhead and a little time with my mom before I caught the bus the next morning and started that long and dreary ride to Altus. It was a terrible and lonely trip. I tried to stay in touch with the redhead, but she and her family were truly white trash and disappeared.

By the time I returned to Altus, I discovered that two other fellows from Georgia had been assigned to our communications unit, and we became great friends. I don't recall the name of the older one, who was a good bit older than me. He had apparently gotten a divorce and lost his job, and that motivated him to reenlist in the Air Force. The other boy, Delmus Knight, was about my age. I have a picture of the three of us taken on a large lake during an outing near Altus. The event was hosted and sponsored by our company commander and was attended by the whole company, including wives and children.

After several months at Altus, a few of us began to get antsy

*Here I am at left with some of my fellow Georgians at
Altus Air Force Base in Altus, Oklahoma.*

and started watching the Teletypes that came in with new posting opportunities. If a posting came across on the Teletype and you had the right skill set, you put your name in the hat and waited to see what happened. One day, my staff sergeant buddy brought to my attention an opportunity that would give us both the chance to rotate to Greenham Common in Southern England. The jobs on that posting fit both of our skill sets, so we put our names in. A few days later, orders came across sending us on our way to Greenham Common via Manhattan Air Base, located near Coney Island, New York. We waited there until we were assigned to a ship for the crossing to England.

CHAPTER SEVEN

Headed Across the Pond

Before heading to England, we got a pretty generous leave, so I went to Atlanta and Newnan to check on my mother, who was more or less on her own again and not doing too well. I also decided to spend some time with the Hopkinses since they had been so nice to me. One of their neighbors had a really pretty blond daughter, so here we go again. Rather than get on to Newnan as I had promised, I hung around College Park a few days and spent some time with her. I don't recall being with my dad very long, as I had to get on to Manhattan Beach. When I arrived at the Air Force base, we had to wait several days before being assigned to a ship.

When the day came for us to board the *William O. Darby*, I was better prepared for the voyage than most of my shipmates, as my staff sergeant buddy had made a few crossings before and knew the drill. He told me that as soon as I got on board the ship, I should volunteer for "light kitchen duty," which I did. And was I glad I did, as the guys who tried to dodge doing anything got some tough and nasty assignments, like cleaning the decks and worse. It was a bit crowded with hammock-type beds about three deep and not much space to hang clothes. I have forgotten how many people were on the ship, but it was loaded. The officers and their families were segregated on another deck.

One of the most interesting aspects of the trip occurred when we landed in Southampton. Keep in mind, my arrival occurred in 1954, not too many years after World War II, and England was still recovering from the war. They must have had a couple of hundred longshoremen helping get the ship docked and unloaded. Hundreds of us were standing on the bridge, watching all that was going on down below. Several of our guys were throwing cigarettes and money to the Englishmen. I noticed right away they all had their bicycles with them. They finally got us off the boat and took us to a rail yard, where they tried to assemble us by destination or base assigned. It took a long time for the people running this operation to sort out the people and the baggage. After many hours, this work was finally completed, and we caught our trains with our luggage. Greenham Common was only a few hours from Southampton, so we got there after just a few hours on the train.

Greenham Common was a US Air Force Strategic Air Command (SAC) base, but at that time, the only aircraft based there were KC-97 refueling aircraft. As expected, I was assigned to the communications unit and primarily handled the coding and decoding of communications of B-47 and B-57 bombers based in Northern England. Almost every night, these bombers made "pretend bomb runs" over Russian targets, and we had to code their reports and send them to SAC headquarters and the Pentagon. Occasionally I worked as a telephone operator when we were short of help.

Overall it was a good experience, as the guys in my barracks got along well, as did those I worked with in the communications center. We had a couple of older guys who gave us young kids a lot of guidance and showed us how to have a good time when we went into town. The town, by the way, was a typical British village with great pubs and was pretty dependent on the Air Force base to support their economy. There were lots of pretty girls in town, but the single guys from the base outnumbered the girls by two to one, and that, combined with my limited funds, meant I didn't have any dates with the local girls.

Not long after I arrived at Greenham Common, a couple of my older buddies and I decided to go into London for a long weekend. We rode the train in and got a hotel room in an inexpensive place near Piccadilly Circus. The hotel was also very near the Douglas House, a special hospitality center for US servicemen and women. After we settled into our rooms, we went to a nearby pub for an English beer and hopefully to meet some ladies. Afterward, we went to the Douglas House to meet some of our other friends and spent the rest of the night drinking and having fun.

On the way back to Greenham Common, I met a young man who was in the English air force, and we hit it off right away. He lived in London and was on his way to an English air force base near Reading. He gave me his phone number, and the next time we both had leave, we arranged to meet in London for the week-end. He introduced me to a lot of local people, and I became good friends with some of them. After I left Greenham Common, I lost contact with him and never heard from him again.

While there were many good things associated with my tour of duty at Greenham Common, it wasn't all rosy. In addition to the Air Force refueling squadron, there was also an army engineering battalion based at Greenham Common. Its mission was to rebuild the runways so the Air Force could base a B-52 heavy bomber squadron there.

The enlisted guys attached to the engineering battalion were mostly rough construction types who resented the Air Force guys for being a bunch of "softies." Unfortunately, the mess hall was run by the engineering battalion, including the sergeant, the supervisor of the mess hall. The local rules required everyone below airman first class or Army corporal to pull KP duty a certain number of days each quarter, and these Army sergeants always gave us poor Air Force guys the nastiest and dirtiest jobs. Everyone in my squadron complained to our first sergeant about it, but he just laughed at us.

While I enjoyed being in the Air Force, things were getting pretty bad for my mom, financially and otherwise. I met with my first sergeant to bring him up to speed on my personal situation, and he encouraged me to file for a hardship discharge so I could go home and help my mother. I took his advice, and after about six weeks of them investigating my mother's circumstances, I was approved for a hardship discharge and traveled back to the US when my discharge was processed.

After I arrived in Atlanta, I searched for a job and a place to live, as my mom was living in a boardinghouse. I initially moved in with my old friends in the Hopkins family until I found a job as a stock clerk at an A&P Supermarket. I soon found a small apartment and bought an old '52 Chevrolet. A few weeks later, I called my old friend Wayne Nash, and he advised me that Pye Barker had an opening for a delivery truck driver in their welding supply division. This position paid more than I was making at the supermarket. With Wayne's assistance, I was hired by Pye Barker and started work almost immediately.

The extra pay and the location of the Pye Barker office made it possible for me to move back to the East Point/College Park area near my mom. I soon found an affordable furnished garage apartment in College Park. I continued to help my mom pay her living expenses, as she was not working.

A couple of months after I started the new job, my uncle Tom Richards, who had worked for Delta, suggested that I apply for a job there, as the pay and working conditions were much better than my current job.

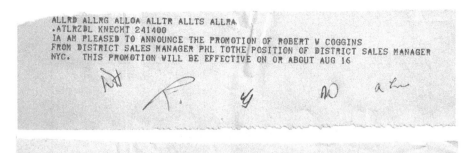

ALLRD ALLRG ALLOA ALLTR ALLTS ALLRA
.ATLRZDL KNECHT 241400
IA AM PLEASED TO ANNOUNCE THE PROMOTION OF ROBERT W COGGINS
FROM DISTRICT SALES MANAGER PHL TOTHE POSITION OF DISTRICT SALES MANAGER
NYC. THIS PROMOTION WILL BE EFFECTIVE ON OR ABOUT AUG 16

NYCRDDL JFKOADL EWROADL NYCRADL EWRRGDL MSG 14
ATLRZDL KNECHT ATLOZDL HAMNER 011800

CONGRATULATIONS TO ALL NYC AND EWR PERSONNEL FOR THE NEW BOARDING
RECORD THAT YOU ESTABLISHED IN AUGUST. YOU FINALLY TOPPED THAT RECORD
SET DURING THE STRIKE OF 66. BY ENPLANING 48,578 PASSENGERS
YOU ESTABLISHED A NEW RECORD. PLEASE EXPRESS OUR APPRECIATION TO
ALL YOUR PEOPLE

These are just two of the many Teletypes I saved over the course of my Delta career.

I did apply for a job at Delta, and about two weeks later, I received a letter inviting me to come in for an interview. I was interviewed by Mr. Horace Messer, Delta's director of personnel. A couple of days later, I was offered a job as a ramp service agent, provided that I could start work the following Wednesday, in just four days. This was a challenge, as I was sure Pye Barker would want two weeks' notice. While I fretted over what to do, Delta informed me that if I accepted the job, I would work the "swing shift" for the first three to four weeks. I immediately accepted the job, as the swing shift allowed me to give Pye Barker the necessary two-week notice and work a full day for them and work for Delta that evening. That development also provided me with two paychecks for two weeks. Once again, God was looking out for me.

I think my experience as an Air Force communications specialist might have influenced Mr. Messer's decision to offer me a position at Delta, as the airlines relied on Teletype systems for most of their communications in the 1950s.

I regret that my uncle Tom Richards passed away before I could express my appreciation for his advice to apply for a job at Delta.

A photo of myself early in my Delta career.

CHAPTER EIGHT

Launching My Career with Delta

I began my Delta career as a ramp service agent in April 1956 and retired from Delta in May of 1998 as executive vice president of marketing and technology. During that forty-two years, I held a number of positions, which I have listed in Appendix 4.

Based on my limited education and background, I thought my job as a ramp service agent was the perfect job, and that was where I would work for the rest of my working life. It didn't take long for me to understand that because of the culture created by Delta's founder, C. E. Woolman, a person's future at Delta was limited only by their willingness to put forth that extra effort and an openness to taking on any job or task that came their way. Possession of these attributes, combined with a person's willingness to relocate to wherever Delta needed them to work, had the potential of turning this entry-level job into something almost unimaginable. You might say I am a poster child for how far a person could go at Delta if they demonstrated all these attributes. It is sometimes hard for me to believe I was hired as a ramp service agent and retired as an executive vice president. I want to acknowledge again that God was with me every step of the way. He kept me from making bad decisions, and he opened the doors to many opportunities, including meeting and marrying Millie.

In Appendix 5, I have described the Delta operation and the

When I began my career with Delta, I couldn't have imagined that I would get to enjoy amazing opportunities such as playing eighteen holes of golf with Willie Nelson at a charity event in Austin, Texas.

area around the Atlanta airport when I started to work for Delta in April of 1956.

I enjoyed many incredible, once-in-a-lifetime experiences during my Delta career, and they were certainly experiences beyond anything I could have ever imagined. My most unforgettable personal experiences during my Delta career included:

- Meeting and marrying Millie after I became a Delta sales representative in the Washington, DC, sales office.

- Experiencing the birth of our son, Jeff, which also occurred in Washington.

- Taking my dad and stepmother, Vera, to the 1969 World Series to see the New York Mets play the Baltimore Orioles. This was very important to me, as my dad was an avid baseball fan who never imagined he would someday go to a World Series game.

- Being at the 1977 World Series game with Millie and Jeff when Reggie Jackson hit three home runs in the sixth game of the World Series against the Los Angeles Dodgers.

- Riding in the cockpit of a British Airways Concord all the way from New York to London. Not many nonpilots can lay claim to that great experience.

- Having people on my Delta Planning Department team who had the talent, skills, and determination to develop and implement the technology platform that the department needed to manage the many pricing and scheduling challenges created by deregulation.

- Accompanying Wayne Smith, founder of the Friendship Force, on a trip to Russia in 1991, shortly after the Iron Curtain fell. Millie and I made this trip together, and our mission was to deliver money donated by Newnan Presbyterian Church to a Russian orphanage that badly needed the funding to clothe and feed children.

- Enjoying significant involvement in the 1996 Olympic Games, including flying to Athens, Greece, to pick up the Olympic Torch and being part of the team that carried the torch from Los Angeles to Atlanta.
- Having Richard Branson and family as guests in our home for three days during the 1996 Olympics.
- Being promoted to Delta's executive vice president of marketing.
- Experiencing the very last flight of the "Spirit of Delta" in 2006. Millie and I both were invited to join this flight, which included a low flight over the Atlanta airport.
- Being one of the first travel industry executives inducted into the Business Travel Hall of Fame, along with Bob Crandall, retired CEO of American Airlines, and Gordon Bethune, retired CEO of Continental.
- Playing eighteen holes of golf with Willie Nelson at a charity event in Austin, Texas.
- Traveling all over the world.

As time went by, I also learned that a person can have all the skills, work ethic, and commitment needed to succeed, but being in the right place at the right time also plays a major role in the success a person achieves.

Being in the right place at the right time certainly played a major role in several of the opportunities that came my way during my Delta career. Just a couple of years after I joined Delta in 1956, the industry entered a very fast-moving phase of evolution. In 1958, Boeing introduced the Boeing 707, followed by the Douglas DC-8. In the early 1960s, IBM introduced the first fully computerized reservations system.

The evolution of the industry was beyond anything it had ever experienced, and some airline executives were better prepared for the evolution than others. In Appendix 6, I have detailed the various phases of the airline evolution. My career was certainly impacted by this evolution, as the challenges I faced gave me many opportunities to demonstrate my ability to adapt to and manage change.

As early as 1960, it was clear that Delta's evolution would be tied to the development and implementation of technology. Delta's failure to embrace and develop a clear technology strategy during this period would have a negative impact on our ability to adapt to phases of evolution that were driven by technology.

Starting pay as a ramp service agent in April of 1956 was $250 per month, about $90 in take-home pay twice a month. To supplement my base salary, I took advantage of every opportunity to work overtime, especially on my days off. This worked out well for me. I made extra money, and my willingness to work those extra hours soon came to the attention of Mr. Jody Brown, the Atlanta station manager. My willingness to work overtime had a huge influence on my being promoted to station agent in Montgomery.

My first job as a ramp service agent or "ramp rat" involved working in the baggage make-up room on the swing shift, and all I had to do was load the outbound bags on the appropriate cart. We also helped clean the aircraft.

During the six months I worked on the Atlanta ramp, I had many interesting experiences, some of them driven by Delta's new routes to the Northeast, which resulted in more flights serving Atlanta. This expansion increased the conflict with Eastern Air Lines over the use of ramp space. The ramp congestion was occasionally a big issue between the two carriers, as both airlines tried to use every inch of what they considered their ramp space.

Another example of the issues related to Delta's growth in Atlanta concerned the shortage of newer ground equipment, including the newer tugs. This issue was serious enough that some of the guys whose primary job involved driving those tugs would come to work early to be sure they had access to one of the newer tugs.

When Delta received authority to fly to the Northeast markets, we didn't have many spare aircraft, and all of the other airlines that also received new route authority quickly bought the few aircraft that were on the market. Delta needed additional aircraft to implement the new service, and the only aircraft they could find were some old Lockheed Constellations that Pan American Airways had taken out of service due to age and maintenance costs, but they were the only option. Ironically, C&S Airways owned some relatively new Connies at the time of the merger. Mr. Woolman and several other Delta officers didn't want to add another aircraft type to the fleet, so Delta leased these aircraft to another airline. Unfortunately, when Delta made the decision to lease the aircraft, Delta management had no way of knowing that they would be awarded those routes to the Northeast a few years later.

During the time I was on the Atlanta ramp, I worked with some really great people. When the guys I worked with found out that Tom Richards was my uncle, they were anxious to find out if I was cut from the same cloth as Uncle Tom. They were probably disappointed since I didn't quite have his flare for practical jokes or drinking. Apparently he kept a bottle of whiskey hidden in his locker in the old break room.

Driving the tugs that pulled the baggage carts was one of the most sought-after jobs and was generally assigned to the most senior ramp rats. That job basically required the tug driver to run carts of bags between the baggage make-up room and the appropriate aircraft flight, or they would deliver them to the baggage claim area. Many of these senior guys rarely got off the tug to help load or unload bags. There were, of course, exceptions, and Bill Mathis was a real exception.

As you can imagine, lots of flight attendants lived around the airport in those days, and they were all single, or at least claimed to be, as you couldn't work as a flight attendant after you were married. (That was a strange rule.)

A number of apartment complexes were located around the airport, and in many instances, they were almost totally occupied by airline personnel, with the majority being flight attendants. I recall a few occasions when parties around the swimming pools would go on for days. As one group sobered up to go to work, another group would be coming in off of their flights.

I naturally had many adventures on the ramp, everything from stealing a kiss from a flight attendant I'd hung out with the night before to taking leftover food off an aircraft that had just come in from the West Coast. This, by the way, was a no-no. But the adventure that almost got me fired involved a forklift I was driving.

I had been asked to use a forklift to take a large piece of freight to a flight and load it in the rear bin of a CV-440. This aircraft was parked right in front of the observation platform where people came to watch aircraft come in and take off. As I approached the aircraft, I noticed a couple of especially pretty young ladies standing on the observation deck and watching what I was doing. I decided to put on a little show for them, and rather than just drive the forklift straight up to the cargo bin, I decided to make the lift do a figure eight as I approached the aircraft.

Unfortunately, I had the lift up about eight feet with the cargo on it, and when I tried to do the figure eight, the forklift almost tipped over onto the aircraft. By some miracle, I got the lift under control, and it didn't hit the aircraft. The girls thought this was all part of my act and applauded. If I'd had a clean set of underwear with me, I would have changed, as it scared me so bad.

One day Jody Brown, the Atlanta station manager, called me into his office and asked if I would like to be promoted to station agent and transferred to Montgomery, Alabama. It didn't take ten seconds for me to say yes. Before I could get the job, I had to fly over to Montgomery and be interviewed by Fred West, the station manager. Except for my trip back to the US from England, I had never been on an airplane before. I was almost as excited about flying to Montgomery for the interview with Fred West as I was about the new job opportunity. Fred gave me the green light and asked that I report to Montgomery ready to work in approximately two weeks.

While Delta was a big part of my life in those days, I still had time to spend with my mother and the rest of my family. Though my dad was still unhappy with me for leaving him to join the Air Force, I went to Newnan to visit my family from time to time, as I really loved all of them, especially my grandmother Coggin, who cared for me during much of my early years. I also liked to hunt and fish with Uncle Asa and Uncle Raymond.

Before I moved to Montgomery, I took my mother to Whitesburg to see Mama Richards. I supported my mother financially but didn't spend that much time with her.

As I was making the move to Montgomery, my aunt Opal, who lived in Hurtsboro, Alabama, asked my mother to move to Hurtsboro and help her run a hotel that the family owned. About that same time, my brother Gary, also known as Joe, joined the Navy, so it all worked out pretty well.

CHAPTER NINE

First Promotion and a Move to Montgomery

When I reported to Montgomery, there were four other agents assigned there plus Fred West, the station manager, so I was agent number five. Those four consisted of the unofficial senior agent, Wink Peterson, and Charlie Powell, Eddie Cooper, and a new hire whose name I don't recall. Shortly after I reported to Montgomery, Fred West got a call from Delta's personnel department and was advised that he would have to fire the new hire. That hire was replaced by David Poole, a great addition who had a great career with Delta. Wink and Charlie had been around a while, and Eddie Cooper had also been there long enough to know his way around. Between the three of them, it didn't take long for us new guys to pick up on how to handle the operation.

Working as a station agent in Montgomery was quite a change versus working the Atlanta ramp. In a small station like Montgomery, we were required to do many different tasks, including working the ticket counter, taking reservations over the phone, maintaining radio contact with the flights, working the air freight, doing the paperwork on air express, handling lost bags, fueling the aircraft, and the list went on and on. I immediately had to junk my old ramp uniforms and buy some black pants, a black coat, white shirts, and black ties.

In 1956, the Montgomery terminal was little more than a shack with a restaurant in front of the terminal, with the Eastern ticket counter on the left-hand side and the Delta counter on the right. The normal level of activity at the airport was so small that many of the passengers parked right in front of the terminal.

Segregation was still the law of the land in Alabama in those days, so we had segregated waiting rooms of sorts on the ramp side of the ticket counters. Most of the African Americans would not go in the waiting room but just stood around outside and waited for the boarding process to start. Most of the white passengers would stand around in the small lobby area until we started boarding their flight.

Since Eastern had more flights and handled more passengers than Delta, their ticket counter was larger. With Delta having only four flights per day—two of them operated with DC-3s—we didn't need much ticket counter space. Working the ticket counter was not a complex process, as fares were relatively simple. The only challenge occurred when a ticket counter agent had to reissue a ticket or collect excess baggage fees. The boarding process was the simplest part of the job, as the aircraft was usually parked no more than fifty yards from the terminal. An agent stood at the gate and collected the tickets as the passengers boarded the aircraft.

Martin Luther King Jr. and the civil rights movement were really just getting cranked up in Montgomery when I moved there. As a matter of fact, the Rosa Parks bus incident took place shortly after I arrived. Martin Luther King Jr. and some of his team flew over to Atlanta fairly frequently.

Shortly after I arrived in Montgomery, I enrolled in Alabama Christian College, where I took marketing courses for about a year. I didn't have much of a personal life back then, as I had a small apartment in a lady's home in downtown Montgomery and had only a few social contacts. Wink and some of the other guys occasionally invited me over for dinner.

Delta only had four flights per day, and two of them were Douglas DC-3s and two were Convair 340/440s. Both of the westbound flights served Montgomery from Atlanta and Columbus, and one of the eastbound flights originated in Dallas and the other in New Orleans. With the limited air service out of Montgomery, these flights were always heavily booked, mostly with business travelers and military personnel.

The downline stations sent "load messages" to all the stations on a flight's itinerary. These load messages provided information on how many pieces of luggage, mail, express, and freight they had boarded for a particular station. On a good day, they would also tell you in which bins your bags and cargo had been loaded. Before a flight landed, we took the load message info and created an "off sheet" so we would know exactly what to look for when we started unloading the flight.

Soon after Jimmy Dunn began to work with us, we had a rash of lost luggage. One day after Jimmy had worked Flight 416, which came in from the west, Wink Peterson double-checked one of the cargo bins and found two Montgomery bags that Jimmy had failed to unload. Wink had a discussion with him about his work and discovered that when Jimmy worked a flight, he quit looking for any more Montgomery bags after he'd found the number of bags on the "off sheet." Almost at once, our lost-bag epidemic was solved. Shortly after that, Jimmy was gone.

Most of the operations at Montgomery were routine, but we did have a little excitement one morning when the captain on Flight 409 called in on the radio and told Fred to have an ambulance waiting, as a flight attendant was having an appendicitis attack. We made the call, and shortly after the flight arrived, the ambulance took her to the hospital. We had a real dilemma, however, as the flight had to go on to Dallas, but there was no flight attendant on board, so I was selected to get on the flight and serve the passengers.

After I'd made a couple of trips up and down the aisles while trying to serve coffee, the captain called me on the aircraft intercom and told me to sit my ass down until we landed in Jackson, because every time I walked toward the front of the aircraft, both pilots had to pull up on the controls to keep the flight level, and every time I walked to the back of the aircraft, they had to push down on the controls. Needless to say, when the flight arrived in Jackson, they took me off the flight and replaced me with a ninety-pound female ticket agent. Under the current rules, the FAA would have required Delta to cancel the flight due to my not having the necessary safety training.

The Eastern Air Lines morning flight to Atlanta was with a Constellation, which competed with our poor little DC-3. One morning, the Eastern Constellation had a mechanical issue, and the flight was going to be delayed. When I made the departure announcement for our Atlanta flight, I said, "Delta's dependable DC-3 service is now departing for Atlanta." Later that day, all the Eastern agents harassed me for making that announcement.

After being promoted to station agent in Montgomery, I continued to go back to Georgia on some of my days off to visit with my Coggin family, especially during hunting season, as I still enjoyed hunting with Uncle Raymond and Uncle Asa. My mom was living in Hurtsboro, Alabama, so it was a short ride over to see her, but I didn't go there often.

Due to the high load factors on our existing service, Delta decided to add a couple of additional flights between Atlanta and

Montgomery that served only the Atlanta-to-Montgomery markets. One was an afternoon flight operated with a CV-440 and departed shortly before the existing afternoon flight. One day we had a mechanical on the flight that operated with a CV-440, and Flight Control replaced it with a DC-3. That smaller aircraft created an oversold situation, and several passengers were angry about having to fly on a DC-3. I'll never forget the comments of a prominent Montgomery businessman as he boarded the flight. He turned to me as he went up the steps of the DC-3 and said, "I bought a ticket for a first-class flight, and you have put me on a third-class fright."

The passenger loads on the new flights did not meet expectations, and about six months after Delta added them, Delta decided to cut back to the original four daily flights.

As a result of the schedule reduction, Montgomery was overstaffed since we had added a couple of staff with the new flights. After the reduction in flights, Fred West was advised that he had to reduce the head count by one, and being the only single person serving Delta in Montgomery, I volunteered to be reassigned.

CHAPTER TEN

Next Stop: Hot Springs, Arkansas

The Delta operation at Hot Springs, Arkansas, needed an additional agent on a temporary basis to help with the extra flights Delta added during the horse racing season. I volunteered to go to Hot Springs with the expectation that Delta would transfer me to Atlanta after horse racing season was over.

It didn't take long for me to pack all my belongings into my 1956 Bel Air convertible and hit the road. On my way to Hot Springs, I drove to Newnan to see my folks, as I wasn't sure when I would be able to get back home again. More than anything, I wanted to see my grandmother Coggin, whom I loved so dearly. After visiting for a day or so, I drove on to Hot Springs. When I arrived, I drove directly to the airport to meet Ed Mayo, the station manager, and the other two agents. One fellow was named Lloyd, and the other was a little guy named Hugh. After I met with the Hot Springs team, I began the search for a place to live and found a room in a nice boardinghouse.

The Hot Springs assignment turned into a much longer tour of duty than I had expected. Hugh was having some health problems, and while he was out on sick leave, the Delta auditor came to Hot Springs to do the annual audit. When he did, he discovered that Hugh had been stealing from the company, and Hugh was subsequently fired. Since I was already there, they put me in his slot, and the assignment lasted a little more than a year.

I certainly experienced a lifestyle change when I transferred from quiet little old Montgomery to Hot Springs. In those days, Hot Springs was wide open with gambling casinos, lots of "retired" New York and Chicago gangsters, plenty of pretty girls, and many good bars.

Delta normally operated only two flights per day at Hot Springs, but during the horse racing season, Delta added a third flight by landing a flight at Hot Springs that normally flew between Chicago and New Orleans via Memphis and St. Louis.

My duties in Hot Springs were similar to those in Montgomery, but the clientele was certainly different, and there were no similarities in the style and personality of the two station managers.

Ed Mayo was a hot-tempered Cajun who made you tow the line, but you always knew where you stood with Ed, as he never held back. Fred West, on the other hand, was a lot quieter but could be deceptive at times. Hot Springs had been a C&S station before the merger with Delta, and we still used many of the forms and procedures that had been used by C&S. Ed Mayo had started his airline career as a C&S employee, and he preferred to use the C&S forms and procedures.

Many of our passengers, especially in the horse racing season, were Jewish, and they lived in Chicago, New York, or another major East Coast city. They came to Hot Springs not only for the racing season but also for the "hot natural baths" offered by some exclusive hotels. When these passengers traveled, they always had excess baggage, and to avoid paying the excess-baggage fees, they would tip the two skycaps and hide their bags until the skycaps could slip tags on them. It didn't take me long to figure out what was going on, and we put a stop to it, much to the frustration of our skycaps, who were getting lots of tip money. On the morning trip, a large number of our passengers were flying Delta to Memphis and connecting to American Airlines before flying to New York City, Philadelphia, and other cities on the East Coast. In those days, very few people carried any bags on the airplanes, which did not have closed storage bins.

The horse racing season at Hot Springs was a big event, and since we were the major airline, one of the races was named the "Delta Race," with someone from Delta posing for pictures with the winning horse, jockey, and owner. The year that I was there for the horse racing season, a Tommy Aycock from Atlanta represented Delta. He was a Delta sales manager based in the General Office. Until I started talking with Tommy during his visit, I hadn't realized that Delta had salespeople calling on customers, as I thought the passenger just happened. After talking with Tommy and finding out more about what he did in Sales, I made up my mind that Sales was where I wanted to work. I wasn't sure how I was going to get from the lowly position of station agent to sales rep, but I knew that was where I wanted to go.

There was no control tower or other air traffic control facility in Hot Springs, so we did our own weather observations for the pilots. At times, this was an interesting experience. A little wooden boxlike structure stood just outside the terminal building, and it was built like a small house with slanted sides so the air could circulate through it. This structure housed the device that gave us the temperature and barometric pressure reading. When a flight was due to land, we went out to the little house and wrote down the number. If the ceiling was the least bit low, we released a balloon and counted the number of seconds before it disappeared into the clouds, and that was how we determined the ceiling level.

We then went back into Operations and called the pilots of the approaching flights to give them our weather observations.

The airport was partially surrounded by Lake Ouachita, which was aligned with our primary runways, and the lake caused us some weather issues, especially in the winter and spring. If the ceiling heights were marginal, we fudged a little and gave them numbers that made it okay to land. I never will forget one day when "Red" Ellers was flying the trip that originated in Houston, and I fudged quite a bit on the ceiling because we had a full flight and I didn't know what in the heck we would do with the passengers if Red decided to overfly Hot Springs. Red shot a couple of approaches before he was finally able to land, and after he parked the aircraft at the gate, he stormed out of the cockpit. He grabbed me by the shoulder and said, "I know you did this, and when I come back through here from Chicago tonight, I'm going to bring you bastards a thousand-foot rope with knots tied every foot so you can count the damn knots when that balloon goes up, as you missed this ceiling by at least three hundred feet."

He did report us, but he never gave us the rope. I should point out that Ed Mayo was not working that day or this would never have happened. As you would expect, after Ellers reported us, Ed was chewed out by our regional manager, and Ed passed the chewing on down the line.

One day the flight from Memphis landed, and as a passenger came into the terminal, he said, "Wow, you guys have sure done a lot of work on this terminal since my visit last year." I said, "No, sir, it's been this way for as long as I can remember." He looked at me and asked, "Am I in Hot Springs, Virginia?" and I said, "No, sir, you're in Arkansas." He went into a rage, as he was supposed to give a speech at some high-level corporate conference that night in Hot Springs, Virginia. He had originated somewhere in the Midwest, and when the agent booked his reservations, they had misunderstood and booked him to Hot Springs, Arkansas, not Virginia. The gate agent in Memphis didn't catch the mistake. I don't remember all the details, but the man got on the phone to Mr. Woolman's office, and Delta arranged a charter with the local fixed-base operator to fly him to Hot Springs, Virginia.

The guy who operated the fixed-base operation and charter service hired me part-time to help with his paperwork, and in return, he agreed to teach me how to fly. I had a couple of flying lessons in Montgomery, but the lessons I had in Hot Springs were serious, as he had his flight instructor give me flying lessons. I was transferred from Hot Springs before I had enough hours to try to get a pilot's license.

I did a lot of work for this gentleman, and when he flew charters, he let me fly with him if I wasn't on duty that day. On one occasion, he had to go to Montgomery to pick up a customer, and I flew over there with him and had an opportunity to visit with my old Delta buddies. Actually, I wasn't that interested in visiting with them. I just wanted to impress them with the fact that I had just flown in on a private aircraft. I'm not sure, but in talking to my Delta colleagues, I might have exaggerated my flying experience and my participation in flying the airplane.

Now my social life did change quite a bit from my time in Montgomery. In addition to hanging out at a couple of bars, the Illinois bar being my favorite, I spent a lot of time at a drive-in restaurant called "Bob's." I got to know Bob pretty well, and we did a little drinking together. When I arrived in Hot Springs, I was driving my black-and-white 1956 Chevrolet convertible, a beautiful car, and the girls loved it. A few months after moving to Hot Springs, I went home to Newnan. Right after I arrived, I passed by a used car lot and saw a red 1958 Chevrolet convertible that I bought, and all the girls were really hot to ride in that car.

Making that change was a big mistake, as I had nothing but trouble with that car from day one, but the girls didn't care about my mechanical problems. They just wanted to be seen sitting with me in my car at Bob's drive-in or be seen riding around town with me. I was kind of a "big shot" in Hot Springs, as I worked for Delta and made lots more money than most of my peers who worked in service stations and similar places. It's rather funny that people thought I made lots of money.

I met one of the local radio station disc jockeys at the drive-in, and we started hanging out together and eventually became roommates. His radio station was experiencing a lot of difficulty getting good weather info, so I got one of my buddies at Delta's Little Rock operation to get me the official weather forecast from the control tower every day and Teletype it to me. I then went on the air three times a day and gave the weather report. That lasted several months until the station was sold and my friend left.

My mother wrote and told me that my brother Gary—or "Joe," as we called him—was still in the Navy and was going to get a furlough and come to Pensacola to visit her and my new step-father, Harley Rigdon. She asked if I could arrange to come see them while he was there. I managed to get a couple of extra days off and flew our Delta flight down to New Orleans then bought a round-trip ticket on National Airlines from New Orleans to Pensacola.

I dated several girls, and some of them were very accommodating. After I left Hot Springs, I went back on a couple of occasions to see a particular girl, but she wanted to get married, and I ended the relationship. I had a couple of other good friends there, including Wayne Nichols. I used to hang out with him a good bit and frequently went to his house and ate dinner with him and his folks. Another guy that I became good friends with was the brother of a girl I was dating. His folks lived in the country, and I would go out to their farm and plow their garden for them. I guess I was homesick to be behind a mule and plow stock.

I had been in Hot Springs less than a year when Delta was awarded authority to serve Orlando. Shortly after the announcement, we received word that Ed Mayo had been named station manager in Orlando, and John Brinkley, the chief radio operator at Little Rock, would replace Ed as station manager in Hot Springs.

Not long after the announcement about Mayo's promotion, a system-wide Teletype message came across the network seeking a volunteer who would relocate to Brunswick, Georgia, as station agent. Since I was already a bit restless and wasn't excited about working for John, I immediately put my name in the hat. Brunswick was much closer to home, and that also influenced my decision to volunteer so quickly.

In a few days, our regional managers called Ed and told him I was being transferred to Brunswick to fill that slot. As soon as I got the word, I went around to all of my friends to tell them goodbye, and we had some pretty wild parties those last few days prior to my departure. I promised all my friends that I would use my pass privileges and come back as often as I could, and I did go back a couple of times.

CHAPTER ELEVEN

Reporting to Brunswick

The Brunswick airport was actually on St. Simons Island, which was connected to Brunswick by a causeway. The airport was twenty to thirty minutes from downtown Brunswick, and Sea Island was only a few minutes' drive from the airport. Sea Island was the crown jewel of the South and home of The Cloister hotel complex. The Cloister was a favorite vacation spot for folks in the Northeast, many of whom owned homes on Sea Island.

When I reported to St. Simons, the station was staffed by Rufus Warren, the station manager, and two station agents, including Bill Truett and another person whose name I can't recall. Rufus was quiet and easygoing but focused on making sure that we abided by all the rules. As I'd expected, the operation and duties were similar to what I had experienced in Montgomery and Hot Springs.

Now when I was born, I was named Robert Wilmer Coggin. As far back as I can remember, my nickname was Bill, and Bill stuck until I was transferred to St. Simons. Since there was already a Bill Truett on staff, Rufus wanted me to go by Bob to save some confusion about which Bill he was talking to. I agreed to that, but the next time I was in Newnan visiting the Coggins, my three-year-old nephew, Mitch Coggin, became a little confused and started calling me "Bill/Bob," and that is what most of the Coggin grandchildren, nephews, nieces, and cousins call me today.

In my new job, Delta's primary customers were individuals who were guests at one of the upscale resorts and businesspeople who worked on St. Simons or in Brunswick. Many people from the Northeast drove down in late fall and spent the winter at The Cloister, and they frequently looked for someone they could pay to drive their cars back home. One gentleman hired me to drive his car to Manhattan, and what an experience that was for this old country boy.

When I arrived in St. Simons, Delta served the destinations with three flights per day. Two of the flights originated in Atlanta and served St. Simons via Savannah. One of the flights terminated at St. Simons, and the other flight flew on to Jacksonville with a return to Atlanta via St. Simons and Savannah. The flight that was a St. Simons turnaround had a four-hour layover in St. Simons. All these flights were operated with DC-3s. Eastern was our competition, with two round trips that originated in Charlotte and terminated somewhere in Florida. Eastern had a staff of three people, including the station manager, Frank Gay.

Since the two airlines were so thinly staffed, we tried to help each other out when we could, including answering each other's airline phone when everyone was out on the ramp working a flight. When we answered the other airline's phone, we took a message so the appropriate airline could return the call. One day when Frank and his crew were out working their flight, I answered the phone, and the person on the other end of the line wanted to speak with Frank. When I told him Frank was out working the flight, he wanted to know who I was, and I told him I was a Delta agent. It turned out the caller was from the Eastern Air Lines General Office, and when Frank came in from working the flight, he called the guy back and caught hell for letting a Delta person answer for him. That was the end of helping each other out with the phones.

When I first moved to St. Simons, I rented a garage apartment from a lady who also rented rooms in her house to schoolteachers. I met one of the schoolteachers and dated her a few times. I can't recall her name, and she was a little too stiff for me, but she introduced me to a young man named Wallace Phillips, who had recently been discharged from the Navy and was working at a plant on the island. Wallace and I became best friends, and his mother frequently had me over to their house to eat. When I had to have some minor surgery, Wallace's mother insisted I stay with them while I recuperated. Later, when Delta promoted me and moved me from Jackson, Mississippi, to Philadelphia, Pennsylvania, Millie and I drove from Jackson to Philadelphia, and I made it a point to go via St. Simons on our way to Philadelphia so I could introduce her to Mrs. Phillips and visit with her and Wallace again. That was the last time I saw either of them, as Mrs. Phillips died not long after that, and Wallace reenlisted in the Navy.

St. Simons was also a popular vacation spot for folks who lived in the Atlanta area and for Georgia in general. I met a lot of nice people in the bars, but they were mostly college kids. Between Wallace and me, we knew just about all the local people on the island, especially the young ones.

St. Simons was small enough that you had to be careful who you dated, as word got around pretty quickly. There was one local girl I really wanted to date, but she would never date me, so one day when we were both in the downtown coffee shop, I just flat-out asked her why she wouldn't date me. She said the word was out that I took every girl I dated to bed, and she was just trying to protect her reputation. I'm afraid my reputation far exceeded reality.

I had been living on St. Simons for about four months when I found out that Georgia Power had transferred Richard Tenney to their Brunswick Power Plant. I knew Richard and his family back when I was still living in Newnan. I contacted him and arranged to meet and have a drink, and we hit it off so well we decided to become roommates. We rented a nice two-bedroom apartment not far from where I was living at the time.

Richard had a girlfriend he was crazy about, and she had a friend she wanted me to date, so I finally agreed to go on a blind date with this girl. We were going to double-date with Richard and his girlfriend, and since I had never seen this girl, I arranged for us to go to this small bowling alley that was hardly ever used by any of the local young people. I did that to protect my reputation in case this girl turned out to be a pig.

When we got to her house to pick her up, I was shocked when she walked out the door, or maybe I should say "waddled" out the door. "Short, fat, and ugly" is the best way to describe her. I was so relieved that I'd had the foresight to say we were going to the bowling alley. We arrived, and a half dozen of my friends were there, including a good-looking gal I had been trying to date. When we sat down in our chairs to bowl, I wouldn't even sit by my date. I sat behind her. The next day, as I expected, my phone began to ring off the wall with callers wanting to know where I picked up that "honey."

Because one of our flights had a four-hour layover, and since it was only four hours, the company didn't make any accommodations for the crew. They were expected to hang out at the airport. On days when I was working, I let them use my car, and Richard and I let them use our apartment if they wanted to change clothes and go to the beach. As a result of extending this hospitality, I made some lifelong friendships with these pilots and flight attendants. On my days off, I would hang out with them if I didn't have other plans.

Another Georgia Power guy, Bobby Garner, had gone to school with me. He worked in the same office as Richard Tenney, and I used to go over to their office to have lunch and visit with them. The guy who ran the office spent a lot of time with us, and one day he said he'd like to introduce me to his sister. I agreed to go to their house one evening for dinner. I forget who his dad worked for, but he was an engineer making pretty good money and had a house on the entrance to the coastal waterway. I met his sister, and we hit it off right away. I dated her off and on for a long time, but like most of the girls I dated, she was anxious to get married. Not many months after I met her, I moved back to Montgomery, but we stayed in touch.

While the routine work in my life was going on, I met the famous tobacco heir and billionaire R. J. Reynolds. He was living on Sapelo Island, which he owned. He was also one of the largest Delta shareholders at the time. He became good friends with Miles Baker, who ran the local FAA office at the St. Simons airport. One day Mr. Reynolds met with Miles Baker and asked him to quit working for the FAA and launch and operate an airline for him. Golden Isles Airlines would have its headquarters at the St. Simons airport and would serve a number of cities in Florida. Somewhere along the way, Mr. Reynolds had also met a Jacksonville-based Delta reservations supervisor who had a marketing degree, and he hired this fellow to head up sales and marketing for Golden Isles Airlines. Miles Baker had gotten to know me pretty well and thought I would be an asset to the new company. He made me a job offer, and I couldn't turn it down for a couple of reasons, one being the salary and the other being an opportunity to work in airline sales. I saw this as my big opportunity to move

In 1960, I went to work in sales for Golden Isles Airlines, which was founded by tobacco heir and billionaire R. J. Reynolds in Brunswick, Georgia.

up the ladder.

Golden Isles started with a half dozen de Havilland Dove aircraft and had some seasoned pilots to fly them. Mr. Reynolds also allowed Miles to build a major maintenance facility so they could accept work from third parties.

So I went to work for Golden Isles Airlines as the sales guy, and in the meantime, Richard Tenney had moved back to Brunswick to get married. Miles Baker had hired a chief mechanic who was single and had moved from Texas to St. Simons. The two of us decided to become roommates and rented a nicer apartment than the one I had shared with Richard.

In my new capacity as head of sales for Golden Isles Airlines, I worked closely with the fellow R. J. and Miles had hired from Delta Reservations. The first couple of weeks, the two of us made some joint calls, then I branched out on my own and was making calls in Brunswick, Gainesville, Jacksonville, and Tampa. All was going well, and I got some favorable responses to my calls, as many people felt that we were providing a much-needed service.

One day I got a call from Miles, and he told me to stop whatever I was doing and go to headquarters for a meeting the next morning. When we all assembled, Miles announced that Mr. Reynolds had married again and had decided to live in Italy. He didn't want to continue to operate the airline, and in one week, we would be shutting down.

Everyone was in shock, as things had appeared to be going so well. It was devastating to so many people, and many of us had given up good jobs to come work for Mr. Reynolds. We thought Golden Isles Airlines was going to be a great success. Miles called me into his office and told me that Mr. Reynolds had called Mr. Woolman and had arranged for me to be reinstated at Delta with

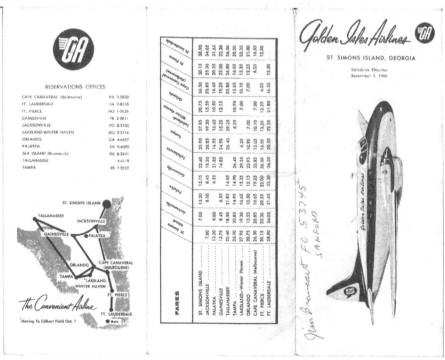

This Golden Isles Airlines schedule features an image of one of the company's de Havilland Dove aircraft.

no loss of seniority, and I had a job in Montgomery as a station agent.

So here I go again from Big-Time Airline Sales Guy back to station agent. You can't imagine how relieved I was to find out that Delta would take me back, especially without any loss of seniority. Thankfully for all those people who had quit other jobs to work in the maintenance facility, Miles Baker also convinced Mr. Reynolds to keep operating that facility, which they did for several months before finally closing it down.

When I left Delta to work for Golden Isles, many people told me that I was crazy, as it was much too risky. I now realize that my leaving Delta for Golden Isles was another example of God steering me in the right direction. If I hadn't left Delta to work for Golden Isles, I have no idea what my life might have been like. As a result of that move, I went back to Montgomery, where I met Jack Sweigart, who played a major role in my being promoted to a position as a Delta sales representative. That promotion was the stepping-stone to the rest of my Delta career.

So once again, I was telling everyone goodbye as I prepared to move back to Montgomery. I didn't have any strong romantic or other ties, so it was just a matter of packing up and moving on.

CHAPTER TWELVE

A Return to Montgomery

When I arrived back in Montgomery in April of 1960, things had changed quite a bit in terms of both the facilities and the people. One of the most significant changes was the new terminal, which was a major improvement over the old terminal, which could only be described as a shack. The new terminal had modern facilities and a fuel truck so you didn't have to drag that fuel hose out to the aircraft. Fred West was still the station manager, and Wink Peterson, David Poole, and Eddie Cooper were still there. Wink had officially been promoted to senior agent. My best friend, Charlie Powell, had been promoted to senior agent in Dallas. There were several new people since my last tour of duty in Montgomery, and Fred had also added a porter to the staff. Fred had not changed at all and still went out of his way to avoid any controversy.

A few months before I went back to Montgomery, Delta had decided to create a sales manager position and had promoted Jack Sweigart from sales rep in Atlanta to the new sales manager position in Montgomery. I was encouraged that Delta was placing more emphasis on sales, as I felt that this might give me an opportunity to learn and help me achieve my goal of getting into sales.

Typically Delta would cover only three days in hotel/motel expenses when I reported to my new job in Montgomery. Fortunately

I met Bill Riggins on my first day on the job, and he told me he had an extra bedroom in his apartment and that I could move in with him. I moved in right away, and we got on very well. Bill grew up not far from Montgomery and visited his family on most of his days off, so I frequently had the apartment to myself. On a few occasions, I went with him to visit his parents.

While Montgomery had a fancy new terminal, the Delta operation was mostly unchanged from my previous tour of duty, except that all four of the current flights were operated with CV-440s, as was a new fifth round-trip to and from Atlanta. I was in Montgomery the first time one of our round-trips was operated with a DC-3. Since we were no longer flying DC-3s, Delta had stopped serving Selma and Hattiesburg.

In 1960, the local Delta stations were still handling the local reservations calls, as was the case in all of the smaller stations. Delta did have "call centers," reservations offices in all of the larger markets such as Chicago, Atlanta, and New York. If the telephone booking involved a connecting flight, we had to call reservations control to get availability for the connecting flights versus going to the old manual availability charts.

The Delta operation at Montgomery was pretty routine, but in the late fifties, the industry began requiring that passengers reconfirm their reservations at least twenty-four hours before departure. Typically when a business traveler deplaned in Montgomery, they stopped by the ticket counter to reconfirm the next leg of their trip. If we had several passengers reconfirming their flights, it was not unusual to take the reservations records for several flights out to the ticket counter so we could expedite the process. Once we had finished reconfirming, we would refile the reservations cards.

On at least one occasion, when I had reconfirmed a large number of reservations, I misfiled all of the reservations cards for a specific flight on a specific date. When we discovered what I had done, we had just about double-booked that flight. Luckily Fred West was able to convince Flight Control to operate an extra section on this flight, otherwise there would have been big problems—including me most likely getting fired.

When I worked in Montgomery the first time, I became friends with all the Eastern agents. When I was there the second time, I reconnected with the people I knew and met some new people, including a single guy named Spencer Baird, and we became good friends and double-dated a lot. Not long after I met him, Spence found a nice furnished house for rent in a residential section of Montgomery. Bill Riggins and I decided to team up with Spence and rent this house.

About this time, I became good friends with a guy who had worked for the police department and was currently working as a private detective. His wife was a beautician, and she introduced me to a young lady who worked with her. Unfortunately it has been so long ago that I can't recall any of their names, but the detective and I spent a good bit of time together.

One night, my private detective friend asked me to go with him, and we rode all the way up to Lake Martin, where we parked outside of a motel. We sat there about an hour, and he wouldn't give me any details about who we were looking for. An hour later, I was shocked to see his wife come out of a motel room with another man. I'm not sure I would have gone with him if I had known he was following his own wife, as I would have been concerned about what he might do. As it turned out, we just drove away. Needless to say, they divorced, and he moved to Orlando, where he went to work for the company that provided security coverage for NASA. We stayed in contact for a long time, but over the years I lost touch with him. As a side benefit of this friendship,

I got to know a lot of the senior people on the Montgomery police force.

In spite of the joint calls with Jack, my work schedule, and social activity, I managed to make a few trips to Georgia to spend time with Dad and my Coggin relatives. My mother was still living in Hurtsboro, Alabama, helping Aunt Opal run their hotel. She met Harley Rigdon, who was a guest in the hotel and a heavy equipment operator working a job in the Hurtsboro area. They dated for a while and got married about the time Harley was finishing the Hurtsboro job. After Harley finished, they moved to his home in Pensacola. Harley was a good man, and I was so pleased that my mom had finally found such a solid person and married him. I visited them at least every two or three months, and they came up to Montgomery a couple of times to see me.

I had been living with Spence and crew in the rental property for a few months when I discovered that both Bob Kirby and Dave Poole had bought houses in a new subdivision on the "Old Selma" highway, only a few miles from the airport. I talked to the Realtor they had dealt with and found out I could get a nice three-bed-room house with almost no money down using my GI benefits. There was just one small issue. Back in those days, the mortgage companies wouldn't lend to a single person, and that was about to kill the deal. My Realtor checked into it and discovered that I could get the mortgage if I were about to get married.

The Realtor told me all I had to do was get a female to sign a statement that we were engaged and going to get married. While I obviously knew many young ladies in Montgomery, I was not about to ask one of them to sign that kind of agreement. Just about the time I was going to walk away from the deal, a Mont-gomery policeman whom I had double-dated with asked his girl-friend to sign the document. We both signed it, and I was on my way to being a happy homeowner for the first time.

The timing was good, as Spence Baird and the other Eastern Air Lines guy I lived with were being transferred to Orlando, and I was going to have to make other arrangements. I also had to deal with the fact that I didn't have much money to buy furniture for my new house. I talked to my mother and stepfather, Harley, and they agreed to loan me five hundred dollars to help with furnishings.

Shortly after I closed on the house, I drove to Pensacola so Mother and Harley could help me shop for used furniture for the bedrooms, living room, den, and kitchen. Harley had a full-size pickup truck, so we loaded the furniture on his truck and drove to Montgomery. Fortunately the house came with major appliances, so that wasn't an issue. I had a record player and later found a good used TV. I had a couple of roommates right off, as Spencer wasn't going to Orlando for a few months, and shortly after I moved in, my good friend Nick Bixby moved in with me. Nick didn't have a car, just a motorcycle, and on cold and rainy days, I let him use my car or drove him where he wanted to go.

One of the ladies who worked for Eastern said she had a beautiful niece that she wanted me to meet, so one night she threw a party at her house and invited several of us from the airport, along with her niece and a few other people. As promised, the niece was one good-looking hot chick, and we dated nonstop for several weeks.

One day she called me at work and said she needed to borrow my car that day, as hers was in the shop. She said she would be back at 4 p.m. to pick me up when my shift ended. So at 4 p.m., I went out front to wait on her, and it got to be 5 p.m., then 5:30, so I called her aunt to see if she knew what was going on. It turned out the niece had written a bunch of bad checks and a warrant had been issued for her arrest, so to avoid being arrested, she had driven my car to Las Vegas. After I worked with the police and her family, she finally agreed to drive the car back to Montgomery, and her brother would meet her and return my car. Needless to say, I never saw her again. The car this "lady" hijacked was my brand-new 1961 Impala convertible.

CHAPTER THIRTEEN

A Life-Changing Move to Washington, DC

Delta DC sales rep
June 1961–April 1965

Based on my brief sales experience at Golden Isles and my contact with Tommy Aycock when he came to the horse races in Hot Springs, I was determined to secure a sales job at Delta.

My key objective was to learn more about what Delta expected from a salesperson. While a lot of other stuff was going on in my life, I took advantage of Jack Sweigart's offer to let me make sales calls with him on my days off. I couldn't do it all the time, but I did it as often as I could in order to pursue my ambition to achieve a career in sales at Delta. Jack was apparently impressed with how I handled myself on these calls and began working on Charlie Knecht, Delta's assistant vice president of sales, and Charlie Mashburn, manager of sales administration, to secure an appointment for me to go over to the General Office and be interviewed for a sales rep position.

It took a little while to secure the appointment, but I was finally invited to Atlanta for an interview. The process was a bit tedious and included a session with Dr. Janus, a psychologist Delta had just begun using to determine whether an applicant had the aptitude for the job and was mentally qualified. I think this whole process started as part of Delta's effort to make sure pilots were mentally stable. I'm not sure Charlie Knecht was impressed, but I could tell right away that Mashburn liked me. Before I went to Atlanta for the interview, I had bought a suit, white shirt, ties, and so forth, as I didn't own a stitch of dress clothes.

The interview apparently came about as a result of a sales rep position being open in Washington, DC. Ernie Massey, a DC sales rep, had been promoted to a military and government sales position in the General Office. The sales rep position had been open a few months since Delta had not been able to find a qualified person who was interested in the position or in relocating to Washington. This fact played a big role in my getting the job. The location of the position was not an issue with me. I just wanted the opportunity.

As part of this interview process, Charlie Mashburn had me fly up to Baltimore for an interview with Ed Mallard, Delta's sales manager there. Prior to his promotion to sales manager, Ed was a sales rep in DC. Charlie Mashburn apparently felt that Ed would have a good feeling for my ability to handle the job in DC.

The interviews with Knecht, Mashburn, and Mallard must have gone well, as a few weeks later, Charlie Mashburn called Sweigart and told him to have me go to DC for an interview with Osgood Willis, the Delta district sales manager in Washington. Shortly after that call from Mashburn, I flew to DC for my interview with Mr. Willis. The Washington sales office was on K Street, right behind the City Ticket Office, and to get to the sales office, you had to ask a ticket agent to announce you. When I went into the ticket office, I was so nervous that I asked to see Willis Osgood instead of Osgood Willis.

The young lady behind the counter smiled and asked, "Do you mean Mr. Osgood Willis?"

I blushed and said, "Yes, please."

I can only assume my interview with Osgood went well, as a couple of weeks later, I was offered the job. The fact that Delta had difficulty finding someone to take that sales job made me more determined to do a great job.

When I first began interviewing for the sales job, I talked with Jimmy Meyers, who worked with me at Delta in Montgomery, about buying my house or just taking over the mortgage if I was successful in securing the new job. We basically cut a deal that included my furniture, as I wasn't sure what my housing situation would be in DC.

My second tour of duty in Montgomery had lasted about fifteen months, a time of some interesting and rewarding adventures filled with some great experiences. I crammed about two years of normal living into those fifteen months, as I was on the go every day.

When I departed Montgomery for my new job in DC, some great memories and new friendships were the most important things I had to show for my time in Montgomery. Once again, I was packing my meager belongings into my car, and off I went.

The five things I value most about my tour of duty as a sales rep in DC are:

- Meeting and marrying Millie.
- Millie giving birth to Jeff.
- The opportunity I had to get to know Shorty Rogers and so many other NASA folks, including several astronauts.
- The friendships I developed with many of the Piedmont Airlines people I worked with, especially Lionel Anders and Sherl Folger.
- The opportunity to demonstrate my sales and management skills.

When I left for DC, I didn't have any idea where I would live.

Before I departed Montgomery, I called Rita Royston, the Washington sales office secretary, and asked her to help me find a furnished room in a boardinghouse. After a little searching, she found me a room about twenty blocks north of the sales office.

The staff in the DC sales office consisted of Osgood Willis, the district sales manager; Rita Royston, the secretary; and John Coleman and George Potter, both sales reps. Rita was a nice lady who did a great job of supporting the sales staff.

Delta also had a government affairs office and a reservations office located on Connecticut Avenue, just a couple of blocks from the sales office. Mr. Bob Griffith was the vice president of government affairs, and Millie Shell was his secretary. The reservations office was managed by Dave James and had a staff of about twenty-five reservations agents and supervisors.

Shortly after I reported to DC, Mr. Willis took me over to meet Mr. Griffith, Millie, and the reservations staff. My visit to Mr. Griffith's office was the first time I met Millie, and I think I recall that she winked at me during that visit, but she will of course deny that.

A few days after I reported to DC, Eastern Air Lines, our major competitor, and a couple of other airlines went on strike. As you can imagine, the Delta reservations office in DC was overwhelmed with additional calls. Since our reservations staff wasn't able to handle the call volume, there wasn't much point in George, John, and me going out on sales calls, and we were assigned to assist the reservations staff in handling the heavy call volume. My experience in handling reservations calls came in handy.

Mr. Griffith's office was just down the hall from the reservations office, and to walk from Mr. Griffith's office to the restrooms, a person had to walk right past the reservations office. I didn't think much about it at the time, but Millie sure made a lot of trips

Getting to meet astronauts like Alan Shepard, center, was one of the highlights of my time as a Delta sales rep in Washington, DC.

to the ladies' room during the couple of weeks I worked in Reservations. I can still see that wink she would flash at me as she walked by. I am just kidding, as I was the one doing the winking.

Since the DC sales office was short a sales rep, George Potter and John Coleman had been covering the key accounts in that territory. I spent the first few days getting my feet on the ground, but beginning the second week, George and John took me around to introduce me to my major accounts. Those intro calls lasted two or three weeks.

George and Helen Potter lived in Arlington, Virginia, and when I first arrived in DC, they took me under their wing. They had a daughter who was born after I moved to Washington, about the same time my son, Jeff, was born.

John Coleman and his wife, Jackie, had two or three girls and lived in Maryland. I didn't have much contact with Jackie in the early days. John and I did make a few joint calls, mostly during my training.

Shortly after I arrived, Osgood expanded my territory and added Central and Western Maryland, Southern Virginia, and part of West Virginia. These areas had been mostly neglected over the last few years.

My major accounts in DC included big government agencies like the Department of Agriculture, Department of Commerce, NASA, the Government Printing Office, the Department of Health, the Department of Education, the National Institutes of Health, a couple of Air Force offices, and some large travel agencies. My accounts outside of DC included several large travel agencies and Piedmont Airlines. Piedmont connected a large number of passengers to Delta at our Atlanta hub.

In the 1950s, the airline industry developed a credit card called an Air Travel Plan or "ATP." Bank credit cards and the American Express credit card weren't yet widely used. One of the best ways for a sales rep to get on the Big Boss's radar was to convince a business account to sign up for an ATP account. One day a guy called the office and wanted to talk with someone about opening an ATP account, and I happened to be standing at Rita's desk when she took the call. I immediately told her I would take care of it.

I briefed the man on all the details of the card and arranged to meet him for lunch, and hopefully he would sign a contract. He said he wasn't ready to do the deal at that moment and would get back to me. A week or so went by before he called to invite me to join him and his girlfriend at the swimming pool of the Marriott on Fourteenth Street. He said to bring a date!

There were a few ladies I could have invited, but I had been looking for an opportunity to ask Millie for a date, so I called and asked if she would go with me, and she said yes. I picked her up at her apartment, and we drove over to the Marriott. Much to my surprise, she had on a red-and-white bikini underneath whatever she was wearing. Needless to say, I was smitten, and we began to date occasionally.

I had grown weary of my room in the rooming house, and I think they had grown weary of me. While I was working in Reservations, I met a nice young man named Jon Smith. Jon had a two-bedroom apartment in Arlington and was looking for a roommate, so I moved in with Jon.

Now in those days at Delta, Eastern was our major competitor, as they overlapped us on almost every route we flew out of Washington National and Baltimore. They also had the advantage of serving a number of points in Florida and the Northeast that Delta didn't service out of DC, making them more important to the major accounts. American, United, Allegheny, and TWA were also marginal competitors, but we didn't compete head-to-head with them as we did with Eastern Air Lines.

Delta had an account record called a "House Record Card," and the sales rep was required to create a House Record Card on all of their accounts. The rep was required to list the names of the key people along with their title, phone numbers, the destinations their travelers visited most frequently, and if we could get this information, their volume of travel. Depending on their volume of travel, we were also assigned a frequency of calls on that account. The norm was to call on a very large account every thirty days and a marginal account maybe every ninety days or every six months. Each time we called on the account, we made a note of the date, the purpose of the call, and what was accomplished.

Some reps foolishly made notes on the House Record Card about people in the account that they didn't like. When you were planning your calls for that week, you would line up your House

Record Cards, or HRCs, for each day, and that would be your plan for the week. I know some of my peers and competitors faked some of their calls, and occasionally, when I got involved with George Potter and his extended lunch hour or early cocktail hour, I did the same thing. After being in a territory long enough, a good rep could make their calls without ever taking their HRCs with them. My ability to recall what was on the HRCs actually helped get me promoted.

After my indoctrination, I started getting involved in my new job and got better acquainted with my accounts. All of the government agencies had a travel department that managed their travel and booked their reservations. These were the people that I concentrated on as I sought to learn more about my accounts.

In some of the larger military and government agencies, the airlines operated ticketing offices called JAMTOs, or joint airline/military traffic offices. It was important to pay attention to the personnel in these offices, as they had a huge influence on which airline the travelers chose. I spent a lot of time with these folks, including taking them to lunch.

It didn't take me long to figure out which of my government accounts were the most important based on the markets Delta served and the travel patterns of their travelers. For example, many people in the agriculture department flew to points in the Southeast, Delta's bread and butter, so I paid a lot of attention to the Department of Agriculture. The Department of Commerce had very little travel to the Southeast, so I made only periodic courtesy calls on these folks. Since the Centers for Disease Control (CDC) were located in Atlanta, there was a ton of travel to Atlanta by the CDC and the National Institutes of Health (NIH).

My best account and the one I enjoyed calling on most was NASA. They often traveled to Houston and other points in the

Southeast and Southwest. I had a special relationship with the ladies who managed most of the NASA travel. To support them, when key NASA people were flying with Delta, I went to the Baltimore airport to make sure the NASA officials received excellent service. My counterpart at Eastern didn't bother to go this extra mile.

Both NASA and the Department of Agriculture had offices in Maryland that I called on frequently. The NASA guys were all scientists and very serious. The only thing they wanted to talk about was our service and the need for more flights to Houston. The agriculture office was quite different and my second favorite account. Both of the ladies who worked in the travel office, Doris and Sara, liked to have a two-hour lunch with several drinks. Occasionally I would ask George Potter to go with me, as handling these two ladies alone was a real challenge. There were times that I didn't remember how I got back to the office, and on other occasions, I remember helping Doris back to her office or to her car so she could go home.

On a sad note, I was at lunch with these ladies the day that President Kennedy was assassinated, and we were so deep into our drinks that we were not aware of it until I took them back to their office. That was such a sad day that everything just came to a halt.

The National Institutes of Health (NIH) was another great account, as the staff—especially the lady who ran the travel department—was partial to Delta and very nice to me. I spent a lot of time with them, as they controlled much of the CDC travel to Atlanta. Osgood Willis and I took her to lunch one day at a fancy restaurant in Bethesda. Both Osgood and I thought the other had come prepared to pick up the check, but unfortunately, we didn't have enough cash between us to pay it. Things were about to get embarrassing when Osgood remembered that he had a sample ATP card in his wallet, and many of the more expensive restaurants accepted the ATP card. The waiter charged our lunch to Osgood's card, and that was it. I took the NIH lady to her office, and Osgood went back to the sales office and cashed a check. Then he returned to the restaurant, paid the bill, and tore up the ATP charge. Thank goodness for the ATP card.

Like most Delta sales reps, I was responsible for calling on cargo accounts as well as passenger accounts. Out at the Delta freight office at the airport, I went through the airway bills to identify our best airfreight customers. I discovered that the US Government printing office was shipping a lot of material on Delta to the West Coast. After some research, I identified the general manager who made the decision on which airline to use for certain shipments. I called to thank him for all the business they were giving Delta to the West Coast. He said, "What do you mean those idiots in Shipping are putting these shipments on Delta? I'll put a stop to that nonsense." The lesson I learned was, "If you see that you are getting business you shouldn't be getting, just keep your mouth shut."

Eastern West Virginia was now in my territory, and there were a couple of larger travel agencies in Charleston, West Virginia, that no one in the Washington sales office had ever called on. I got some business passes on Lake Central Airlines to fly to Charleston and visit these accounts, so I made appointments to see them. I tried twice to make the trip, and both times the weather in Charleston was so bad the flights were canceled. The DC-3s that Lake Central flew didn't have sophisticated navigation equipment. After two attempts, I gave up on Charleston to focus on those accounts that I could reach more easily. Two of those accounts were large travel agencies in Hagerstown, Maryland, and both of them required a lot of attention. They were on my quarterly call frequency list. When I called on these agencies, I also called on a couple of corporate accounts in Western Maryland.

Some of our larger travel agencies were located in Central Virginia, and when their business was combined with the volume of connecting traffic generated by Piedmont, this area was a high priority, so I spent a lot of time there. To increase the volume of connecting traffic, I also "courted" the Piedmont sales managers in that area. I succeeded in developing a great relationship with the Piedmont sales managers in Roanoke, Lynchburg, and Richmond. Lionel Anders, Piedmont's sales manager in Roanoke, was the most supportive. It didn't take long for George Shed, Delta's manager of interline sales, to become aware that the volume of interline sales from Piedmont via Delta's Atlanta hub had increased significantly. He apparently did a little research and determined that the traffic was coming from the markets where I had such a good relationship with the Piedmont folks. When he understood what was happening, he put a few stars in my crown.

By the fall of 1961, Millie and I were dating pretty seriously and even talking about getting married. Once we decided to marry, we debated about telling Millie's parents our plans, as they were living in Dayton, Ohio, and weren't in a position to host a wedding. It would have been difficult for us to take that much time off, so we decided not to tell anyone and just elope, which we did on November 1, 1961. We got our marriage license at the courthouse in Arlington, Virginia, and were married by Dr. Miden, a justice of the peace. Prior to our decision to get married, we had found a furnished apartment near Arlington, and after the wedding, we moved in that afternoon.

Over the next few weeks, we made arrangements to visit our respective parents and introduce them to their new daughter-in-law or son-in-law. Millie's mom and dad made me feel like part of the family right from the first meeting. My parents were also excited that I had met a very beautiful young lady and was going to settle down.

After living in the furnished apartment for several months, we wanted a nicer place and some furniture of our own. We found a place in a small but nice apartment building in Arlington. Millie had saved five hundred dollars in cash, and we used it to buy several pieces of furniture. We also arranged to meet Millie's mom and dad in their Tennessee home to pick up some furniture Millie had bought when she was living at home. Our new apartment was much closer to DC, which made our commute easier. In September of 1962, Millie became pregnant with Jeff but continued to work until a few weeks before he was born. We have a great picture of a very pregnant Millie when we visited my mom and Harley in Pensacola.

When Millie called her doctor and told him she was having contractions, he told her to be at the hospital at noon. We did as the doctor said and got into a room about 1 p.m. I had planned to stay with Millie until Jeff was born, but later that evening, the doctor called and told me to go home and said he would let me know when the baby was born. Early in the morning, I got a call that I had a healthy baby boy who weighed eight pounds. We were all set up for mommy and baby in our little one-bedroom apartment. Millie's mom came to help her with Jeff. We were also very cramped in the one-bedroom apartment, so we started looking for a two-bedroom apartment and found one not far from where we were living.

Our families were excited about Jeff, and we made a few trips to see our parents so they could spend some time with him. As Christmas of 1963 approached, Millie and I really wanted to have a Christmas tree for Jeff. A few weeks before Christmas, I got a part-time job after work in a department store that sold Christmas decorations, and we bought our decorations at a discount. We still use some of these original Christmas decorations on our tree.

While much was happening in my personal life, a couple of important things occurred that influenced my career. My current boss, Osgood Willis, was promoted to director of meeting and convention sales, based in the General Office, and he was succeeded by Pat Bernal. Pat was Delta's district sales manager in Jackson, Mississippi, a position he had held for many years. It was going to take Pat a few weeks to make the move, and I was temporarily put in charge of the DC sales office, which I took as a vote of confidence. Shortly after Pat arrived in DC, George Potter resigned to accept a position at the Air Transport Association (ATA). The Pentagon was one of Potter's major accounts, and Pat asked me to add the Pentagon to my long list of accounts. I jumped at the opportunity, as the Pentagon was our single most important account. Pat and I hit it off well, and after he settled in, I began taking him around to meet a number of our key accounts. He adapted quickly.

When I started calling on the Pentagon, I met Ed Maloney, manager of the Pentagon JAMTO (joint airline/military traffic office) operation, and I was impressed with him, as he really knew the government business. As our friendship developed, I told him that if a sales rep position came available in the DC office, I would recommend that he be interviewed for the position if he was interested. He told me he would welcome the opportunity, so I told Pat about Ed.

One day, I received a call from Ernie Massey advising me that he wanted to come up to DC so we could do a joint call on the Pentagon and some of my other accounts. That morning when I left the office, I forgot to put my House Record Cards in my briefcase. While I was worried about Ernie's reaction to my forgetting my HRCs, it ended up being a positive and not a negative development. Ernie was blown away that I knew every person we called on, where they were located, and everything we needed to know about their business.

It wasn't long after those joint calls with Ernie that Pat Bernal called me into his office and told me that Delta Vice President of Sales Charlie Knecht had called and wanted me to consider taking the district sales manager job in either Chattanooga or Jackson. The Jackson position was open because Tommy Aycock, who had replaced Pat Bernal as district sales manager in Jackson, had not worked out. Since Millie's parents lived near Knoxville, just a couple of hours from Chattanooga, I was tempted to take that position, but everyone told me that would be a mistake since Jackson was so much larger and so important to Delta.

So I said I would go to Jackson if that was what they wanted me to do. In a couple of days, Pat told me I had the Jackson job and a sixty-dollar-a-month raise. Millie worked in an office next door to the Delta sales office, and I called and told her to meet me in the coffee shop and that I had some great news. We were both excited about this new opportunity and the salary increase. Pat told me later that having Ed Maloney waiting in the wings to replace me as a sales rep in the DC office moved things along much quicker than normal. Ed had a long and successful career with Delta and retired as director of military and government sales.

CHAPTER FOURTEEN

A New Job in Jackson, Mississippi

Delta Sales Manager–Jackson, Mississippi
April 1965–September 1967

Since my replacement had already been selected, I was free to make my initial trip to Jackson. I quickly made arrangements to visit and learn more about the city and the Delta staff. Since Millie needed to be at home to take care of Jeff, we decided I would start the house hunting during my visit to Jackson. We also decided that if I found the right place on this initial trip, I could make the deal without Millie seeing the house. Fortunately for us, a large number of FHA-repossessed houses were on the market in Jackson, and the real estate broker that Pat Bernal had introduced me to found the perfect house for us in a couple of days. The best part was that I didn't have to make a down payment. The monthly payment— including principal, interest, and insurance—was $117.

When Millie came down to see the house, she loved it. With my $60-per-month salary increase, my new salary was $600 a month, and with the low house payment, we had enough money to live comfortably. We were also blessed with good neighbors, especially Ted and Betty Blackburn and their two daughters, one of whom was just a couple of years older than Jeff.

My office was attached to the Delta City Ticket Office in the

ORCHIDS IN JACKSON

Jackson's 10,000th passenger for the month of June, Mrs. D. C. Lutken, shown boarding a Delta CV-880 to New York, receives a complimentary Delta orchid. On hand for the occasion are, from left, Captain Tom Turner, Jackson Airport manager; Mrs. Lutken, daughter Melissa, husband Mr. D. C. Lutken, and R. W. Coggin, Jackson sales manager for Delta.

DELTA DIGEST · 27

Heidelberg Hotel, only twenty minutes from our house. The Heidelberg was in the center of downtown Jackson, near the offices of many of our key customers and civic contacts.

The City Ticket Office was staffed by three ladies who were also my administrative support. Frances Lutz was the supervisor and the most senior of the three. The City Ticket Office (CTO) was very busy, as many people came to the CTO to make reservations and buy tickets.

After a couple of months, Millie decided to go back to work. We found a nice older lady to look after Jeff while Millie worked. Millie secured a great administrative position in the executive office with MPI, the largest company in Jackson. Since she was my wife, Millie took a little heat from the MPI management staff when they were unhappy with Delta, but she hung in there and continued working for them right up to the time of our next move.

Though on a much smaller scale than Atlanta, the Jackson area had evolved as a transportation and business hub due to its geographic location, the North-South and East-West highway system, and good rail service. Delta played a major role in the economy, as we had a large operation at Jackson, with flights to all points up and down the Mississippi Valley from Chicago/Detroit to New Orleans/Houston plus frequent service between Dallas and Atlanta. Our most prized service was a one-stop Convair 880 jet flight from Jackson to Newark, New Jersey, via Birmingham. Delta's only competition consisted of Southern Airways and Trans Texas. Both had very few flights, which they operated with DC-3s.

My tour of duty in Jackson was a rewarding experience in which I learned a great deal about managing people and representing Delta outside the sales area. I also learned that when you replace a person who has been in that position for a long time and has grown stale, you find many opportunities to be creative if you're willing to put forth the time and effort. I also learned quickly that in the environment that had been created in Jackson, there was great resistance to change.

One example of this resistance to change occurred when I put a large display in the window of the City Ticket Office, announcing that Delta would be replacing our propeller service to New Orleans and Chicago with new DC-9 jet aircraft. The CTO staff was shocked that I would place such a commercial display in the window. They considered it crude and unsophisticated. It wasn't long before they realized this was a great way to get the message out about our new DC-9 jet service.

The manager of Jackson's largest travel agency was so impressed with the attention the CTO display received that she asked me if I could design a window display for her agency, which was just up the street. Delta had cut a deal with the Atlanta Braves involving discounted ticket prices, and I worked out a deal where a person could get a round-trip airfare and ticket to a Braves game for $64. I used that deal to create a window display for the agency, and she loved it.

As the district sales manager, I was the Delta go-to person, and I had many responsibilities not related to sales. Some of those responsibilities included:

- I was responsible for the reservations office or "call center," as it is called today. I appreciated how important it was for a person in my position to be visible to the folks who worked in Reservations, and I made it a priority to visit the reservations office frequently.
- I managed Delta's relationship with Tom Turner, the state-appointed manager of the Jackson airport. Tom was a tough guy to deal with. He felt that Delta's strong position at Jackson was the primary reason the other major airlines wouldn't include Jackson in their request for new markets during the Southern Transcontinental Route Case.
- It was very important that I maintain a close relationship with Ray Minks, Delta's Jackson station manager. I spent a good bit of time with Ray and his senior staff. Ray was a great guy.
- I was also responsible for lobbying the state legislature and state officials. As part of that responsibility, I worked closely with Bud Moore, director of the Mississippi State Department of Aviation. I had a great relationship with Bud thanks to the great relationship Pat Bernal had developed. Bud and Ray Minks were good friends, and Millie and I

occasionally had dinner with Bud and the Minkses.

- One of my most challenging responsibilities involved representing Delta with the Jackson Chamber of Commerce. They were not always Delta friendly, as they also felt that Delta's dominance in the Jackson market kept other major airlines from trying to secure approval to add new service at Jackson.

- The other major issue I had to deal with was the number of people who claimed to be Mr. Woolman's "best friends." Believe me, there were lots of those folks in Jackson, and some of them actually were his friends. Any time one of these people had a complaint about Delta service or a lost or damaged bag, the issue frequently ended up on my desk, with the person threatening to go to Mr. Woolman if I didn't resolve the issue to their satisfaction.

One day I received a call from my boss, Charlie Knecht, vice president of sales. He called to tell me that Mr. Woolman had gotten a complaint about me from a friend of Pat Bernal. This gentleman told Mr. Woolman that I was very unfriendly and wouldn't take the time to sit in the lobby of the Heidelberg Hotel and play checkers with him and his friends as Pat had done over the years. Mr. Knecht told me that was a great compliment, and we both laughed about it. I don't think Mr. Knecht ever mentioned this to Pat, but I certainly kidded Pat about it on several occasions.

One of our largest accounts outside of Jackson was the US Army Corps of Engineers in Vicksburg, and I visited them as frequently as my schedule permitted. Shortly after I reported to my new job in Jackson, Delta took delivery of our first DC-9s, and Jackson was one of the first cities to be served with these new jets. The new aircraft greatly improved the service on the routes it flew and made a favorable impression on the community, which helped

It was big news when Delta offered its inaugural DC-9 service in Jackson, Mississippi, and here I am celebrating the arrival of these new jets with Ray Minks, Delta's Jackson station manager.

to ease some of the tension related to Delta's strong position in the market.

When we took delivery of the DC-9s, we used one of these first aircraft to replace a DC-7 on the Chicago, St. Louis, Memphis, and Jackson to New Orleans flights. The DC-9 cut more than an hour off the elapsed time between Jackson and Chicago due to the significantly reduced ground times and, of course, the faster speed.

I leveraged the new DC-9 service to improve our relationship with community business and civic leaders. Basically, I used the DC-9 service to demonstrate how Delta was improving air service to Jackson. The night we inaugurated the service with the DC-9, Tom Miller, Delta's senior vice president of sales and marketing, visited Jackson to cut the ribbon of the first DC-9 flight. I have some great pictures of that event.

Geographically, my territory was quite large and included all of Central Mississippi, east to Meridian, west to Vicksburg and Monroe, Louisiana, and Southern Arkansas. Servicing my major accounts in and around the Jackson area combined with all of my other responsibilities didn't leave me much time to call on accounts in remote areas. But I did call on key accounts in Vicksburg, Meridian, and Monroe as frequently as my schedule permitted. Vicksburg was a priority, as the Corps of Engineers had a large facility there and frequently traveled to Washington.

I enjoyed working with the Monroe and Meridian station managers, who did a great job of representing Delta. My primary justification for going to Monroe was the fact that several major Delta shareholder families lived there, including the Biedenharns. Delta's annual shareholder meeting was also held in Monroe.

During my time in Jackson, a number of funny incidents involved my predecessor, Pat Bernal. In reviewing Pat's House Record Cards, I discovered that he had been calling on the John

Deere parts distributor on a regular basis, as they were one of our better cargo accounts. Since it appeared that Pat had been regularly calling on the owner of the business, I decided I had better make a call, especially since no one had called on them since Pat moved to DC. I drove out to their office, walked up to the counter, and asked the lady there if I could speak to Mr. Johnson. No sooner had the words come out of my mouth than she went into hysterics, crying and sobbing. A man came over and said, "You'll have to forgive her, as you just asked for her late husband, who died a couple of years ago, and just the mention of his name sets her off." I apologized profusely, explained who I was and why I was there, and asked them to please call me if they ever needed assistance.

After I made contact with our key accounts in the metro Jackson area, my next priority was to call on those key accounts outside of Jackson. I reviewed Pat's House Record Cards to identify the key accounts north and east of Jackson. According to Pat's HRCs, one of our best customers was Superior Coach Company, located about fifty miles north of Jackson. When I developed my call list, I put Mr. Reynolds, the president of Superior Coach, at the top of my list. When I entered their offices, I gave the receptionist my business card and told her I would like to see Mr. Reynolds. She went into his office. In a few seconds, he came rushing out and wanted to know if there had been a crash and whether any of his people had been killed. I was so taken aback I stammered for a few minutes and said, "No, sir, I'm just here to tell you how much we appreciate your business and want to know if we're serving your needs."

He got this strange look on his face and said, "Are you telling me that airlines call on their customers to thank them for their business?"

I replied, "Yes, sir, Delta does."

He just stood there and laughed for a moment and invited me

The sales promotion that I created in a window at our City Ticket Office in Jackson, Mississippi, was so effective that I was asked to create one for the Rightway Travel Agency just up the street.

to join him for a cup of coffee. We had a great relationship even after I moved away.

Another story related to Pat involves a lunch I had with the lady who ran the IRS office in Jackson. Supervisor Frances Lutz and the other two young ladies were aware that I was taking this female customer to lunch, and when I came out of my office, Francis asked, "Which one of us do you want to join you for lunch?"

I replied, "What in the heck are you talking about?"

She said, "Oh, anytime Mr. Bernal took a lady to lunch, he

asked one of us to go with him. People in Jackson tend to gossip when they see a married man or lady having lunch with a male or female companion who is not their husband or wife unless there's a third person joining them."

I told Frances and the other ladies they could just forget that idea, as I was very comfortable taking a female customer to lunch without a chaperone.

Pat was active in the Jackson Rotary Club, and I had not been there long before I was asked to join. It was the number one civic organization for the key businesspeople in Jackson, so I joined. I leveraged my membership in the Jackson Rotary Club to attend Rotary meetings around Mississippi and the Northern Louisiana area, which gave me the opportunity to meet key business leaders in the smaller towns. Most of them had never seen an airline sales-person before and spent a lot of time talking to me.

The day the president of the Jackson Rotary Club announced that I had been promoted and would be moving to Philadelphia, two elderly longtime members came over and said, "You are going to like Neshoba County, as it is a great place." They thought I was moving to Philadelphia, Mississippi, as they could not conceive of anyone moving from Jackson to Philadelphia, Pennsylvania.

While I spent a lot of time on my work life in Jackson, my per-sonal life was also great. Millie and I spent as much time with Jeff as we could, as he was growing up so fast. Fortunately, we had a nice big backyard, and Jeff spent a lot of time playing in the sand-box. We also took advantage of every opportunity for him to see his grandparents, as they all loved him so much.

All three sets of parents visited us, and it was a great and un-expected pleasure to have Millie's mom and dad come down from Tennessee to visit. My mother and stepfather, Harley, drove over from Pensacola a couple of times, and my mom really enjoyed spending time with Jeff.

Also during this time, one of my neighbors talked me into umpiring a Little League Baseball game that his son was playing in. In the second inning, I called a runner safe at home plate in a very close play. All of the parents and the manager of the other team went wild, hollering and accusing me of making a bad call. I took the umpire gear off, threw it on the ground, and walked off the field, never to go back. I never umpired another Little League Baseball game.

One day, I received a call from my boss, Charlie Knecht, asking if I would consider taking the district sales manager job in Philadelphia. The job was available because Wayne Schweitzer, the district sales manager there, had been promoted to district sales manager in New York City.

We had been in Jackson almost two years and had met lots of nice people, both personally and professionally, and we also had wonderful neighbors. We had spent a lot of money upgrading our house and were happy living there.

Jackson was also a convenient location for my parents and other relatives to visit. For all those reasons, we were prepared to live in Jackson for a long time. These factors made my decision to accept the Philadelphia job very difficult, but after lots of discussions with Millie about the pros and cons of taking the job, we decided that I should accept it. I called Mr. Knecht and told him I would take the job.

CHAPTER FIFTEEN

On to Philadelphia

District Sales Manager
Philadelphia, Pennsylvania
Fall of 1966 to Summer of 1968

After officially being named Delta's Philadelphia district sales manager, I scheduled a trip to Philadelphia to meet the staff and learn about their responsibilities.

The Philadelphia staff consisted of an excellent secretary, Mary Ann Lofthouse; the sales assistant, Ellen; and three sales reps, Peggy Kane, Jim Ramage, and Ernie Giverton. The staff at the City Ticket Office included a supervisor and one agent. The CTO was

R. W. Coggin   J. J. Sedlacek   J. F. Donohue
THESE MEN made business news last week: Robert W. Coggin was named Philadelphia district sales manager for Delta Air Lines, succeeding Wayne Schweitzer, who becomes district sales manager, New York . . . John J. Sedlacek was promoted to Mid-Atlantic area sales manager, I-T-E Circuit Breaker Co. . . . John F. Donohue was appointed general manager of the Bellevue-Stratford Hotel.

The Philadelphia Sunday Bulletin *and the* Philadelphia Daily News *announce my promotion to Philadelphia district sales manager.*

in a hotel lobby across the street from the sales office.

After a couple of weeks in Philadelphia, I had the impression that my responsibilities and workload in Philadelphia were going to be a walk in the park compared to my responsibilities in Jackson. In Jackson, I was "Mr. Everything," and in Philadelphia, I was "Bob Who?" But the personal side of life was a little more challenging here, because Jackson had a much less expensive cost of living.

One of the most significant differences in the two markets was that Delta had lots of competitors in Philadelphia versus almost none in Jackson. Delta was a small player in the Philadelphia market, with about 10 percent of the airline service, and our primary markets were Atlanta, New Orleans, Houston, and the connecting opportunities via our Atlanta hub.

My territory included all of Eastern and Central Pennsylvania and as far west as Penn State, Southern New Jersey north to Princeton, and all of Delaware. A number of major corporate accounts were in my area, including companies such as DuPont. In the 1960s, several major pharmaceutical companies were also headquartered in Philadelphia.

For the most part, I inherited a good sales staff that did an acceptable job managing their accounts. There were, of course, several major travel agency accounts that required a lot of attention.

When I started exploring where we would live, it didn't take much time to figure out that on my Delta salary, we couldn't afford to live on the Philadelphia side of the Delaware River, so I started looking in New Jersey, where both Peggy Kane and Jim Ramage lived. It was obvious that we would have to sell the house in Jackson before we could even think about looking for a house or apartment in Philadelphia. After I returned from the first Philadelphia visit, we put our house on the market, hoping to walk away with a minimum of three thousand dollars in cash, as we had made a number of improvements since buying the house. The housing market in Jackson was still tough for sellers, and fortunately for us, a couple soon came by and looked at the house. We were anxious to sell so we could move on to Philadelphia, and we accepted their offer, but in the end, we didn't have sufficient funds to make a down payment on a house in the Philadelphia/New Jersey area.

On my next trip, I looked at an apartment complex in Stratford, New Jersey, which Peggy Kane had recommended, and I found a nice ground-floor apartment that I really liked. I arranged for Millie to fly up and look at the apartment, and we decided that was where we would live. Stratford was a good location, as it was just a few miles across the river from my office, pretty close to the airport, and near some nice shopping areas. The apartment was also close to where Peggy and Jim lived. We enjoyed living there, as we had some great neighbors and made many lasting friendships.

One thing I'll never forget about the move to Philadelphia was the phone call I received on my second visit there. A friend was calling to let me know that Mr. Woolman had passed away. That was truly a sad and depressing day and really put a damper on any excitement I had related to the promotion.

While Delta was a smaller player in Philadelphia, we were fortunate that the Delta customer service in Philadelphia was far better than Eastern's. In those days, customer service was key to success, as there were no Frequent Flyer programs to drive loyalty, and we operated our flights with reasonably high load factors.

After I settled into my new office and got acquainted with my staff and key accounts, the next task on my to-do list was getting to know the Delta team at the airport. I had already heard some interesting stories about Bill Farris, the Delta station manager, and his long lunch hours with his friend Robert Baker, the American

Airlines city manager. They apparently did lunch frequently, and according to the rumor mill, they usually spent most of the lunch hour enjoying a beverage and not eating. Again according to the rumor mill, my predecessor, Wayne Schweitzer, joined them occasionally. My staff shared stories with me of how he would bounce off the wall when he came through the office door after a lunch with these two guys.

About the second or third time I visited with Bill Farris, the Delta station manager, he invited me to join him and Baker for lunch at their favorite local tavern. It turned into a three-hour lunch, and most of the time was spent enjoying a few choice beverages.

Delta had a very senior crew at the Philadelphia airport, and some were quite good, especially at the ticket counter. A gentleman by the name of Carlos Augsotrazi was the ticket counter supervisor, and he did a great job. One day when I visited the airport to talk to Carlos, he was very busy, as Eastern had a delayed Atlanta flight that departed about the same time as a Delta flight to Atlanta. The Eastern passengers were standing in a line at the boarding gate, waiting for more information on their delayed flight. Carlos went over to the Eastern gate and quietly worked his way down the line, telling the Eastern passengers that Delta had seats on their next flight to Atlanta, and several people got out of line and went over to Delta. Back in those days, tickets were not so restricted and were easily interchangeable.

The airline community in Philadelphia was relatively small, and I quickly became friends with most of my peers. I had a special friendship with Wally Rice, the American Airlines district sales manager. It was while I was in Philadelphia that I became acquainted with a travel industry organization called SKAL. It was difficult to become a member of SKAL, as you had to be in a key management position, and they took a limited number of members from each industry sector. I was invited to join after I had been in Philadelphia about six months.

At home, our personal life was centered on the great friends we had made in the apartment complex where we lived. Since the grandparents were always so anxious to see Jeff, we did make a few trips to visit our parents, but none of them visited us during our relatively short tour of duty in Philadelphia. They knew we were living in a small apartment and didn't have a lot of room for company, and except for my mother and Harley, none of them had ever stayed in a hotel or motel.

Through my connections with the sales managers of some of the radio stations, we were invited to go to some Phillies games and Eagles football games. Millie, Jeff, and I spent most of our leisure time with the two couples who became our best friends. Lots of children lived in the apartment complex, and Jeff didn't have any trouble finding friends to spend time with.

I enjoyed working with my sales team and had some interesting experiences and a few challenging ones. A couple that I remember involved Jim Ramage. The first time I made joint calls with Jim that we had arranged for him, he was to pick me up at the apartment, and we were going to make sales calls in Dover. When I got in his car, I discovered that most of the floorboard was missing below the front passenger seat. I kept my feet pulled up all the way to Dover and made sure I didn't drop anything. On another occasion, Jim was working with Talmadge Travel on a group who planned to attend the Super Bowl in New Orleans, and Jim had committed to securing the Super Bowl tickets. We got right up to the date before the group was supposed to travel to New Orleans to attend the Super Bowl, and Jim had failed to secure any tickets to the game. I don't recall all the details, but I made some phone calls and secured the tickets. It all worked out, but I could have been nasty.

I arranged to make joint calls with Ernie Giverton in Eastern and Central Pennsylvania, including Harrisburg, where we had several important accounts. We also made calls in the area around Penn State. We drove through the coal-mining region, where the coal in the mines had been burning for several years, and that was quite interesting.

Ernie was okay but not always as thorough with his follow-up as I required, and I probably demanded more of him than my predecessor. Subsequently, Ernie decided that he would resign and explore other opportunities. I replaced Ernie with a great young man named Jerry DeShong. Most of my calls with Peggy Kane were in the city or in our New Jersey territory. Peggy had a great relationship with her accounts, and I rarely needed to give her much direction.

I enjoyed my time in Philadelphia. I made some great friends and also learned a lot about how the advertising industry operated, especially as it related to radio and the newspaper business. The knowledge I gained helped me when I was promoted to district sales manager and later director of sales and marketing in New York. I had great friends in both of those areas, with the sales guy at the *Philadelphia Enquirer* becoming one of my best friends. He lived in the country, and on a couple of occasions, he invited me to hunt pheasants with him and his two sons.

By the summer of 1968, I had been in Philadelphia almost two years, and we were looking at the possibility of buying a house in Haddonfield, New Jersey. Jeff was almost four years old, and we were exploring the options for him to go to kindergarten. With all of that in the works, combined with the expectation that I would have a long tour of duty in Philadelphia, I wasn't prepared for the life-changing call I received from my regional manager, Johnny Shad.

Johnny called to let me know that Wayne Schweitzer, the district director of New York sales and marketing, was being promoted to a new government affairs position in the General Office, and Johnny said I was a strong candidate to replace Wayne in New York. My first and immediate reaction to Johnny's suggestion that I consider taking the job wasn't no, it was "Hell no!"

We wanted to buy a house, and I knew that based on Delta's salary policies, and considering the cost of real estate in the New York City area, we would never be able to buy a house if I took the New York job. I was also concerned that I didn't have the skills and experience to handle the job.

I called my good friend Whit Hawkins—like Johnny, he was also a regional sales manager—and asked him to try to protect me if management decided to punish me for not taking the New York job. A few days passed, and I began to question my decision to turn down an opportunity to run one of the largest field sales operations in the Delta system, plus a very large reservations office/call center.

(FOR INTRA COMPANY CORRESPONDENCE ONLY)

DATE: July 31, 1968

TO: Mr. Robert W. Coggin
District Sales Manager - PHL

FROM: Senior Vice President-Administration

SUBJECT:

Dear Bob:

Congratulations on your promotion to DSM-NYC! You have some
illustrious folks to follow there, but I'm sure that under
your direction our business will boom.

Please don't hesitate to call on me if I can ever help.

Cordially,

Tom

WTB-hst   W. T. Beebe

(FOR INTRACOMPANY   DELTA   CORRESPONDENCE ONLY)

CONFIDENTIAL

DATE: September 9, 1969

TO: District Director - Traffic and Sales - NYC

FROM: Regional Sales Manager - Eastern

SUBJECT: Personal

Dear Bob:

This will merely confirm our phone conversation of the
other day when I informed you of your promotion to District Director - Traffic and Sales and a $75 per month
salary increase effective September 1, 1969.

I have a conviction you understand your new responsibilities and that you will follow the dual management
concept to the letter and as it is envisioned. A
periodic review of S.P. 46 is encouraged and perhaps
it should be done jointly by you and your ADSM/DSM.

I'm certain you fully realize the large job ahead for
all of us, and particularly in the New York area. It
means a great deal to me to know you are running the
show in New York. Congratulations again on your well
deserved promotion.

Best regards,

John J. Shad

JJS/mh

cc: Employment (For personnel file of Robert W. Coggin)

CHAPTER SIXTEEN

My Tour of Duty in New York City

District Sales Manager and later Director of Sales and Marketing New York City Spring 1968 to June 1979

I strongly believe that God sent me to New York so that I would have the opportunity to gain the knowledge and experience that would prepare me for the many challenges I would face in the years ahead. My time in New York would have quite a favorable impact on my Delta career.

I called Whit and told him if the New York job was still available, I wanted it, and I asked for his assistance in getting me a reasonable salary increase. What a pipe dream that was. Johnny Shad called and said I had the job and my salary would be increased by less than one hundred dollars per month. When I accepted the job with that small salary increase, I wasn't aware that I would be paying both New York State and New York City income taxes as a result of our offices being in Manhattan.

After I accepted the New York job, finding a home or apartment we could afford was obviously a priority. Part of that search involved getting recommendations from the New York and New Jersey staff concerning the best and least expensive places to live in the New York area. I quickly determined there was no way I could afford to live in Manhattan. At the suggestion of some of the ladies in the New York City sales office, I decided to look in Connecticut. I arranged for Jim Madigan, the sales rep who covered Connecticut and all of New England, to drive me around and let me look at housing in Southern Connecticut. It didn't take long to find out that I couldn't afford to live there either.

After we spent several hours looking at houses and apartments, Jim suggested we take a break and have lunch. It was almost 1 p.m. when we arrived at his favorite eating spot, which appeared to be a neighborhood tavern. As soon as we walked in the door, these blue-collar truck driver types sat around the bar, staring and hollering at Jim and saying, "Where the hell have you been? You know we meet at noon every day." They all had a big glass of beer sitting in front of them. That set off alarm bells. I wondered, "How can he cover Connecticut and all of New England and do lunch frequently with these guys?"

Meanwhile, I stayed focused on my search for housing. Millie and I did some research on the cost of housing and commuting if we lived on Long Island or in Northern New Jersey, and we quickly determined that these areas were also out of our price range. We were about to give up on finding a place we could afford when a friend who lived near us in South Jersey suggested we look in the Hightstown-East Windsor area, as rents there were reasonable, and it was convenient to Princeton Junction Railroad Station. We found an apartment that we could afford, and the monthly train tickets between Princeton Junction and Manhattan cost less than forty dollars per month. It was also a reasonable drive to the Newark airport, which would be our airport of choice for personal travel.

The apartment was also close to the school that Jeff would attend and very near a shopping area and medical complex. And for the record, one of the first things I did when I became an officer at Delta was to lobby for changes in our salary structure, taking into consideration the cost of living when we promoted or assigned someone to a market like New York. It took a while, but we finally made it happen.

When we moved to East Windsor, we had only one car, so Millie had to drive me to and from the train station every day. Shortly after we moved into the apartment, I saw an ad in the local paper indicating that a Princeton professor wanted to sell an old green four-door Chevrolet for one hundred dollars. Millie took me over to his house to look at the car, as we needed another car so badly. We bought the car that afternoon without even test-driving it, and when Jeff saw it, he named it the "Green Goose."

New Jersey had strict emission testing regulations, and the first time I took the car to be tested, it failed. A friend suggested I leave the car near the testing facility during the day and take it for testing after I got home from work, as the emissions levels would be low when the engine was still relatively cool. I took their advice, and the car passed the test.

When I accepted the position as district director in New York, I never dreamed I would be there eleven-plus years. I also had no idea of the challenges I would have to deal with to make the operation meet my expectations. On the positive side, it never occurred to me that I would have so many opportunities to enrich my Delta career or my personal life.

It's hard to describe the magnitude of the change to my personal life or the increase in my Delta responsibilities when I moved from Philadelphia to New York. In Philadelphia, I was responsible for a small sales office and one City Ticket Office. In New York, I was responsible for a large sales operation, a reservations center, and six City Ticket Offices. While it wasn't in my job description,

I also took it upon myself to build and improve the relationships between Delta's airport management teams and its reservations and sales groups. If you used a scale of 1 to 10 to measure the magnitude of the changes in my responsibilities in Philadelphia versus the ones in New York, Philadelphia would have been a 3 and New York would have been a 9. That ranking is based on someone really focusing on and identifying all of the issues that needed to be fixed.

There was no indication that any of my predecessors addressed many or any of these challenges very effectively. That was certainly not all bad, as accepting the New York job in its present state and addressing and fixing these challenges was the launching pad for the opportunities and success I would achieve over the next twenty-plus years. I want to emphasize that I didn't make the improvements in the New York sales operation alone. I will always be thankful for the encouragement and support I received from my wife, Millie, Whit Hawkins, Charlie Mashburn, Hank Ross, and Ed Preston.

The one person to whom I owe a great deal of credit for the success I achieved during my time in New York is Ed Preston. Ed became my regional manager four or five months after I moved to New York, and he was my boss until I was promoted to regional sales manager and moved to Atlanta in 1979. He was a real motivator, an incredible supporter and advocate. All of this support made the move to New York much more manageable, regardless of the initial hardships I faced. I also must compliment two of my administrative assistants. Betty Malloy did a great job and helped me navigate the many bumps in the road that I encountered when I first reported to New York. Pat Hamilton, my administrative assistant before and after the Northeast merger, also did an outstanding job of assisting me with my schedule and my workload.

I'm also thankful for the support and encouragement I received from Glenn Verrill and his team at BBDO, the Delta advertising agency. They let me have a strong voice in how our New York advertising dollars were spent, and that gave me a lot of clout and leverage with the New York radio stations and newspapers.

When I first moved to New York, the Delta sales office was located in Rockefeller Center, right on Fifth Avenue at Fiftieth Street, a great midtown location. The only downside for me was the fact that it was about fourteen blocks from Penn Station, where my train arrived and departed. I occasionally used the Suburban Transit bus service, which arrived at the Port Authority bus station near Penn Station. About a year after I reported to New York, our lease on our office expired, and we moved the sales office down the street to Forty-Fifth Street and Fifth Avenue. This space was okay but not great. The best part was the fact that I was five blocks closer to Penn Station and the Port Authority bus station.

There were almost a hundred people in my area of responsibility, including twenty people in the Manhattan and Newark sales offices.

Based on my experience with Jim Madigan, the sales rep who apparently was a regular at a neighborhood tavern, my first priority once the housing issue was resolved was to schedule a meeting with Sales Manager Ed Dean and members of the New York sales team so I could better understand the challenges and opportunities they thought needed to be addressed. As Delta's New York district director of sales and marketing, I found it was my responsibility to make the improvements happen.

My earlier experience with Madigan caused me to be concerned about the overall operation and management of the New York sales office. Within a few days of getting familiar with my staff, I told Ed Dean to have Jim report to the office the next day with all of his most recent daily sales plans and all of his House Record Cards. As I suspected, Jim showed up empty-handed. He didn't have any House Record Cards or daily sales plans. It wasn't long before Jim was out the door. Ed Dean had been in the sales manager position for over a year, and why he wasn't aware of the situation with Madigan puzzled me, as I had a hard time believing a sales manager would not know that one of their salespeople did not have contact information on all of their accounts.

A few days later, I met with Ed to discuss his failure to manage the situation with Madigan, and I also wanted more information about Madigan's poor performance. Ed's response to me was, "I was not hired to be a policeman and spy on my people." Ed's reaction to the Madigan situation really set off my alarm bells and confirmed my concerns that I had inherited a dysfunctional organization with a sales manager who didn't have a clue about managing a sales team.

In reality, it was much more Delta's fault than Ed's, as it was so hard to get people to move to New York that Delta promoted the first person who raised their hand, regardless of their qualifications. Ed just happened to be one of the few people who would take that New York sales manager job when it became available. Ed apparently had never worked for anyone who held him accountable for his performance or for managing people.

In little more than a year after I became district director, about half of the people who worked in the New York sales office had resigned, been fired, or been reassigned. I replaced them with a combination of great Delta people that I recruited from one of the airports, the reservations office, or the best talent I could find outside Delta. As part of that restructuring, I worked with Charlie Mashburn to find Ed Dean a job he was more qualified to handle, and I replaced him with Jack Sweigart, who was Delta's district sales manager in Charlotte, North Carolina, prior to coming to New York. I had known Jack for some time, as he was Delta's sales manager in Montgomery when I worked there as a station agent. With Jack's assistance, I basically built a sales organization that was the envy of my Delta peers and most of our New York and New Jersey competitors.

———————————————

On the home front, Millie, Jeff, and I lived in the apartment only a few months before we found a house we really liked, but we didn't have sufficient funds to make the required down payment. Millie's mom and dad came to our rescue and gave us the money for the down payment so we could buy the house.

This house was only a few blocks from our apartment, which made it an easy move. That old green Chevrolet played a key role in the move from the apartment to our new house, as I used it to move many of our possessions, especially clothing and smaller items. I made many trips between the apartment and our new house, but we finally got most of it moved.

We became close friends with several of our new neighbors, including Jean and George Miller, John and Ann Heaney, and Bob and Pattie Rice. Millie also joined a ladies group called the Junior Friday Club, which helped her get into the East Windsor social circle. I will never forget an occasion when we attended a Junior Friday event, and several of us were standing in the kitchen, where some were talking about the colleges they had attended. I didn't say very much, and this one arrogant lady who was a Princeton graduate turned to me and asked, "And what college did you attend?"

I replied, "The School of Hard Knocks," and she said, "Oh, that sounds very interesting. And what was your major?"

Our house on Charred Oak Lane had a large area in the back where we always had a great garden, which Millie and Jeff spent hours maintaining. They grew tomatoes and other vegetables, and to this day, Jeff says his mother taught him all he knows about growing tomatoes.

The okra Millie grew in the garden became quite popular, as most of our neighbors had never heard of okra. They all loved it so much that people began requesting fried okra to serve as hors d'oeuvres.

The other big event that occurred while we lived at Charred Oak Lane was our acquisition of an antique sleigh. It was a beautiful red one-horse sleigh, which we put in the front yard and decorated each Christmas. We still have the sleigh and still decorate it at Christmas.

While being Delta's senior representative in New York had many challenges, it wasn't all bad, as my family and I enjoyed some unbelievable personal and family experiences that only occurred because I accepted the New York job. During the years that I was in New York, we participated in some incredible events and trips.

- We were at the Yankees World Series game and sitting right behind the Yankees dugout when Reggie Jackson hit three home runs to win that game.

- Millie and I took advantage of the opportunity to go to Berlin and other German cities with the New York Chapter of the American Society of Travel Agents (ASTA). This trip occurred about five or six years before the Berlin Wall fell. We actually were allowed to go to East Berlin and have lunch.

- We also went with ASTA to Turkey before it became a real tourist destination. We saw many great historical sites and traveled to remote areas of the country. The Turks extended VIP treatment to the group. Our visit to Turkey happened to occur when they were doing a countrywide census, and every Turk was required to stay at home that day. We were the only people allowed on the streets and highways.

- While we enjoyed the trips to Berlin and Turkey, our favorite ASTA trip was to Ireland. That was our first trip to Ireland, and it was great. Over the last twenty-five years, we have made many trips to Ireland after that wonderful experience.

- Some of my radio and newspaper contacts arranged for us to see exciting Broadway shows. What Jeff liked most was the great restaurants, especially the ones in Manhattan. It made him even happier when he was able to bring along one of his friends.

- The list of exciting events, meals, and trips goes on and on, but this gives you an idea of just how fortunate we were.

Some humorous artwork notes the pressure I was under when Delta started flying new service from LaGuardia and new service to Houston. We had already been flying from New York to Atlanta out of JFK and Newark for several years.

Delta had this Statue of Liberty portrait created for New York Mayor Abe Beame. He autographed this photo: "To Bob W. Coggin, With my very best wishes, Abe Beame."

During my time as Delta's district director in New York, our sales office recognized the JFK freight personnel for being the first to board one million pounds of air freight during a given month.

CHAPTER SEVENTEEN

Creative Opportunities in New York

I soon discovered that New York offered many opportunities to think outside the box, which really got my creative juices flowing. Implementing some of my creative ideas helped generate new business for Delta and very effectively promote the Delta brand.

When I was district sales manager in Jackson, I became aware

Here I am at left as Delta is holding a ribbon cutting for the City Ticket Office on Fifth Avenue in New York.

of how frequently the independent retail clothing merchants flew to New York for trade shows. As a result of my relationship with radio station WHN, I was invited to join WHN and some other clients for a cruise around Manhattan on Roy Cohn's yacht. During that cruise, it occurred to me that offering an evening on Mr. Cohn's yacht would be a great way to reach out to those merchants in the Southeast who flew to New York for trade shows.

I made arrangements to use Mr. Cohn's yacht, and I worked with the Delta sales managers in some of the smaller southern markets and with some of my Jewish contacts to develop a list of people who were coming to New York for trade shows. We sent invitations to about fifty of these merchants, inviting them to join us on Mr. Cohn's yacht. Wow, that was an amazing success! Most of these people were from small Southern cities and had never seen a yacht, let alone experienced a ride around Manhattan on one. I think it's fair to say we made Delta some real friends and loyal customers. We did this three or four times, but we didn't invite the same people every time. We kind of spread it around, but it had a real impact on these customers and took a lot of business from Eastern Air Lines and American Airlines.

Prior to deregulation, airlines were restricted as to the markets they could serve. In many cases, it was necessary for the passenger to fly Airline A to a connecting point and Airline B to their destination. We referred to those passengers as "interline bookings." Most of the international airlines that served JFK depended on US domestic carriers to provide the service to a passenger's final destination. Every six months or so, I had Joe Pallo, who called on the international airlines, to organize a group of us to go out to JFK in the evening and personally visit with the international airline personnel. We'd give them some little Delta memento. Our competition didn't do anything like this, which made it a very effective campaign.

The second step in the interline process involved a team of us, including myself, visiting all of the airline reservations offices in the New York area on Labor Day and passing out New Orleans–made pralines, something many of these people had never seen before. The fact that a Delta management team took the time on Labor Day to visit their reservations offices made a great impression on the airline reservations agents we met.

I also had responsibility for the Delta reservations office and the City Ticket Offices. Since the reservations office was such a critical part of our operation, I spent a good bit of time working with and supporting Tom Bauer, the reservations manager. The reservations operation was a twenty-four seven operation staffed by fifty-plus people, including four or five supervisors. Many of our corporate accounts received their tickets through a process we called "tele-ticketing."

We had a small staff that worked in a secure area and literally created and transmitted paper tickets to the corporate account for their corporate travelers. The Delta team did an excellent job with tele-ticketing and efficiently handled the high volume of traffic at the Delta City Ticket Offices. As a result, Delta's travel agency sales were much lower than those of most of the other airlines. It was all about the superior customer service culture that existed at Delta.

After the merger with Northeast, our New York area call volume increased so significantly that we had to reroute a large volume of the calls to the Boston reservations office, as our New York office wasn't large enough to handle the volume. Shortly after the merger with Northeast was approved, we began to search for a new facility that could house a much larger reservations office and our New York sales office.

In New York, the City Ticket Office operation was very important, as CTOs were the primary ticketing option for many of our major corporate accounts if they didn't use the tele-ticketing option or a travel agent. To ensure that we served those travelers based in Manhattan and Newark, we had six CTO locations in Manhattan and one in Newark. Some of the CTOs, like the one Delta opened on Fifth Avenue in Rockefeller Center, also served as an advertising venue. We placed elaborate window displays in the Fifth Avenue CTO to promote various Delta products and services.

Hank Ross and the Delta advertising department, in combination with BBDO, the Delta advertising agency, involved me in their decision-making process regarding the best media buys for the New York markets. Some of my recommendations were influenced by the promotional support we received from various radio stations and newspapers. The relationship I had with radio station WHN was a great example of how that worked.

As I had learned in Philadelphia, the SKAL club was one of the most prestigious organizations in the travel industry. Securing membership was difficult, as it was restricted to a specific number of people in each sector of the travel industry, and you had to hold a senior position in your company. In New York, there was a long waiting list of people who wanted to join SKAL. Back in the sixties and seventies, many of the leading cruise lines, US-based travel companies, and airlines were headquartered in New York, and many of these senior executives wanted membership in SKAL. I don't know how I pulled it off, but after less than a year in New York, I was invited to join the New York SKAL club, and in my second year, I served the first of two terms as president and later became a regional vice president of SKAL.

In my role as Delta's senior manager in the New York market, I was invited to attend many major civic and charity events. I met and established business relationships with lots of prominent busi-

When my term as president of the New York Chapter of SKAL Club ended, I received this plaque from my successor, Harry Kidd of Canadian National Railways.

ness leaders, politicians, and travel industry executives. Any time I became aware that an event would honor a high-ranking political or business leader, I involved Delta as a sponsor so I could sit at the head table with the high-level business executives. This is how I met leaders like George Steinbrenner, Steve Forbes, American Express CEO James Robinson, and members of the Rockefeller family.

In New York, I gained exposure to some creative, visionary, aggressive, and demanding executives. Some of the things I learned as a result of my exposure to these individuals included:

1. The knowledge I gained related to how these executives managed their businesses was much more beneficial to my future than any college degree would have been.
2. The insight I gained into the business world by meeting leaders at the George Steinbrenner level put me ahead of most of my peers at Delta.

3. Delta's conservative approach to business, especially where finance was concerned, had built a firm foundation that served the shareholders and employees well for many years. As I observed how the business world was changing, I was concerned that Delta's management did not appreciate how rapidly the business world was evolving during the late seventies and early eighties. This included how much the airline industry would change if deregulation were fully implemented. Delta spent a significant amount of resources fighting deregulation versus preparing for it. As I was now exposed to many elements of this evolution, I believed Delta needed to take a more aggressive approach in planning for the changes that could and most likely would occur. As one of Delta's youngest district directors, if not the youngest, I was determined to break that mold. I approached my responsibilities with a vision and determination to improve the effectiveness of not only Delta's New York sales operation but also, hopefully, Delta's entire field sales organization.

4. I knew that many of the Fortune 500 companies, such as American Express and American Airlines, were focused on the use of technology to operate their business, and I was concerned that Delta's "laid-back" approach to technology must change if we wanted to be competitive. Many of the people who knew me back then will acknowledge that I never missed an opportunity to point out how Delta's poor focus on technology was hurting the company in so many ways.

Role Models

In spite of the success I was achieving in my role as Delta's senior manager in New York, I felt that I could achieve more if I could identify a couple of good role models to learn from. I recalled *The Proud Tower*, a book written by Barbara Tuchman, a great writer of historic and biographical novels. *The Proud Tower* was a historical account of events that took place in the twenty-plus years leading up to World War I. Tuchman documented the actions of the politicians and military and social leaders of that era.

One of the most profound leaders she wrote about in *The Proud Tower* was Sir John Fisher, First Sea Lord of the British Navy from 1904 until 1910. While modernizing and restoring the British Navy to its former status as a world power, he aggressively demanded that everyone deliver on their responsibilities, and he was famous for getting rid of those who didn't perform. What really caught my attention was the fact that his peers and subordinates described him as "a fierce broom" sweeping away obsolescence. That description fit my view of what we had to do at Delta in the years ahead, and I advocated doing it sooner rather than later.

My actions related to restructuring the sales staff during my first eighteen months as Delta's district director in New York were motivated to some degree by what I had read about Sir John and his broom. In fact, I frequently used Sir John's "broom" as I moved up the corporate ladder.

Another person who inspired me was Vince Lombardi, the general manager and head coach of the great Green Bay Packers football team. Vince operated with a very simple philosophy: "You don't play to win some of the time, you play to win all of the time." This advice from Coach Lombardi was a great inspiration to me and became one of my guiding lights going forward.

In my role as Delta's district director in New York, I found that my first real opportunity to demonstrate my ability to respond to significant challenges occurred within just a few months. Delta decided to inaugurate our initial service at LaGuardia with nonstop service to Atlanta. With this new LaGuardia-to-Atlanta service, we were competing with Eastern Air Lines, which served Atlanta and a number of other destinations out of LaGuardia. This competitive environment required an aggressive sales effort and creative promotional ideas.

LaGuardia was the preferred airport for most of the business travelers in Manhattan. Our strategy involved having the New York sales team identify all those accounts with significant travel to Atlanta and other points in the Southeast. We conducted a blitz on all these accounts, and in addition to our local sales team, I arranged to bring in sales reps from other Delta cities to assist my team in blitzing these accounts. We also focused on the travel agents who handled large corporate accounts. Most of the radio stations we used provided us with items we could offer as incentives with the travel agencies to promote our new LaGuardia service.

In the fall of 1969, shortly after we started the LaGuardia service, Delta decided to inaugurate our first nonstop service between New York (JFK) and Houston. Eastern dominated the New York-to-Houston market with two and sometimes three nonstop flights per day.

As part of our promotional effort to increase awareness of Delta's new service with our corporate customers, we had hired Fran Tarkenton to be a spokesperson for Delta, and Fran participated at events and receptions. He was a great asset.

I'm sure I inherited this from my mother, but I have always been a person who was quick to identify a unique promotional opportunity. A good example was the creative way I decided to promote this new service between New York and Houston. I rented the stagecoach we had used in an earlier promotion and had it travel throughout Manhattan with a large sign reading, "This stagecoach doesn't fly to Houston, but Delta does." To add insult

Fran Tarkenton was hired as a spokesperson for Delta, and he was a great asset in helping us promote Delta with our corporate customers.

Several times while I was in New York, I hired a stagecoach as a publicity stunt for Delta. We promoted our flights to Florida by proclaiming, "No champagne on this coach but ... Delta serves champagne on non-stop flights to Florida."

to injury, I had them park the stagecoach in front of Eastern's headquarters in Rockefeller Center and left it there for about an hour. That effort worked well, and we enjoyed an excellent load factor on the Houston flight right from the start.

I need to emphasize again that a lot of the success we achieved in launching our new LaGuardia-to-Houston service was heavily influenced by the support we received from Ed Preston and many other people in the General Office, especially Hank Ross, who ran the Advertising and Sales Promotion Department, and Glen Cowart, who worked for Hank. Both were great guys and very supportive. Jim Ewing, who worked in public relations, was also a strong supporter. Jim was very involved in the press coverage we received on the new LaGuardia-to-Houston service. Jim spent a lot of time with me in New York and frequently let me go with him when he called on key media contacts. Jim always looked for opportunities to call my accomplishments to the attention of senior management.

By the summer of 1972, Jack Sweigart, Ed Schnatterly, and I had the New York City/New Jersey sales operations running smoothly. But we faced a lot of new challenges when Delta merged with Northeast in August of 1972. This merger radically changed Delta's position in the NYC/NJ markets, as it added many new destinations to our portfolio.

Prior to the merger, Delta only offered nonstop service from New York to Charlotte, Atlanta, Birmingham, New Orleans, and Houston. After the Northeast merger, we added nonstop service to Tampa, Palm Beach, Fort Lauderdale, Miami, Nassau and Free-port, Boston, Washington, DC, Montreal, and other cities in New England. Prior to the merger, our customer demographics were largely white male business travelers twenty-five to forty-nine. The Northeast merger greatly expanded the demographics of our customer base, with many of our new customers being somewhat older leisure travelers. Based on our pre-merger customer demographics, I had been accustomed to most of our advertising focusing on the business traveler and was not quite mentally prepared for the amount of our advertising budget that would be directed at the older leisure traveler.

When BBDO committed a big hunk of my advertising budget to the Sunday *New York Times* Travel and Leisure section, I was angry and told BBDO they were wasting Delta's advertising dollars. As it turned out, I was badly mistaken. The first weekend the ad ran, the call volume to the Vacations Sales Desk was so great that we had to call people in on overtime to handle the calls. I was so humbled by the experience that I wrote my *New York Times* rep a letter and told him how wrong I had been and what a great success the ads were. The *Times* was so impressed with my letter in which I explained the success of our ad that they built an advertising campaign featuring me telling how successful the ads were.

The Delta-Northeast merger was another example of my being in the right place at the right time, as it presented me with many challenges and opportunities to demonstrate my management, sales, and creative marketing skills. When I faced major challenges, I turned these challenges into opportunities to create effective solutions. Following are some of these challenges and the solutions we implemented.

Challenge — Addressing Delta's lack of brand identity in the markets we acquired via the Northeast merger.

Solution — I convinced my *New York Daily News* rep to have the *Daily News* publish a special edition with a front-page headline and article announcing the Delta-Northeast merger and the new markets Delta would be serving. To maximize this opportunity, I brought approximately thirty salespeople from around the Delta

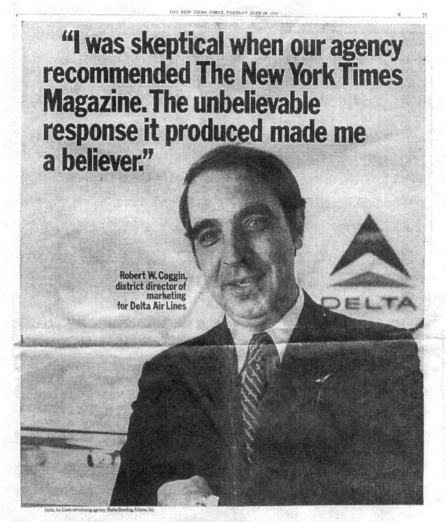

After a successful New York Times *ad had our Delta phones ringing off the hook, I agreed to be part of a testimonial ad for the newspaper.*

system to New York and placed them on the street corners of midtown Manhattan and Wall Street, handing out copies of this edition of the *Daily News*. That effort was successful beyond my wildest expectations and irritated the hell out of both National Airlines and Eastern Air Lines.

Just before the onset of the first winter after the merger, I ordered several thousand windshield scrapers imprinted with a message about all the Florida and Bahamas markets Delta now served. Any time we had snow or an ice storm, I recruited volunteers from Reservations and the airports to take the ice scrapers, go to the commuter rail parking lots, and place them under the windshield wipers of cars parked in the commuter rail parking lots. They did this throughout the New York and New Jersey suburbs.

Northeast didn't have authority to fly nonstop from New York to Orlando, and that was a significant gap in the routes we acquired in the merger. To maintain the support of our key travel agents with large volumes of Orlando business, we cut a deal with Alamo Rent A Car to give a free first-day car rental to any customer buying an Orlando package and flying Delta into Tampa. Jim Porter, who was the head of Delta Vacation Sales, and Warren Binder, owner and operator of Creative Travel, are due all the credit for the success of this creative program.

Warren and Jim played an even bigger role

While I was serving as district director of sales and marketing in New York, one of my promotional ideas was to advertise Delta's Florida and Bahamas markets by giving away these windshield scrapers, leaving them on commuters' cars whenever we had snow or an ice storm.

Tom Miller, Delta's senior vice president of sales and marketing, and I celebrate the Delta/Northeast merger by flipping the switch that turned on our lighted billboard in Times Square in New York. This billboard highlighted our new service to Florida.

in our initial success by creating some attractive and inexpensive vacation packages involving hotels in the Fort Lauderdale area. These packages went way beyond anything Northeast had ever done or anything our competitors were doing.

I also rented the same stagecoach I had used to promote our new Houston service to promote Orlando through our Alamo deal via Tampa. We received some great trade press coverage on that promotion.

Challenge — Creating an opportunity for all of the Delta and Northeast personnel who worked at the three airports in Reservations or in Sales to get to know each other. The mission was to build a good rapport between the Delta and Northeast personnel in the city and at the three airports. This was a major challenge, as the airport teams seemed to operate in silos.

Solution — My first initiative to address this issue was to arrange for radio station WHN to host a party on a Manhattan Circle Line boat for all of the Delta and Northeast personnel. I also secured many prizes that would be distributed during the cruise. To make sure everyone got to know their peers, I issued name tags to everyone as they boarded the boat. There were unique matching numbers on all of the name tags. To win a prize, the two people with matching numbers had to find each other. It was a very successful event, and we held a similar event a year later.

Challenge — Develop an identity and good relationships with the key Northeast customers, especially the tour operators and travel agents.

Solution — This was a top priority, and we had a lot of ground to cover, as Delta had treated these agencies as second-tier customers prior to the merger. All of the major leisure airlines courted these agencies with cocktail parties and familiarization or "FAM" trips. Finding the right strategy to get the travel agents to participate in any of our promotional efforts was a challenge. After the success of our employee party boat program, I decided to go a step further and worked out a deal to charter a big Hudson River party boat and invited over two hundred travel agents to a celebration party. This was a very successful event, and a good 90 percent of the invitees participated.

Four of the key radio stations we used in the NYC market agreed to host smaller receptions for a select number of our key travel agents, and these were also well attended, as our radio station partners did it first-class. I arranged to have Ed Preston and other General Office personnel accompany sales reps on calls to key agencies and tour operators. (This was a real learning experience for some of the Delta General Office folks.) With the support of Warren Binder, Jim Porter, and others, we arranged a number of FAM trips to Florida and the Bahamas. These were not just ordinary FAM trips, as our hosts in Florida and the Bahamas made sure these trips, too, were first-class. My friend George Myers, who ran the Nassau Beach Hotel and later the Britannia Beach Hotel on Paradise Island, did an outstanding job of entertaining our travel agents and tour operators.

Challenge — Establishing a strong relationship with individuals who were loyal Northeast customers but did not book their reservations through travel agencies.

Solution — Shortly after the merger, I discovered that the single largest non-agency segment of customers were those people who owned second homes in South Florida and made twenty to thirty trips per year to these homes. Most of these folks were involved in the garment/textile industry at a pretty high level and expected extra service. To secure a larger share of this business, we enhanced and expanded a special reservations desk that was set up to serve this important segment of the market. As a result of this enhanced service, we captured more than our share of this very large market.

Challenge — Provide some unique onboard products and services that neither Eastern nor National Airlines were providing that would appeal to and attract the typical Jewish customer. This was a customer base that was not very familiar with the Delta brand prior to the Northeast merger, and we weren't reaching many of these potential customers through the travel agencies.

Solution — Delta came up with two compelling ideas. First, we started serving bagels in the boarding areas of the Florida flights. Our Florida passengers enjoyed the bagels while waiting to board their flights. Once word was out that Delta was serving free food in the boarding area, some passengers started bringing family members to the airport to eat our free bagels, even though they were not traveling. Second, we started serving steak and champagne in the coach section of our Florida flights. While serving champagne in coach was a big success, we had to deal with the fact that many of these customers were walking off the flight with our champagne glasses.

Challenge — Finding sufficient office space to house the combined Delta and Northeast sales staff and support personnel.

Solution — The Delta sales office at Forty-Fifth Street and Fifth Avenue was too small to house the combined Delta and Northeast sales and administration staff and the three or four people we added after the merger. As a temporary solution, we closed the Northeast City Ticket Office and housed part of the sales staff in that facility.

Challenge — Finding adequate and affordable space that would accommodate a greatly expanded NYC reservations office and the sales staff.

Solution — We needed a reservations facility that would handle four hundred-plus staff and preferably a facility that would also house the sales team and be close to public transportation. Fortunately we had some great Properties people working on this issue, and they found the perfect space at a very good price at One Penn Plaza, literally across the street from Penn Station and very near three subway stations. Around 1974, we acquired this space at a very attractive price, as the US and New York economies were in a deep recession. By leasing two floors at One Penn Plaza and adding approximately four hundred jobs, we received a lot of press and a lot of attention from the politicians, including Mayor

John Lindsay, who participated in the ribbon cutting when we officially occupied the space.

Challenge — Having adequate airport facilities to handle the expanded operation and larger equipment that Delta would operate, especially at LaGuardia.

Solution — With a few adjustments, we were able to make John F. Kennedy and Newark work well, but LaGuardia was a different story. We had a serious problem with the LaGuardia-to-Florida flights that we operated with DC-10s, as the concourses were so narrow and the hold rooms were too small to handle the volume of passengers booked on these flights. I finally convinced Stan Gulick, our LaGuardia station manager, to start the boarding process about thirty-plus minutes earlier than normal to get some of these passengers out of the hold rooms. We of course had to get the cooperation of the In-Flight Department, and they were very supportive. As other airlines added wide-body aircraft at LaGuardia, they also had some of the same issues with the narrow concourses and small hold rooms.

Challenge — The Northeast sales team in New York had illegally deregulated pricing for some of their key accounts before the industry itself was officially deregulated. When I started calling a halt to these deals, I made a lot of tour operators and travel agents very angry, to the point that one major tour operator threatened to put me in the East River in a pair of concrete shoes.

Solution — Fortunately I inherited a pretty good team of salespeople from Northeast, and they helped me get this situation under control without losing too much business. The business we did lose was short-term, as the travel agents soon realized we were going to be a major player in the Florida and Bahamas markets.

About eighteen months after the merger, the situation in New York became even more complex and challenging due to Jack

Sweigart's illness and subsequent death. I didn't have anyone on my New York staff that I felt had the appropriate experience or skills to take on the district sales manager job, and finding a qualified person elsewhere in the Delta system who was willing to move to New York and take on this job was daunting. After several weeks of searching, I was approached by Andy Neiburg, the number two person in Delta's Travel Agency Sales Department in the General Office. I found it appealing that he had so much experience managing Delta's travel agency programs from a corporate perspective. But as is sometimes the case, a person who does a great job in the headquarters environment can't cut it out in the field, where you are dealing directly with the field sales staff and the customers. After Andy had been on the job for about a year, we had some pretty serious discussion about his poor performance, and he decided to pursue other opportunities.

Before Neiburg became New York district sales manager and shortly after the merger, I reorganized the sales group and created two teams with a manager for each team. These teams were managed by Carl Gnirke, the former Northeast district sales manager, and Al Kolakowski, a senior sales representative. Based on the great job Kolakowski was doing as a team manager, I promoted him to district sales manager after Andy's departure.

When we opened the new, much larger New York facility, Tom Bauer, who had been Delta's reservations manager for many years, decided to accept an early retirement package. Pete Conlin, a former Northeast Airlines reservations manager, replaced Bauer as manager of the New York Reservations Office. We grew the operation pretty rapidly and recruited some good people. After promoting Al Kolakowski to district sales manager, I began to spend more time in Reservations.

By late 1978, I had been in New York almost eleven years and had been passed over for a couple of promotions due to concerns that Delta couldn't find the right person to replace me.

Probably the most significant indication that I was doing a very good job as district director of sales and marketing in New York came when all the senior field sales staff attended a two-day meeting in Atlanta. Around lunchtime on the first day, Ben Wells, the Delta district director in Houston, asked if I would have dinner with him and a few of the other senior district directors. I was surprised by that invitation, but I certainly accepted.

After a drink and a few bites of our dinner, Ben said, "Bob, in case you are wondering why we arranged this little get-together, it has to do with the fact that you're creating problems for the rest of us. This group has been talking about you, and I've been asked to let you know that we want you to slow down some and pull back on some of your activities, as you're making us all look bad."

I laughed and said to the group, "You guys must be crazy, as I'm just doing my job, and I certainly will not stop carrying out my responsibilities." It got very quiet around the table, and we finished our dinner and went our separate ways.

I attended many sporting events in New York, especially those held at Madison Square Garden since our offices were across the street. On one occasion, one of my contacts at Madison Square Garden gave me four tickets to a boxing match that was being promoted as a very large event. One of the boxers was from San Juan and the other from the Dominican Republic. Apparently some of the fans were upset about the way the fight was going, and with three rounds to go, a security guy walked over and recommended that we leave, as it was going to be nasty when the fight was over, and we would probably be the target of some violence, so we got the hell out of there.

We frequently took advantage of our Delta pass benefits to

visit our parents, and on a trip to visit the Coggins in 1972, I learned that the widow of Mr. Hewlett South wanted to sell the eighty-seven-acre property that they had owned for many years. I knew the property well, as I used to help Mr. South bale hay and do other farmwork when I was growing up. I really wanted to buy the property, as I wanted to hold on to all of the good memories I had of growing up in that area. And down deep, I wanted to show my dad that I had the means to buy the South property.

Being the avid hunter and fisherman that I was, I also knew the property had a couple of great pond sites and was an ideal place to hunt, as there was lots of natural terrain, including wooded areas and swamps. I made Mrs. South what I considered a reasonable offer, and she accepted. That property became our go-to place for all those years I was in New York. Not long after we bought the property, I arranged for a contractor to build us a five-plus-acre fishing pond. A few months after we built the pond, I found out that a friend's mother who lived in the Orlando area had a small RV that she wanted to sell. I flew to Orlando and checked it out. I liked what I saw, and we agreed on a price. A few weeks later, my stepfather, Harley, towed the RV to what I had begun calling "my farm." With the help of my dad, Uncle Raymond, and Harley, we put the RV on a good foundation, built a screened-in porch, installed a septic tank, and connected it to electricity. Millie, Jeff, and I came to Georgia even more often now that we had our own place to camp out. In the early eighties, when I began thinking about developing some of the land, I built a second pond just below the original one.

While all of this was going on in Georgia, a lot was happening in our personal lives in East Windsor/Hightstown. After we'd spent three or four years in the Charred Oak Lane house, a much nicer house on Shagbark Lane became available, and we decided to buy it. We kept the Charred Oak Lane house as rental property for a couple of years. In addition to being on a beautiful wooded lot, the Shagbark Lane house was in a great neighborhood. Our neighbors included Phil and Marge Alspach and Dee and Earl Diamond.

By the time we moved to Shagbark Lane, Jeff was in the fourth or fifth grade and had gotten involved with the Cub Scouts, including their Pinewood Derby event. Jeff and I spent a lot of time every year carving his car and trying to fix it so it would win. He had also become more involved in Little League Baseball and youth basketball. About the time we moved to Shagbark Lane, Jeff had really gotten into the CB radio craze, which was the thing in the early 1970s.

Hightstown was the home of Peddie, a fine private school that had a great reputation and attracted students from many areas. By the time Jeff was finishing the seventh grade, many of his classmates were planning to go to Peddie the next year. After giving it a lot of thought, we decided that we would send Jeff to Peddie. He did exceptionally well with his schoolwork and made the football and rugby teams.

About the time we moved to Shagbark, Millie had given up her part-time jobs and gone to work as an administrative assistant for Mr. Irvin Greenberg, who owned a commercial real estate business. That job is one of the reasons we were able to send Jeff to Peddie. Mr. Greenberg helped Millie get her real estate license, and she went to work for a local agent. Her first client was a friend of mine, Rick Williams. Rick had moved from Florida to New York due to a job change. He knew where we lived and decided he wanted a house in the Hightstown-Cranbury area. Since we were friends, he asked Millie to be his real estate agent. She accepted the challenge and found him a house in Cranbury that he and his wife loved.

CHAPTER EIGHTEEN
Home to Georgia

My Promotion to Regional Sales Manager
May 1979 to April 1980

In May 1979, a regional sales manager position became available, and Tony McKinnon wanted to promote me to that position, but Whit Hawkins and others in the General Office had a lot of concern about who would replace me. After much consideration, senior management became more comfortable with Al Kolakowski's ability to handle the district director position in New York and New Jersey. So I finally managed to escape New York by being promoted to regional sales manager, which required that I relocate to the Atlanta base in the General Office. The only concern Millie and I had about making a move to Atlanta right away was that Jeff's school year did not end for a few weeks after I was due to report to Atlanta. Our neighbors and good friends Phil and Marge Alspach came to our rescue and invited Jeff to live with them until the school year ended.

The region I was responsible for included all of the East Coast north of Atlanta, Eastern Canada, and Europe. When I assumed responsibility for that region, the only European destination Delta served was London. The tour of duty as a regional sales manager was short and ended in April 1980, when I was promoted to system manager of planning.

When I was promoted to regional sales manager, I expected

153

to spend 60 to 70 percent of my time in the cities in my region, working with the sales manager and staff in order to achieve the results I wanted. My time on the road would be influenced by the time I needed to spend in London, since it was so important to Delta. There were also some personnel issues that needed to be addressed, and I knew I would have to spend a lot of time in London working with and supporting John Lovegrove, the country manager.

As soon as I knew I was moving to Atlanta, we put our house on the market, and it sold in a few weeks. Since we had family in Newnan, there was no question about where we would live. It was just a matter of finding a house we liked and could afford. In the 1979-80 time frame, not a lot of houses were on the market in Newnan, as the Newnan population was only about 12,000. Realtor Tom Farmer showed us a house at 108 LaGrange Street, and we knew the house was going to require some renovation and expansion, but we liked the location and the construction of the house. We made an offer, which the owner accepted, and we closed in a few days. As was the case in all the other places we had lived, we had some great neighbors and very good friends, including J. T. and Norma Haynes, Dr. Earnest and Carolyn Barron, and Hershall and Rochelle Norred. Norma Haynes introduced us to a lot of other people in Newnan. One of our very best neighbors was Mr. Pete Martin, who lived next door. He loved to talk, and he knew the history of that area of Newnan better than anyone else I ever met.

A few months after we moved in, I hired Jack Russell, a contractor I had known for a long time, to build us a big family room, a large new bedroom, and a deck on the back of the house. Jack was a good friend of my dad, and I knew he would do a great job for us. The pioneer-style fireplace he built in our family room was featured in an issue of *Progressive Farmer* magazine. It had a long arm similar to the one the pioneers used to hold a pot over the fire. Back in the good old days when my dad and Uncle Raymond went rabbit hunting, they brought the rabbits to our house and barbecued them in front of the fireplace. Our fireplace has attracted a lot of attention over the years.

Not long after we moved to Newnan, we joined the Newnan Presbyterian Church, where we have been active members for more than thirty years. I have served as a deacon and an elder and chaired several committees over the years. With this move, we also took advantage of being much closer to Millie's mom and dad and visited them more often. Unfortunately, as time went by, Millie had to make several trips to see them, especially as her dad's health declined.

Jeff began his junior year that fall at Newnan High School, where he made the varsity football team. He played on the team in both his junior and senior years. For Jeff, the downside of our move to Newnan was the fact that the education he acquired during his three years at Peddie put him so far ahead of his classmates at Newnan High that high school was a little boring for him. At Peddie, he had already taken many of the classes that they were now studying at Newnan High.

As expected, my travel schedule was a downside for the family, as my job kept me on the road 60 to 70 percent of the time, putting most of the responsibility of raising and managing Jeff on Millie at a time when he needed some strong guidance from his dad. Jeff did like to hunt and fish, so we spent a lot of time on the weekend hunting and fishing down at the farm. One weekend when Millie, Jeff, and I were at the farm, we discovered that the people who had been renting the old Hewlett South house had moved and not taken their dog with them. It was a beautiful black lab, and Jeff immediately adopted the dog and named her "Tar Baby."

The experience I had gained and lessons I had learned as district director in New York were beneficial in my new role as regional sales manager. I don't intend to demean my colleagues or people who had held the regional sales manager position in the past, but after a few weeks into the new job, I got the impression that accountability for the folks in the field was not a priority for some of my peers (except Ed Preston), especially where account management and delivery of revenue were concerned. As was the case in New York, this situation gave me lots of opportunities to implement some accountability.

In defense of my peers, especially those who held or had held the position in the past, Delta's Finance and IT departments had failed to provide the sales organization with the data and tools needed to track and measure how effectively the field sales organizations were performing in terms of securing Delta's share of revenue from the accounts in their territory. This failure had a serious negative impact on the sales organization's ability to set goals or track the performance of the sales staff. You can't place all the blame on the Finance and IT departments, as the senior sales management people should have made IT support for the sales organization a priority.

During a large management meeting hosted by Delta's senior management team in the late 1970s, I raised the finance/technology issue with Delta's CFO during a Q and A session, and he basically told me to sit down and be quiet. That evening before dinner, I was called aside by Charles Knight, the vice president of sales, and told that I was completely out of line with my comments about the lack of the financial information needed by the sales organization.

My time in New York gave me the insight, experience, and the passion to create the focused accountability program I needed to measure many of the activities of the field sales offices in my region. Working with some of my sales managers, we created the basic accountability tools that I needed to improve my ability to track the sales performance of the sales offices and individuals in my region.

CHAPTER NINETEEN

Planning for Change

Promotion to System Manager
April 1979 to 1984

When I assumed the planning responsibilities at Delta in 1980, the airline industry was facing two issues that would have a profound impact on it going forward. Issue number one was deregulation, and issue number two was technology. Some airlines were better prepared than others to deal with these issues.

United and American were in favor of deregulation, while Delta was very much opposed due to concerns about new competition on Delta's monopoly routes and lower fares in general and the negative impact these factors would have on the company's bottom line. Based on this concern, Delta aggressively opposed the legislation that Congress was considering, which would deregulate the airline industry.

In the years leading up to deregulation, Delta was the darling of Wall Street in the airline sector, as Delta was consistently one of the industry's most profitable airlines. Two factors contributed to Delta's profitability: the great relationship Delta enjoyed with its employees and the fact that a large segment of Delta's route network was basically a monopoly, or else we competed with Eastern, which was the next best thing to having a monopoly. As it evolved, deregulation had the anticipated negative impact on Delta's bottom line. All of the legacy airlines experienced a reduction in profitability, but few of them were impacted as much as Delta.

I had a good understanding of how technology was evolving based on the knowledge that I had acquired in New York. My exposure to many industry leaders and the way they conducted business had shown me the important role technology would play in the years ahead.

Technology was evolving rapidly in the airline industry, as it was a critical tool in areas such as marketing and planning (scheduling and pricing). American Airlines was the industry leader in developing and implementing technology in a number of areas. Unfortunately, Delta was at or near the bottom of the list when it came to technology spend and development, especially in marketing. On several occasions, I tried to convince the senior-level decision makers that Delta needed to get on board with technology and have a more focused technology strategy. Since technology was such a critical issue during much of my Delta career, I have written a document on this subject, and it is included as Appendix 7.

My Promotion to System Manager of Planning

I had been in the regional sales manager position about ten months when I received a call from Joe Cooper, senior vice president of marketing, late on a Friday afternoon. Joe called to congratulate me and advise me that I had been promoted to system manager of planning and would replace Ted Maples, as Ted was approaching the mandatory retirement age of seventy and would be retiring in a couple of weeks. My reply to Joe was simply, "Yes, sir," as the call was a surprise. I had heard no rumors related to Ted's retiring or that I was being considered as his replacement. I was in a state of shock after that phone call, as Planning was a critical area of responsibility in which I had little direct experience. I was surprised that anyone in senior management thought the experience I had gained over the last few years qualified me to replace Mr. Maples.

The plan was for me to report to Ted the following Monday and spend some time with him so he could bring me up to speed on the planning process. So much for "succession planning"! During my time with Ted, he shared a lot of information on Planning's relationships with the other departments, such as Maintenance and Flight Ops.

In trying to understand why I was selected to manage the Planning Department, I began pursuing that question with some people who I thought might have been involved and knew what influenced the decision to select me for this position.

The responses I received were related to:

- The issues I had raised concerning Delta preparing for deregulation.
- My questions and concerns about scheduling and pricing.
- The fact that I had requested clarity on some of these issues.
- The validity of the recommendations that I submitted to Ted and others in the Planning Department. These suggestions were related to the New York market and had favorably impacted that market and, later, my region.

Apparently, my questions, requests, and suggestions had given Joe Cooper and the other key decision makers a level of comfort that I was the right person at the right time to handle the planning function in this uncertain environment. While all that might have been true, I sure had to fight a lot of battles to secure the resources I needed to do the job correctly.

After the challenges of deregulation began to emerge, I asked myself, "If Delta's senior management could have foreseen the challenges that would occur over the next five-plus years, would they have put a novice like me in the critical planning job?" One thing is for sure: they couldn't have promoted a Harvard MBA to that position, as Delta didn't have any Harvard MBAs on the payroll. Regardless of what might have been, they put me in the job, and I think history will confirm that I did as good a job as any MBA would have done under the same circumstances, and I must give some key players on my staff a lot of the credit for much of that success.

While I was reasonably confident that I could handle the responsibilities, I continued to be concerned that Delta was unprepared for what we would face as the deregulation process moved forward. My primary concerns were related to Delta not having the necessary technology tools in place for the Planning Department to manage the frequency and volume of changes that would occur in pricing and scheduling as a result of deregulation.

In addition to the knowledge I had gained during my last few years in New York related to what other airlines were doing, I had also read many articles and press releases on how other airlines were preparing for deregulation, especially American and United. Both of these airlines were focused on the development of the appropriate technology needed in this evolving environment.

As head of the Planning Department during the early eighties, I faced numerous challenges, and these were the most significant ones:

1. Learning the planning process and evaluating the staff I inherited.

2. Building a technology team.
3. Understanding deregulation and its impact on pricing and scheduling.
4. Learning about hub development.
5. Understanding PATCO and how we handled the PATCO strike.
6. Developing and implementing a Yield Management system.
7. Leveraging the freedom provided by deregulation to expand and grow Delta's network.
8. Growing Delta's international network in the mid-1980s.
9. Managing the projects I was assigned that were not related to my planning responsibilities.

Based on my concerns about all these challenges and the technology issue, as soon as Ted was out the door, I began developing my plan to address these challenges.

Bucket One — Learning all the details of the planning process and evaluating the staff I inherited

The first item on my agenda was to meet with all the key players in the Planning Department so I could tell them a little about myself and my management style and answer any questions they might have regarding my expectations. Based on the Delta culture, I anticipated that some of the people I inherited had been in their jobs a long time and might not be receptive to change. I hit the nail on the head. After I had briefed the team on the way I conducted business, a very senior guy said, "That's not the way Mr. Maples handled these issues." I looked this guy right in the eye and said, "The next person who tells me how Mr. Maples handled something is going to be reassigned to the Atlanta ramp." Needless to say, I never heard that comment again.

My second agenda item involved a more detailed meeting with the scheduling team. My objective for the meeting was to learn how they used technology in the scheduling process. After a little small talk, I asked if they would give me a demonstration of how they were using technology. Everyone started giggling and laughing.

Mike Bell, a scheduling analyst, stood and said, "Follow me around this wall, and I'll show you an example of the technology we're currently using." Mike paused, pointed at an electric pencil sharpener, and said, "That electric pencil sharpener represents the extent of our technology."

I didn't expect them to have state-of-the-art technology, but I was surprised to learn that the Delta scheduling staff didn't use any technology. As I suspected, the pricing function was as archaic as Scheduling where the use of technology was concerned.

While I knew from experience that Delta was far behind the industry in developing technology resources, I was both surprised and shocked to learn that Delta was so far behind the industry in using technology in the scheduling and pricing areas, especially with total deregulation just around the corner.

Bucket Two — Building a Technology Team

After learning that Planning had zero technology to support our scheduling and pricing, I arranged a meeting with Delta's IT to see if they would help me acquire the technology that Planning needed. What a runaround they gave me, including an estimate that it would take two thousand-plus man-years to develop a system like the one used by American. Basically, I didn't make any progress with the Delta IT management team.

In response, I decided that every time I added or replaced an analyst in the planning area, the new person would have to possess programming and IT development skills as well as the appropriate pricing or scheduling skills. Three of my best hires were Jimmy McCullough, Doug Blissit, and later, Adolfo Salas.

As I have mentioned several times, God was with me during my Delta career. Management's decision to close the Economic Development Department and move those talented people to Planning is another good example of God looking out for me. That was a windfall, as there was a lot of IT talent in that group, especially Dean Hill, Jim Brown, and Bill Moon. Because of the skills this group possessed, combined with the skills of the new people I hired, we had a talented technology group within Planning. My new technology team accomplished this very difficult task of automating many of the planning functions in little more than a year. They not only developed much of the programming we needed but also identified third-party software vendors that we could buy software from to further enhance our mission. Building this technology team was one of my top achievements during my Delta career.

Bucket Three — Deregulation (a deep bucket)

This challenge started to evolve in early 1980, when the first meaningful phase of deregulation was implemented, dramatically changing how business was being conducted by the US commercial airline industry. The initial and subsequent events surrounding deregulation made my other challenges pale in comparison.

Full deregulation gave the airlines unlimited freedom to select the domestic routes they would serve and almost total freedom in pricing so long as the airline followed the basic rules the Civil Aeronautics Board (CAB) and later the Department of Transportation (DOT) put in place.

By early 1981, the industry was well on its way to being fully deregulated, creating many challenges for Delta in both scheduling and pricing. I believe Delta was more negatively impacted by deregulation in the short term than any of the other legacy airlines, primarily due to new competition on many routes that were previously monopoly routes, plus the new competition and low fares on many of our other routes.

While the increased competition from the start-ups and the legacy airlines was definitely an issue for the industry, the pricing freedom allowed by deregulation was an even bigger issue. This was especially true for Delta, as deregulation emphasized the critical need to have the technology tools and programs to allow Planning to quickly analyze and respond intelligently to any competitive pricing action. We were much too slow in our response to competitive pricing, and that really impacted Delta's bottom line.

The pricing issue had become so critical that I had become very involved in many of Delta's pricing decisions. A *Wall Street Journal* writer who followed the airline industry found out how involved I had become in Delta's pricing decisions. He wrote a front-page article in the *Journal* about me and the state of airlines' pricing. He described me as a "Burly Framed, Devilish, Hard-Bitten Shirt-Sleeve Antacid Addict."

In addition to the technology issues, most of the pricing staff had been in their same positions for many years and were accustomed to doing pricing by the book or the way Ted Maples had told them to do it. There was little if any creativity in pricing. This is another area where Sir John Fisher's "clean-sweeping broom" became an absolute necessity.

My colleagues created a humorous poster after this description of me appeared in a Wall Street Journal *article.*

Thanks to Delta's unsophisticated pricing tools, some poor pricing decisions, and increased competition, Delta's 1982 fiscal year profits plummeted 85 percent to $20.8 million, compared to $146.5 million the year before. In the first quarter of 1982, Delta lost $18.4 million, the first quarterly loss in 27 years.

In 1982, I finally used Sir John Fisher's broom and swept obsolescence out of the Pricing Department. Earlier that year, Delta recruited attorney Bob Cross from the Texas Aeronautics Commission to work in Delta's Legal Department. Not long after joining

Delta, Bob was moved to the Sales and Marketing Division. About the same time, Delta Manager of Pricing John Damhorst and I were discussing his discomfort with the way airline pricing was evolving and the significant pressure on him to improve our pricing strategy. As a result of these discussions, John decided that after twenty years as manager of Delta's Pricing, he would retire.

When Vice President of Sales Tony McKinnon became aware of John's decision to retire, he suggested I consider replacing John with Bob Cross, who was very analytical and technology savvy. I met with Bob and briefed him on all the challenges we faced in Pricing. Rather than being turned off by these challenges, he expressed a strong interest in the position. A few days later, Tony and I met with Bob and offered him the position, and Bob did an outstanding job of making changes and improving the pricing process.

Bucket Four — The History of Delta's Hubs

Deregulation had negatively impacted Delta and all the legacy airlines in many ways, but for the legacy airlines, one positive aspect of deregulation was the ability it gave us to grow established hubs and build new hubs.

The Atlanta hub — Delta was ahead of the game where hubs were concerned. As many airline industry historians have acknowledged, prior to deregulation, Delta's Atlanta hub was the only true hub and spoke being operated by any US airline. A factor in the size and scope of Delta's Atlanta hub prior to deregulation included the invention of the Owly Bird and Early Bird complexes by Tom Miller, Delta's senior vice president of marketing. This concept added more frequency in some key markets and helped overcome fleet limitations of that time, allowing Delta to significantly increase the utilization of its existing fleet.

With the freedom provided by deregulation, the Delta Scheduling Team continued to grow the Atlanta hub and was selective in adding new markets. Over the next few years, the Atlanta hub grew as fast as the fleet plan would allow. In December 2017, Delta was operating more than 1,000 flights per day to 219 domestic and international destinations.

The Dallas hub — When Delta Air Service was launched as an airline in 1929, Dallas was one of the early cities served. When the Dallas and Fort Worth airline service was consolidated at the new Dallas-Fort Worth (DFW) airport, Dallas became a Delta hub. When Braniff Airways ceased operations in 1982, Ron Allen and I made a commitment to build DFW into a major hub. Over the

Delta CEO Ron Allen and I spent a lot of time building the Dallas hub, and here we're hosting an event for our customers in Dallas.

next few years, the DFW operation grew to 250 flights per day. With this level of operation, Delta had captured 35 percent of the Dallas-Fort Worth market in 1991.

The Memphis hub — The Memphis hub as it existed prior to deregulation would not meet my definition of a hub. It was primarily a point-to-point operation with a small amount of connecting traffic since only about twenty-two feeder markets were spread out along the Mississippi Valley. Deregulation changed the Memphis operation, with Delta adding new service to Memphis, including nonstop service to Atlanta and some of our other larger Delta markets. As Delta grew its Memphis operation, it slowly achieved limited hub status but was still primarily a point-to-point operation.

Creation of the Cincinnati hub, 1984-85 — Tom Kerns, Mike Bell, and I had been looking closely at the poor performance of several of our Memphis flights and began reviewing opportunities to reallocate these resources. After a lot of research, we decided that due to the limited competition, the need for Delta to have a greater presence in the Midwest, and the number of Fortune 500 companies located in the Cincinnati area, Cincinnati was the ideal spot for a new Delta hub. I am proud to say the Cincinnati hub was profitable almost from the outset.

We implemented the first phase of the new hub in the 1984-85 time frame, and we had to start small, as additional concourses and gates were being built to accommodate our long-range plan. The Western merger in 1987 gave us a good opportunity to grow the hub even faster than we had originally envisioned. By 1992, Cincinnati had become Delta's second-largest hub, handling over 670 Delta and Delta Connection daily flights. By 2005, Delta served over 130 destinations from Cincinnati. We offered daily nonstop flights to Honolulu and Anchorage, London (Gatwick), Frankfurt, and when you included the service offered by our alliance partners, we also served Amsterdam, Brussels, Munich, Paris, Rome, and Zürich. During this period, Cincinnati was ranked as the world's fourth largest hub served by a single airline.

The Orlando hub — While it was a very important point-to-point market for Delta, Orlando wasn't a significant Delta hub. Some connecting opportunities developed over time, but it was more a destination for Delta, with many long-haul flights from almost every major city in the US.

Becoming the official airline of Disney World changed Delta's focus on Orlando, as we were operating approximately 29 flights per day in early 1987. That number increased to 71 flights per day after we did the Disney deal in July 1987. For over a decade beginning in 1987-88, Delta was the dominant carrier at Orlando, but a combination of events resulted in a reduction of Delta service at Orlando.

The Salt Lake City hub — The Salt Lake City hub was already in place when Delta merged with Western Airlines in 1987. Its geographic location and the large number of feeder-type markets north and west of Salt Lake created a great opportunity for Delta to capitalize on the large volume of traffic to these secondary markets via our Atlanta, Dallas, and Cincinnati hubs. A few months into the merger, we realized there was a large market we called "the double connect market." These were markets like Columbia, South Carolina, where a person who wanted to fly from Columbia to Billings, Montana, had few options.

The network created by the Delta-Western merger addressed that issue and gave Delta access to a large market with little competition. The demand grew to a point that we had to fly what we called double daily flights out of our Atlanta and Cincinnati hubs to Salt Lake City. A double daily is when you schedule two flights to the same destination departing on the same departure bank. I can take credit for introducing the double daily concept at Delta, but I stole the idea from a competitor who was at a travel industry meeting and bragged about how they were using that concept.

Beginning in the early 1990s, a number of factors including the recession had a negative impact on some of Delta's hubs. This resulted in hubs such as Dallas, Orlando, and Cincinnati losing their hub status. The aircraft committed to these hubs were reallocated to growth in other markets.

Bucket Five — PATCO Strike, August 3, 1981
(another deep bucket)

While we were still dealing with various aspects of deregulation, another major challenge occurred when the air traffic controllers union (the Professional Air Traffic Controllers Organization, or PATCO) went on strike. Since it is illegal for federal workers to strike, President Ronald Reagan gave the union 48 hours to return to work. They didn't, and on August 5, 1981, over 11,000 air traffic controllers were terminated. Because of the PATCO strike, the industry faced severe scheduling restrictions at most large airports around the country. The FAA ordered airlines to reduce flights at major airports by 50 percent during peak hours. The first weeks were organized chaos. To get through the first few days of the strike, my scheduling team worked long hours without any days off, canceling the required number of flights and coordinating these changes with Delta's operational departments. At the same time, they were working hard to develop more organized schedules to be flown going forward. These schedules had to be continually adjusted due to changing capacity limitations imposed by the FAA. To the credit of the FAA, they appeared to make every effort to help the airlines operate as many flights as possible. Since a big piece of Delta's network was in monopoly markets and smaller cities, we probably weren't as negatively impacted by the strike as some of the other airlines.

During the early stages of the strike, the FAA organized industry meetings to further allocate available capacity at slot-controlled airports and at larger cities. I attended dozens of these industry meetings, some of which were marathon five- to six-day meetings. Delta was usually represented by me, Richard Johnson, my manager of schedules, or Russ Crawford, director of flight control. Initially one or more of Delta's attorneys also attended these meetings, but as time went by, their participation declined. Not having the attorneys there all the time was a benefit, as my team knew how to quietly work solutions versus engaging in arguments. We fought fiercely for the slots made available, but we also worked in cooperation with other airlines to effect solutions.

At one meeting, for example, Delta and Eastern negotiated an agreement to reschedule their flights to Atlanta, a hub for both airlines, to eliminate some of the hub overlaps and to reduce strain on the air traffic system. This cooperative effort gave the air traffic controllers the incentive to increase the total number of flights Delta and Eastern could fly into Atlanta each day. This agreement actually continued for several years after the PATCO strike, which was a win for the FAA and the airlines.

I made sure Richard Johnson and the scheduling team took calculated risks and scheduled a few additional flights beyond the official FAA limits into some constrained airports. We simply waited to see if we would be challenged by the FAA, which rarely happened. It took many months for the situation to stabilize enough for us to consider attempting to restore schedules to the pre-PATCO level. The FAA says it took about ten years before overall controller staffing returned to normal. I must compliment and commend those controllers who stayed on the job and rose to the occasion in the difficult months following the PATCO strike. These people worked hard and clearly excelled.

Slot controls were eventually eliminated for all cities except the original big four: New York-LaGuardia, Chicago-O'Hare, Washington National, and New York-JFK. PATCO was decertified on October 22, 1981, and the strike was broken by the Reagan Administration.

Bucket Six — Development and implementation of Delta's Revenue Management System (Yield Management)

Soon after Bob Cross was promoted to manager of pricing, I received a call from a sweet-sounding young lady who advised me that she represented Control Data, and she said they had developed a technology product that they would like to demo. She said this new technology would be a game changer in the way we priced our seats and allocated our inventories.

She said that Republic Airline had been using this technology very successfully, but the unions had forced Republic to stop using it, as it threatened the job security of the union employees. She also said their research indicated that implementing this product as part of our pricing process would generate more than ten million dollars in incremental revenue on an annual basis. I told her, "The product sounds very nice, but I don't have time to see you." She wouldn't take no for an answer and continued to press me to give them just an hour to demo their product. I finally relented and agreed to meet with their team. I invited Bob Cross, Vice President of Purchasing Doug Dunn, a person from Finance, and a couple of other people.

To put the existing revenue management process into perspective, it's helpful to have a little history on how our seat allocation or revenue management system was working at that time. Typically, on Monday morning, I would receive a call from Joe Cooper, senior vice president of marketing, after he had looked at the loads for the past week and seen that the load factor had fallen. He would tell me, "Coggin, get some more discount seats in the market. The loads have gone to hell." A couple of weeks would go by, and I would receive another call from Joe. He would say, "Coggin, the damn yield has gone to hell. Reduce the number of discount seats in the market." I will admit I have dramatized the situation a bit, but this kind of communication went on for months.

We held our meeting with Control Data, and when it was over, they had convinced us their system was real and could deliver incremental revenue. The biggest challenge we faced was the fact that we had to ship our booking data to their data center in Cleveland every night for them to analyze booking trends and more. Keep in mind that in the early eighties, there was no way to transmit this data electronically.

The guys in Finance, Legal, and IT were very much opposed to shipping this confidential data to a third party. Bob Cross and I met with Tony McKinnon and Doug Dunn, vice president of purchasing, and pleaded with them to help us secure Delta CEO David Garrett's permission to send this info to Control Data. Doug and Tony convinced Mr. Garrett to let us do it.

The next big challenge related to the new revenue management system concerned the staff and system Delta used on a day-to-day basis to set inventories. Since the managers and staff in that area were "old school" and slow to adapt to new ways of doing business, I had to again use Sir John Fisher's "broom" to sweep out the old system. I convinced senior management to have this function report to me, as it had unofficially become a part of the pricing department. Making changes and bringing in some people with the necessary skills was not an easy task. Bob Cross did a very good job of moving people around and finding some good people with the appropriate talent to work in Revenue Management.

After using the Control Data system for one year, Bob Cross and Delta's Finance Department estimated that the new yield management program had produced more than $140 million in incremental revenue, well beyond the $10 million my initial contact at Control Data had promised. The number could have been even higher if we had been able to access all the historical data and found more staffing with better revenue management skills. In the years following this initial implementation of revenue management, we continued to improve and enhance the program. This improvement continued after I retired, and I suspect it is still evolving today.

Being the wise young man that he was, Bob Cross saw so much potential in revenue management that he left Delta in 1984 and formed his own company, which he sold several years later for a significant amount of money. When he left Delta, he took Steve Swope, one of our brightest young team members, with him. Steve later formed his own company and also sold it for a significant amount of money. The departure of both Bob Cross and Steve Swope created a real problem for me, as we didn't have people with their vision and technology skills who could effectively fill their shoes. Consequently, we struggled for a while in the revenue management area.

Bucket Seven — Securing approval to expand Delta's international route network

When I was promoted and moved to the planning position, Delta's only long-haul international routes were limited to Atlanta-to-London and Atlanta-to-Frankfurt. Expanding our international network became more difficult when we launched our Atlanta-to-Paris service, which caused some individuals in Delta senior management to express concerns that Tony McKinnon and I were moving too fast with our international expansion. Since all the long-haul international routes we were flying at that time were profitable, our strategy was to take advantage of this window of opportunity.

With the encouragement and support of Tony McKinnon and Whit Hawkins—plus the assistance of a great staff that included Dean Hill, Richard Johnson, and Mike Bell—we began laying the groundwork for our future international expansion, which included Atlanta-to-Shannon, Ireland and Atlanta-to-Bermuda. Several people in senior management thought I had lost my mind when I presented a plan to expand Delta's Atlanta international service to include these cities. Both the Shannon and Bermuda flights were profitable from day one and continued to be profitable in the April to October time frame. Some of the Delta people who were not familiar with the Bermuda market were shocked when they saw the early load factors and P&Ls on this flight. We leveraged the success of these new routes to continue growing the international network.

When we started focusing on Asia, our opportunities were limited, as the bilateral agreements between the US and most of the Asian countries were very restricted. We discovered there was an opportunity to serve several Asian markets via the Portland gateway, as no other airline was using the existing authority out of Portland. We took advantage of the opportunity to use Portland as a gateway and added service out of Portland to Seoul, Taiwan, and Bangkok and later added Los Angeles-to-Hong Kong.

Bucket Eight — Assignments not related to my planning responsibilities

Some of the challenges management tasked me with were outside my normal area of responsibility. I was tasked with negotiating the "Walt Disney World's Official Airline" agreement, and I took the lead in negotiating our codeshare alliances with Swiss Air and a few other deals. (A codeshare arrangement is one in

A group of flight attendants led "Project 767," a campaign which resulted in Delta employees voluntarily contributing funds to purchase the company's first Boeing 767-200 aircraft, which was named "The Spirit of Delta."

Delta CEO Richard Anderson, second from left, greets me along with former Georgia Bulldogs Coach Vince Dooley and Atlanta Mayor Kasim Reed at the Grand Reopening of the Delta Flight Museum on June 17, 2014.

which two or more airlines share the same flight.) Neither of these tasks were related to my planning responsibilities, but I finally understood that I had become the go-to guy when Joe Cooper, Whit Hawkins, or Tony McKinnon wanted to be sure a deal was handled timely, properly, and with Delta's best interests in mind.

The Spirit of Delta, 1982 — The losses that Delta experienced in 1982 prompted a small group of flight attendants to spearhead "Project 767" with the intent to engage all Delta employees in a campaign to buy Delta's first Boeing 767-200 aircraft. The campaign worked, and the employees met the challenge and raised the funds through payroll deductions. This effort received national and international attention and contributed to Delta's reputation as a unique culture of dedicated employees. On more than one occasion, I was visited by Japanese business executives who were very interested in knowing how Delta had developed so much loyalty from its employees. I explained to them that it all started with Mr. Woolman, which only added to their puzzlement.

When the "Spirit of Delta" was retired in February 2006, it was moved to the Delta Flight Museum, and since then, it has been the premier attraction in the museum. When Richard Anderson became Delta's CEO in 2007, he made upgrading and enhancing the Delta Flight Museum, including the Spirit of Delta, a very high priority, and during 2013-2014, the two original 1940s hangars were renovated. This resulted in the Spirit of Delta becoming the cornerstone exhibit in the museum, which had a Grand Reopening on June 17, 2014, the 85th anniversary of Delta passenger service.

—————————

While all of this change was going on at Delta, my personal life was also moving along well. Our son, Jeff, had graduated from high school and was attending Georgia Tech. While he was at Tech, Alamo Rent A Car offered him a job as a rental agent, and he accepted the position.

He turned this job into a long and successful career. In a little more than a year, he was promoted from rental agent to city manager in Charleston, South Carolina, and later to sales manager in Dallas. Not long after he moved to Dallas, he bought a house in the M Street section, which is near Southern Methodist University. Millie and I made several trips to Dallas to help him make repairs and renovate the house.

A few years after we moved to Newnan, Millie's dad passed away, and a couple of years later, her mom decided to move to Newnan. Millie and I had been wanting to live out on our farm, and after we moved Mrs. Shell into a nice apartment in Newnan, we rented our home in Newnan to a couple and moved to a log cabin we had built on our farm. We loved living out there, but unfortunately, about two years after we moved, Millie's mom began having more health problems, and we moved back to Newnan so Millie could help take care of her.

Millie's mom passed away about a year after we moved back to town, and we decided to look for a nicer house. A beautiful house was available on Alpine Drive, just down the street from our LaGrange Street house. We bought it and have lived there for the past twenty-plus years.

After I was promoted to senior vice president, my responsibilities at Delta required that I spend most of my time at Delta or traveling around the world, but Millie and I did manage to spend time with my dad and Vera. We tried to see them a couple of times a month, and occasionally they would come down to the farm when we were down there fishing or entertaining friends. I had an opportunity to take Dad to a couple of Atlanta Falcons games, and he really enjoyed that experience, especially seated on the fifty-yard line. As my dad grew older, we spent more time with them and helped them with the maintenance of their home and other issues. In 1997, he passed away from a massive heart attack. My stepmother, Vera, lived a couple of more years, and having been a smoker, she passed away due to a lung infection.

Since my mother and Harley lived in Fort Walton Beach, Florida, about a five-hour drive away, we didn't see them as often, but we would occasionally go down for a long weekend. There were several great discount clothing stores in Fort Walton, and one of our favorite ways to spend time there was to go shopping. There were also a couple of good antique shops in Fort Walton, and we bought some great antiques. I would occasionally go fishing on one of the many "party boats" that were based in Fort Walton, and that was always a lot of fun. Harley had done a lot of work to help us set up the camper we bought, and Mother and Harley enjoyed staying in the camper when they came up to visit. My mom was a very heavy smoker, resulting in congestive heart failure, and was in her mid-seventies when she passed away. Harley continued to live in their house for about three more years before he passed away.

CHAPTER TWENTY

Delta and My New Challenges

1984-1987

My next series of challenges occurred when my good friend Chuck Poulton, director of Delta's traffic department, passed away in 1984 due to a massive heart attack. Chuck's responsibilities included Delta's call center/traffic department, City Ticket Offices, and the group that was developing Delta's computer reservations system (CRS).

Since there was no replacement for Chuck waiting in the wings, senior management restructured Marketing and reassigned segments of Chuck's responsibilities to me and Al Kolakowski. At the time of Chuck's death, Al was primarily responsible for the field sales organization and the Frequent Flyer program, and I of course was responsible for the Planning Department. In the restructuring, Al was given responsibility for all of Chuck's Traffic Department functions and retained his field sales responsibilities as well. To balance Al's workload, I was given responsibility for the Frequent Flyer program, and I was also given responsibility for managing Delta's computer reservations system (CRS) product.

The computer reservations system (CRS) was basically a system the airlines were installing in travel agencies to permit the travel agents to book their clients' travel reservations online, directly with the participating supplier. Installing the systems in travel agencies was a very competitive environment, as the airline installing the CRS in an agency could significantly increase their share of that agency's business. The host airline also collected a "distribution fee" from any supplier whose services were booked by the travel agency through their CRS.

So my new responsibilities, along with my planning and other responsibilities, gave me a full plate. I was thankful that Whit Hawkins and Tony McKinnon were involved in the CRS issue.

Both the Frequent Flyer and CRS programs were very technology dependent in order to deliver a good product. Delta's failure to focus on developing the technology needed to support the sales and marketing division was a costly mistake that continued for many years.

The Frequent Flyer Program

The Frequent Flyer concept was initially launched in 1979 by American Airlines and Trans Texas. Other major airlines, including Delta, implemented Frequent Flyer programs over the next couple of years.

The fact that Mr. Garrett thought the Frequent Flyer program would be short-lived may have contributed to that responsibility being given to me. I base that assumption on a conversation I had with Mike Boynton, the day-to-day manager of Delta's Frequent Flyer program in the early days of the program. Mike told me about a conversation he had with Mr. Garrett related to the Frequent Flyer program in which Mr. Garrett asked, "So when do you think we can wind down this Frequent Flyer promotion and get away from providing free flights?" This is another example of how some of Delta's senior management team failed to under-stand that the Frequent Flyer program was a reflection of how the airline industry was evolving.

Just like anything else at Delta that relied on technology to deliver a good product, we were far behind most if not all of our competitors in automated tracking of Frequent Flyer activity. Del-ta's Frequent Flyer had to send Delta their boarding pass so the Delta team could manually record their activity. When I assumed responsibility for the Frequent Flyer program, I discovered that we filed these boarding passes in shoeboxes so we could keep up with them. I fought hard for automated tracking of our Frequent Flyer activity, but as usual, my efforts fell on deaf ears. When Fre-quent Flyer tracking was finally automated, it was an unplanned byproduct of programming that was developed that would pro-vide the Stations Department with the ability to more effectively manage the check-in process. A trusted individual involved in this project told me that the Stations Department would not have suc-ceeded in getting this technology project on the IT project list if all the senior vice presidents had not aggressively pushed for this program development.

The Frequent Flyer program did not go away, and a new ele-ment was introduced in the 1987-88 time frame, when American Airlines and Citibank began offering credit cards to American's Frequent Flyers. The card allowed American's Frequent Flyers to accrue additional miles based on their purchases with the Citibank credit card. This gave American a significant advantage over all of their competitors. In response to the American Citibank deal, my team put together a proposal that Delta would seek a partner to create a similar credit card program in order to compete with American in this space.

Whit Hawkins, whom I reported to, approved my proposal

and sent it on to Finance, which quickly rejected the idea of a co-branded credit card. By the time Finance rejected our proposal, the issue had become more critical, as Eastern had followed American and negotiated a co-branded credit card with another bank. Obviously Whit and I were concerned about our competitive position. Based on the feedback we were receiving from our sales team and customers, I recommended to Whit that we improve our competitive position by launching a triple mileage program that would reward our best customers with triple miles. Since Finance had no control over what Marketing did with the Frequent Flyer program, we moved forward with triple miles. While this was an expensive strategy for Delta, in many cases this was a better deal for our Frequent Flyers than a co-branded credit card. We caught a lot of flak from the Finance Department, but we continued that program from early 1988 until sometime in 1989. We ended it when Finance finally backed off of their opposition to Delta participating in a co-branded credit card.

In 1989-1990, American Express launched a mileage-based credit card program that was available to a number of airlines, including Delta, but wasn't exclusive to any specific airline. We continued to participate in the broader program until Paul Matsen and I negotiated an exclusive co-branded credit card agreement with American Express in 1994. Negotiating a deal with Amex that was acceptable to Delta was a lengthy and challenging process that involved many meetings and phone calls.

This co-branded credit card has proven to be a great financial success for Delta, as we negotiated a revenue guarantee of $1 billion, and I recently saw information on the internet that indicates Delta could realize $3.5 billion in revenue from the Sky Miles card in 2017, and the number is projected to increase to $4 billion by 2021.

My involvement in the Frequent Flyer program was reduced significantly when responsibility for the program was moved to the Advertising and Sales Promotion Department. However, I became very involved again following one of my promotions.

Delta's Travel Agency Computer Reservations System (CRS)

While very involved in the evolution of the Frequent Flyer program and fighting the branded credit card battle, I was also trying to fully understand Delta's position as a CRS provider. Delta's poor competitive position in the "CRS Battle" is another example of Delta's failure to embrace and create a marketing-focused technology strategy. It put the company far behind our major competitors where the CRS was concerned. We simply could not go to market with an internally developed CRS product in a timely manner. We had to take some creative action to compete with American's Sabre and Eastern's System One CRS systems, as they were out there in the marketplace, rapidly installing their CRS systems in travel agencies.

In a strategy to quickly address the issue, Whit Hawkins and Tony McKinnon cut a deal with United Airlines, which was not a significant Delta competitor at that time, to "white label" or partner with the United Apollo computer reservations system and sell it as our own CRS product. We branded our CRS product "Datas." Since American and Eastern were aggressively selling their version of the CRS product, being in the market with Datas was very important to Delta in many ways.

As we were cutting the deal to white label/partner with Apollo, we had already begun developing our own product. In 1983, we finally came to market with Datas II, our "home-grown" CRS product.

While we were engaged in building Datas II, the Delta sales team was out in the marketplace doing an incredible job of selling the Delta Datas CRS. Gary Swanson, a sales rep in Boston at the time, was the best CRS salesperson on the Delta team.

While working frantically to better manage my CRS responsibilities, I continued to do my day job in Planning, which included closely monitoring the utilization and overall performance of the various aircraft in the Delta fleet. The aircraft we monitored very closely was our small fleet of thirteen stretch DC-8s. My team had developed some compelling data that reflected how inefficiently we were using them in terms of aircraft and crew utilization and cost.

After a lot of "counseling and advice" from Art Ford, Delta's chief engineer, who had good access to Mr. Garrett, I got enough courage to go directly to Mr. Garrett to discuss this data (without telling any of the people I reported to what I was doing). It was a good example of hoping to get forgiveness if you didn't think you could get permission. My intent was to convince Mr. Garrett that we should sell these aircraft to one of the all-cargo airlines. After he looked at the data I shared, he agreed and set the process in motion to dispose of the stretch DC-8s.

As I was about to leave his office, he said, "By the way, I just saw this staffing report where you have fifty-plus people on the payroll who are working on or selling our Datas II computer reservations system. I have been assured by Finance and the people in Delta Technology that we have one of the best products in the market, and we don't need all these people out there selling Datas, and I want you to downsize this group."

I said, "Mr. Garrett, with all due respect to what these folks have told you, we are at the very bottom when it comes to the CRS product, and if you will give me a day, I will prove it to you."

He agreed to give me some time to come back with the facts. I left his office and went directly to the office of Tom Cauthen, a key player in the Datas II group. I asked Tom to prepare a list of the ten most important functions of the CRS as valued by the travel agents and create a chart that showed where Delta stood on each of these functions versus our competition. When Tom finished this work, it demonstrated that Delta was at or near the bottom on all ten of these key functions. I took this document to Mr. Garrett. After he reviewed it, he called Joe Cooper, Tony McKinnon, and Whit Hawkins to his office and read them the riot act. (I can't remember if I shared this document with the Finance or IT folks, but I am sure Mr. Garrett did.) This incident was yet another great example of how God was holding my hand during my Delta career.

As a result of seeing the data I gave him, Mr. Garrett had Joe, Whit, and Tony call a meeting the next day of all the key people involved in Datas II, and we started collecting data on our competitive position and the work we needed to do to make Datas II a competitive product.

The fact that I didn't consult with Joe Cooper before meeting with Mr. Garrett reflects his lack of engagement concerning technology as it impacted the Marketing Division. I got my ass kicked for going directly to "Mr. G" with this information rather than taking it up the chain of command, but I was concerned that nothing would happen if I went through the chain of command. Even with the improvements and increased focus on our CRS product as a result of these meetings, we were never able to get close to the success of American's Sabre, but we did become more competitive with Eastern and TWA.

Early on, I learned that in markets like Atlanta and Cincinnati, where Delta was a dominant carrier, we could leverage our market strength and encourage our major corporate accounts like Coke and Procter & Gamble to encourage their travel agents to use our "Datas II" system to book their reservations.

In early 1986, we were still far behind in the CRS game, so Whit Hawkins and I arranged to meet with Carl Icahn, the major shareholder and CEO of Trans World Airlines and the PARS computer reservations system. Since TWA's PARS market share wasn't any better than our Datas II market share, Whit and I wanted to test the water to see if Mr. Icahn would consider selling PARS to Delta. He cut the conversation fairly short by putting a significant price tag on the table. But being the shrewd guy he was, he did indicate he was open to negotiating a deal. Whit and I knew this conversation was not going anywhere, and we walked away.

Not too long after the Icahn meeting, Tony and Whit started negotiating with American to merge Sabre and Datas II into a single CRS company. American Airlines was very interested in this concept, but the price American wanted us to pay to make it happen was totally unreasonable. The price, along with the advice from lawyers representing both airlines that we could never get DOJ approval to combine the two CRS products, caused the deal to fall apart. We were back on our own with our inferior product.

Since the efforts to cut a deal with both TWA/PARS and American/Sabre failed, my team, led by Jimmy McCullough, continued to make improvements to Datas II, but we weren't becoming a serious competitive factor in the CRS business until we successfully negotiated a deal with TWA and Northwest Airlines to combine our CRS resources and create a new company called Worldspan.

Changes in Delta's Senior Management Team

A series of senior management retirements and promotions began in April 1985 when Joe Cooper retired as senior vice president of sales and marketing. Whit Hawkins was promoted from vice president of sales to senior vice president of sales and marketing, and Al Kolakowski succeeded Whit as vice president of sales. Some of Al's field sales responsibilities were handed off to me.

While I was already working ten to twelve hours a day to manage my CRS, Frequent Flyer, and Planning responsibilities, my next challenge occurred unexpectedly in early 1987 when I received a call from Whit Hawkins. He told me that Delta had been approached by Disney to consider replacing Eastern as the official airline of Disney World. He said that senior management wanted me to negotiate and manage a deal with Disney. Eastern had been the official airline of Disney World since it opened, and because of Eastern's continuing financial and other problems, Disney didn't want to renew the contract with Eastern.

I was highly motivated to secure the Disney deal, as it would be a major boost to the Orlando hub, which we had been building over the last few years. Shortly after I had a couple of meetings in Atlanta with Disney executive Pete Clark, he arranged for Whit Hawkins and me to meet with the senior-level Disney corporate executives in Los Angeles to finalize the deal. We successfully negotiated the deal with Disney, and on July 1, 1987, we were the official airline of Walt Disney World. The contract was for ten years, ending in June 1997.

A few days after we signed the contract, Delta Chairman and CEO Ron Allen held a press conference in one of the hangars to announce that Delta would become the new official airline of Walt Disney World on July 1. In addition to lots of Delta people and the media, others in attendance included Mickey, Minnie, Donald, Goofy, and a group of senior-level Disney executives including CEO Frank Wells.

The Disney deal gave Delta a great deal of brand recognition

I negotiated the deal that resulted in Delta Air Lines being named the official airline of Walt Disney World. Here, a famous friend helps me celebrate.

thanks to the way the folks on the front line with Delta and Disney handled the Disney opportunities. The Walt Disney World deal also opened the door for Delta to become the official airline of Disneyland in California, which became more important after the merger with Western.

My responsibilities related to Disney continued for a while, as I had to work with Disney to make sure Delta received the appropriate and promised recognition. About two to three months into the deal, the responsibilities for the Disney relationship were handed to Director of Advertising and Sales Promotion Judy Jordan. Dan Doggendorf was given day-to-day responsibility for managing the Disney relationship.

A few years after the contract was signed, Dan discovered that

Disney/MGM Studios was planning to open a studio/theme park in May of 1995 and needed an aircraft interior scene for this studio/theme park. Dan also learned that Delta was looking for a way to shoot onboard advertising and safety videos that wouldn't require taking an aircraft out of service. Dan worked with Delta Maintenance and found an L-1011 fuselage that Disney could use. Dan negotiated an agreement with Disney that if Delta provided them a fuselage for their studio/theme park, they would let Delta shoot the Delta videos in that fuselage.

James Ray, a Delta mechanic, moved the fuselage from Oklahoma to Disney World, and that worked beautifully for both parties. Disney estimated that twenty-six million people a year visited the studio. After the Delta-Disney deal ended in 1996, the fuselage was brought back to Atlanta and has served as the "store" in the Delta Flight Museum for more than fifteen years.

During the ten-plus years of the Delta-Disney relationship, both parties took advantage of the many opportunities produced by the partnership, and both benefited in many ways.

The Western Merger

My life became a little more complicated and my workload increased in 1987 when we acquired Western Airlines, but there were some significant upsides as well as a few downsides to the deal.

Some of the most favorable impacts of the merger with Western included:

1. Western had significantly more resources and focus on technology than Delta.
2. The merger greatly enhanced our presence on the West Coast, which was a big CRS market.

3. The combined volume of the two airlines made Datas II a more attractive CRS alternative for a number of the travel agencies.

4. The Western hub in Salt Lake City complemented and strengthened our hubs in Cincinnati, Dallas, and Atlanta.

The technology talent we inherited from Western, including Cal Rader, Western's chief information officer, combined with our significantly larger networks, motivated Northwest and TWA to reach out to Delta in 1988 to discuss the possibility of combining the two CRS systems. We did the deal, and having Cal Rader available to run the company gave Delta some leverage in negotiating with Northwest and TWA. In early 1990, the three airlines created a new CRS enterprise, Worldspan. All three airlines had two seats on the board, with Delta represented by Al Kolakowski and Jim Matthews, a junior Finance person.

In addition to helping Delta strengthen its CRS customer base, the merger also provided Delta the opportunity to grow the Delta network. My scheduling team, led by Richard Johnson and Mike Bell, moved quickly to grow the Delta brand by increasing our frequencies from our existing major hubs to Los Angeles, San Francisco, Seattle, and Salt Lake City.

More Changes in Delta's Management Team

In August of 1987, Dave Garrett, Delta's chairman of the board and CEO, retired, and Ron Allen, Delta's president, succeeded him. Hollis Harris succeeded Ron Allen as president, a position he held until his retirement in 1990. When Hollis retired, Ron Allen became chairman, CEO, and president.

In 1988, I was promoted to assistant vice president of planning, and in 1990, I was promoted to vice president of planning and advertising.

In May of 1991, Whit Hawkins was promoted to president and chief operating officer, and Al Kolakowski succeeded him as senior vice president of sales and marketing.

Visit to Taipei

When we started flying from Portland to the Asian markets, we contracted with a "general sales agent" in each market to represent Delta with our customers and others as necessary. Since Taipei was our largest market, Whit Hawkins asked Ivan Dezelic and me to organize a meeting with our Taipei GSA. We met with him in his office, and afterward he hosted a dinner for us in his home. He also invited the minister of aviation and two other government officials. While we were eating, our host began the Asian tradition of toasting everyone at the table with a shot of scotch. The tradition required everyone to toast him in return then slam the glass down on the table. After this first toast, all the Asians toasted everyone. By the time of the last toast, we had all consumed a lot of scotch. I can't remember how productive the meeting was.

The next day, we had lunch with the president of Air China and some of his staff. Since we were catching a flight back to Los Angeles that afternoon, and out of fear that our host would do the Asian "toasting" ritual again, we arrived at the restaurant early, gave our waiter a big tip, and told him not to put any alcohol in our glasses if our host started that toasting process. As feared, they did start the toasting, but all we drank was water, and we were able to catch our flight to Los Angeles.

Developing Delta's Alliance Strategies

Appendix 8 contains the details related to the many alliances Delta participated in following our initial alliance with Swiss Air. Delta was one of the most active airlines in forming alliances, and we were viewed as industry leaders in this segment of the airline industry. As part of our strategy to emphasize Delta's alliance leadership role, we hosted a Global Alliance Conference in 1997 at the Waldorf Astoria hotel in New York City. Susie Snider and her team did an outstanding job of planning and executing this three-day event, which was attended by many global airlines.

Eastern Shuts Down

In 1989, Eastern Air Lines, one of Delta's major competitors, experienced a crippling strike that, combined with some serious mismanagement issues and the collapse of the economy, resulted in Eastern being shut down and liquidated in 1991. I became involved in exploring which Eastern markets we should add service to and which of their assets Delta should pursue, including restricted routes they were flying. Due to fleet constraints, Delta was a bit limited on flying any routes we might pick up. With this issue in mind, we immediately focused on their L-1011 fleet as an item of great interest.

I traveled to New York a few times to participate in the bankruptcy process and bid on their assets. The Delta Technical Operations Department was charged with checking out their fleet of L-1011 aircraft to determine if they were airworthy. Based on recommendations from the Technical Ops group, we acquired a few of the Eastern L-1011 aircraft. This turned out to be a bad decision, as these aircraft required a significant amount of additional maintenance, and we incurred a lot of downtime with these aircraft, which hurt our schedule reliability.

While Delta did benefit some from the Eastern shutdown, it didn't return Delta to profitability, as the impact of the economic downturn was so profound. As a matter of fact, a Wall Street group reported that the losses the airlines incurred during the economic downturn were greater than the combined profits the industry had earned since the commercial airline industry began operating in the 1920s.

About the time Eastern was shutting down, Ron Allen decided to transfer the responsibility for advertising and sales promotion from Al Kolakowski to me, and my title was changed to vice president of planning and advertising.

Acquisition of Pan American Airways' Assets

While I was trying to get my arms around my new advertising and sales promotion responsibilities, Delta began discussions with Pan Am to acquire their European routes and the shuttle. As usual, I was very involved in these negotiations and chaired several meetings.

The Pan Am European operation appealed to everyone at Delta who shared my passion for expansion into more European markets. Pan Am served several markets in Europe from their John F. Kennedy and Berlin hubs. Pan Am's Berlin hub was a product of the Cold War, as the US had lots of control over air service in Berlin and Germany following World War II.

Pan Am's Berlin hub produced additional traffic on their transatlantic service, as it was a connecting point to many smaller markets. Delta didn't serve any of these Pan Am European markets from JFK and in many instances didn't serve the markets period.

My team was given the responsibility of determining the value of Pan Am's European operation, which required that I chair several meetings in New York and Atlanta with representatives of Pan Am and Delta. Since Pan Am was already in Chapter 11 bankruptcy, we were also required to have several meetings with the attorneys representing the creditors committee. On a couple of occasions, we held meetings with large groups of creditors and interested parties to update them on our plans for the acquisition, including the price we were willing to pay.

Some of these meetings took place at night and ran into the early hours of the morning. This aspect of the negotiations became more challenging when TWA Chairman Carl Icahn stepped in and offered more money than Delta had offered to pay. The creditors also pressured Delta to acquire the Latin American operation, and to get the creditors' support, Delta agreed to invest several million dollars in debt or in possession financing to support the continued operation of the Latin American network.

While we were negotiating with Pan Am management and the creditors committee, we were also negotiating with the labor unions about the number of Pan Am employees we would offer Delta jobs if and when the acquisition was completed. As part of the negotiations, we had to decide on the number and type of Pan Am aircraft that we would keep. The Airbus A310 was the only aircraft we wanted, and we weren't very enthusiastic about it. The deal was finally consummated in August of 1991 at a cost of $1.39 billion plus a loan to Pan Am so they could continue operating the Latin American network.

I attended and chaired numerous meetings as we negotiated with the various parties. To be sure we left these meetings with the correct information, I kept precise notes on the issues that were discussed at each meeting. This careful note taking came back to bite me later.

A few months after we closed the deal on Pan Am's European assets, Pan Am ran out of the funds needed to continue operating the Latin American service, and Delta refused to put in more cash, resulting in Pan Am shutting down the Latin American operation. That basically meant the end of Pan Am.

Shortly after they shut down the Latin American operation, the creditors committee filed suit against Delta, alleging that we had promised to put more money into the Latin American operation, though we had not. The creditors' attorneys filed the usual discovery request to secure copies of all documents and communications related to the entire transaction. In the discovery process, I submitted the notebook that I had used to record key discussion points in all of the various meetings I attended or chaired.

As is usual in this kind of lawsuit, the creditors' attorney served notice that they wanted to depose several Delta people who had participated in the transaction. I was on that list because of my notes. I was deposed for almost five days since my notes were so extensive. Our attorneys did a good job of preparing me for the deposition, and while it was tedious, tiring, and stressful, it all worked out okay, as I didn't reveal anything of benefit to the creditors. When the case went to trial, I was also called by the creditors as a witness to testify on commitments made by Delta. In the end, Delta prevailed.

While both Ron Allen and I were criticized by several people for doing the Pan Am deal, the truth is that had we not acquired those European routes and grown the airline, Delta likely would have been swallowed up in one of the mergers that have taken place over the past fifteen years, and the Delta name would have disappeared.

As the Pan Am deal was winding down, the relationship between Ron Allen and Al Kolakowski, which was never very good, got worse, and in the fall of 1991, Ron and Whit demoted Al back to vice president of sales, and I was promoted to senior vice president of sales and marketing.

When we acquired the Pan American assets, each department head had the opportunity to check out the key Pan Am employees to see if they wanted to bring them on board. As I was having discussions with some of the Pan Am people I trusted, one of them recommended I talk with Tamer Ozmen, a young man from Turkey who had a good reputation for forecasting and analytical work. Since we needed those skills, I reached out to see if he was interested in working for Delta. When I tried to contact him, I discovered that since he was a Turkish citizen, he still had to serve his mandatory military tour of duty. When I tracked him down, I told him that I was interested in talking to him about joining Delta. He got released from his military duty, came to Atlanta for an interview, and was hired.

As Tamer and I discussed Turkey, he convinced me that I should visit. A year or so later, my Delta colleague Marty Braham and I had to attend an alliance meeting in Switzerland, and Millie accompanied me. Marty and I decided that since we were going to be so close to Turkey, we should visit, and I arranged for Tamer to meet us there. We connected with Tamer in Marmaris and stayed in a nice hotel near the Aegean Sea. Tamer's uncle had arranged for us to spend the next day on a yacht, and we had a great time. After that experience in Turkey, we chartered a large sailboat with a full crew every summer for the next six years. The Brahams and three or four other couples joined us on these "sailboat excursions," and Tamer frequently participated.

On each of these trips, we always arranged to stay in Istanbul for two or three days, as there was so much ancient history, great food, and some great shopping, including the Grand Bazaar. We saw some incredible ancient historic sites, including many dating back to the Romans and earlier. One interesting site we visited was the church where St. Nicholas was the priest. In the village near St. Nicholas's Church, there were fifty or more shops and a large number of street vendors selling Christmas decorations.

Changes at Worldspan

When I became Delta's senior vice president of sales and marketing, Worldspan was one of the first issues I focused on, as the CRS issue had become a more critical element of the airline industry, and Worldspan wasn't delivering on product development, securing new clients, or generating revenues. Al Kolakowski and Jim Matthews still represented Delta on the Worldspan board of directors, and they were obviously not doing a good job of monitoring or influencing Worldspan's performance. One of my first actions was to replace Al and Jim as Delta's representatives on the Worldspan board. I recruited Rex McClelland, senior vice president of administration, to replace Matthews, and I took Al's seat.

When I took my seat on the Worldspan board, Mike Levine, my counterpart at Northwest Airlines, was one of Northwest's reps on the board, and he was involved in many of the decisions being made about Worldspan's strategy. TWA's key board member was Mike Palumbo, and he rarely engaged in any serious discussions or decision-making. At the first meeting I attended, Mike Levine gave Cal Rader, the Worldspan CEO, a list of IT development projects he wanted Worldspan to work on for Northwest. I said, "Excuse me, is this software development for Worldspan or Northwest?" and he responded that it was for Northwest. I asked Cal if Worldspan was being compensated for doing this development work for

Northwest. Cal replied that Worldspan wasn't being compensated for doing this work, and I said very harshly that there was no way in hell Worldspan was going to continue doing this software development for Northwest without being paid for it.

Levine laughed and said, "I wondered how long it would take you dumb asses at Delta to catch on to what was going on here." I also raised the issue that Worldspan didn't have the IT resources to do this development work for Northwest, even if Northwest compensated them for it, since Worldspan was so far behind on their internal IT development. This discussion basically put a stop to Worldspan doing IT development work for Northwest.

Worldspan had some serious personnel/skills issues, which Cal made even more challenging because of some of the people he recruited. In the first quarter of 1995, the board decided we needed to replace Cal based on Worldspan's poor performance over the last three years. I drew the short straw and was given the task of sitting down with Cal and telling him the board felt that it was time to replace him as CEO. We gave Cal a generous severance package, and he handled his departure very well. While I knew that we had to replace Cal, I felt bad about it, as Cal had brought so many good ideas to Delta related to ways we could improve Delta's IT process/product based on what he had achieved at Western.

After the separation was negotiated with Cal, I was asked to chair the process of recruiting his replacement. One of the first names that surfaced was Mike Buckman, who held a senior position at American Express. He had also held a senior position at American Airlines for many years. Mike was highly respected by his peers in the travel industry. In May of 1995, we offered Mike the Worldspan CEO position, and he accepted. Hiring Mike was expensive, but we were confident Mike was worth the investment, as we needed a great leader at Worldspan. The first year, he made significant improvements in every aspect of the operation, including actually making it profitable. With Mike managing Worldspan, supported by people like Sam Galeotos, we were a competitive CRS provider.

I gave Jimmy McCullough the responsibility of assisting Worldspan when Delta needed to be involved in any issues. I also gave Jimmy the responsibility of making sure that Delta provided the tools we needed on our side of the CRS issue. All of this took a lot of pressure off me on a day-to-day basis where Worldspan was concerned.

Over time, both Delta and Northwest expressed interest in selling or merging Worldspan with another CRS. At the time, Worldspan was providing processing support to Abacus, a Singapore-based CRS that served Singapore Airlines and other Asian airlines. Because of the existing business relationship with Abacus and the fact that we knew the Singapore Airlines people so well, we approached them about expanding the relationship. Mike Buckman, Mike Levine, and I flew to Hong Kong to meet with the Abacus team and had some lengthy discussions concerning a business partnership. As it turned out, Abacus was already in discussions with American and Sabre, and based on the deal that American put on the table, Abacus chose to partner with Sabre.

After the failure of the talks with Abacus, we initiated discussions with Amadeus. The boards of the two companies met in New York to review and discuss the terms outlined in the agreement. After that session, the two boards held separate sessions so they could privately discuss the provisions of the agreement.

We reconvened the meeting of the two boards and reached an agreement. As everyone was putting their papers in their briefcases, one of our board members said, "Hold on a minute. We would like two additional concessions included in the agreement." The Amadeus board members were so furious that one of our board members had asked for these additional concessions that they basically said "Go to hell" and walked out of the room. We lost that opportunity to sell Worldspan to Amadeus or merge the two companies.

The internet was becoming so hot that internet start-ups were emerging in every facet of the business world. This development created a lot of opportunities for good, experienced internet leaders. Due to the great reputation Mike Buckman had earned as Worldspan's CEO, Mike was recruited in March of 1999 by Realtor.com to be their CEO. When it was announced that Mike was leaving Worldspan, the following statement was printed in one of the travel publications: "Since his appointment as Worldspan CEO in May of 1995, Buckman has led the company through a period of unprecedented growth, profitability, and success." The Worldspan board began the search for Mike's replacement, and that was a real challenge.

On the family front, a couple of years after Jeff moved to Dallas, he met and began dating Cindy Hughes, who worked for American Express, one of Jeff's customers. They were married in 1995, and their wedding in Dallas was a great event. Dr. Harry Barrow, our minister at Newnan Presbyterian Church, performed the ceremony. Several of our Newnan friends flew out to Dallas to attend the wedding. Many of Jeff's colleagues from Alamo, including Mike Egan, also attended, as did many of Cindy's family and friends.

Since we had a limited budget for drinks before the rehearsal dinner, we told the owner of the restaurant to close the bar at

9 p.m. He didn't, and the bar tab was as large as the cost of the dinner. The wedding the next day and the reception afterward were great, and everyone had a wonderful time. After the reception, the Newnan crowd went to the airport to catch our flight home.

In 1996, Jeff was promoted again and moved to Chicago. They bought a house in Park Ridge, which is very convenient to O'Hare. In September of 1996, our first and only grandson, Robby, was born. Millie and I made many trips to Park Ridge to spend time with Robby and attend his baseball games. By the time he was four, he was playing T-ball.

In 1995, we bought our current home, and after some extensive renovation and expansion, we moved into the house in 1996. We built a pool a year or so after we moved in, and Robby loved to come stay a few days with us so he could play in the pool with Lauren and Garrett, his cousins.

About the time we were moving into our new home, our friends the Brahams built a house in western Ireland near the village of Doolin. It was a beautiful home that sat high up on a hill and looked out over the Atlantic, and you could see the Aran Islands. Millie and I made several trips to visit the Brahams and usually did some sightseeing. One of the most interesting sightseeing trips we made was to Achill Island on the extreme west side of Ireland. The views from Achill Island were breathtaking, but the best part for me was the golf course Marty and I played every time we went to the island. It was a self-service golf course where you put your money in a slot, took a handcart, and played as much golf as you wanted. But here's the best part—the course was also a sheep ranch. There were sheep on the course, and yellow ropes were around the greens, apparently to keep the sheep off. Millie's favorite place in Ireland was Rosleague Manor, which was just a few miles from Clifden, another Irish village we love to visit.

Changes in Delta's Sales and Marketing Organization

In addition to the issue that needed to be addressed at Worldspan, it was obvious to me and others in Delta's senior management that some significant changes and improvements had to be made in Delta's sales and marketing organization, both in the General Office and in Field Sales. Over the next three to four months, I evaluated all the management-level people in the organization and gave a lot of thought to how I would address this problem. After consulting with a couple of people outside of Delta who had demonstrated good management skills, I decided to hold a two-day retreat on a Friday and Saturday.

I wanted to have a great facilitator run the meeting, and a person I trusted recommended that I engage Eric Freiburg, a senior partner at McKinsey Consulting, as facilitator. I set the theme for the retreat as "If it is not broken, break it and fix it." At the opening of the retreat, I presented all twenty-five participants with a coffee cup with those words on it. Eric went through all the responsibilities of the Delta sales organization and gave everyone an assignment on Friday and told them to be prepared to present answers to the issues the next day. It was a great session, and all of the people who reported to me came away from the retreat knowing that things were about to change. And changes did occur, as I promoted some people I had confidence in, and as a result of the pressure my new management team and I put on the underperformers, we had several people take early retirement. We also demoted or terminated a few others. I suppose you could say "Sir John's broom" was sweeping away obsolescence again.

I treasure the portrait I received on my retirement from Delta, which pictured me sitting "on top of the world."

While we had made significant progress in improving the performance of the sales organization, we just didn't have the internal talent we needed to take it as far as I wanted it to go.

In 1994, I requested permission to go outside the company and recruit a vice president of sales. Much to my surprise, Ron Allen and the human resources department gave me the green light to recruit from outside the company. With HR's help, I worked with a top recruiting firm to find that person I needed to fill the vice president of sales slot. The search was cut short when I received a call from Tony McKinnon that I should talk to Vince Caminiti, the number two sales guy at American. When I talked to him about the position, Vince was very interested in the Delta job. After

Vince had some rigorous interviews with me and all the other senior officers, including Ron Allen, I hired Vince, and right away he made a huge positive impact.

I was one of those people who really believed in managing by walking around, so I was very visible to all the people who worked for me, both in the General Office and in the field. I also believed in keeping people at all levels informed on what was going on and seeking their input about how we could improve our process. As part of that objective, I scheduled quarterly presentations and invited everyone in Sales and Marketing at a manager level and above to attend. I also invited management staff from the other divisions. I made it a priority to secure good motivational speakers from outside the company. Being the Vince Lombardi fan that I was, I arranged for Bart Starr to be the speaker at one of these events, and he was a real hit with the group. These quarterly events were very successful, and most of the credit goes to Caleb Harkness, who worked in sales promotion, as he did a great job making the arrangements and lining up the speakers. The best part of this process happened after I retired. Vince Caminiti, who was acting chief marketing officer, invited me to come to the next quarterly meeting, and they presented me with a great portrait that reflected me sitting "on top of the world."

Once a month, I also had breakfast with twelve to fourteen of the rank-and-file employees, and I always invited people from other divisions to attend these breakfast sessions. I spent the first ten minutes sharing information related to major projects the company was working on, such as buying new aircraft. Then I gave the participants the opportunity to ask me questions and make comments about how the company was performing. I really enjoyed these sessions.

During the major holidays, I requested that everyone on my

staff at the director level join me in working at Hartsfield to assist with the increased volume of passengers. The Hartsfield staff was appreciative that the marketing management team would do this, especially when no one else in the General Office would show up.

In early 1994, I read articles in a couple of business publications that related to how some large companies were restructuring and consolidating their senior leadership positions in order to keep the key decision makers in the loop, speed up favorable change, and improve overall management. After reading those articles, I talked with Ron Allen about the advantage of forming an executive council and dividing the company into three divisions. I shared with him some examples of other companies that had done this successfully. After several meetings with myself, Maurice Worth, and Harry Alger, Ron decided to form an executive council, with each of us being promoted to executive vice president and having responsibility for roughly one third of the airline, excluding Finance and Legal, which would report to Ron.

The Delta Executive Council included me, executive vice president of marketing; Maurice Worth, executive vice president of administration; and Harry Alger, executive vice president of operations.

CHAPTER TWENTY-ONE

Serving on Delta's Executive Council

Harry Alger was given responsibility for the operating side, which included Flight Ops, In-flight, Ground Operations, and Technical Operations. Maurice Worth was given responsibility for all administrative functions, including Human Resources, Public Relations, and Corporate Security. I was given responsibility for Sales, Marketing, Strategic Planning, Scheduling, Pricing, and IT. Ron kept responsibility for Legal and Finance. This approach worked very well, as the four of us got together frequently to address issues, opportunities, and plans to implement our decisions.

The three new executive vice presidents partnered with Bob Adams, the head of Human Resources, to convince Ron that we needed to provide continuing education opportunities for many of our up-and-coming management staff. This education was necessary, as the majority of those in officer and management positions at Delta were beneficiaries of our "promote from within" culture. Many of the management staff and Delta would benefit significantly from additional education and training to keep pace with a rapidly changing business environment.

This program worked well, and a large number of our management team took advantage of this opportunity to better prepare themselves for the future. I was one of the first to take advantage of the program and attended the executive MBA program being

In 1990, I had the opportunity to participate in the executive development program at Northwestern's Kellogg School of Business.

offered by Northwestern University's Kellogg School of Business. One of the brighter young professors asked me to let him visit Delta for a few days and see how we were using our yield management technology. I arranged for him to spend about a week with our pricing and yield management team. He was most appreciative and said he learned a lot.

In late 1994, Judy Jordan decided to resign as director of advertising and sales promotion and become more involved in the home decorating business she had started. The search firm I used to find Judy's replacement found Paul Matsen, who was working for Young & Rubicam, a large New York–based advertising agency. His primary account was Kentucky Fried Chicken. Paul came down for an interview and to check us out. I offered Paul the position, and after thinking about it for a couple of days, he declined my offer. A couple of weeks later, Paul called and asked if the position was still available. I told him it was and I would be delighted to have him on my team. He accepted, and like Vince, he made a significant impact in that department. I was especially pleased to have him leading the team negotiating the Sky Miles Card contract with American Express. Paul did such a good job in advertising and sales promotion that we promoted him to vice president of strategy and gave him the responsibility of creating and running the unit. When we moved him out of the advertising position, we hired an executive search firm to help us find Paul's replacement, and after talking to several candidates, we recruited Gayle Bock.

Paul remained in the strategic planning position until Leo Mullin became CEO and Mullin's "friend" Warren Jenson wanted to bring someone in from outside of Delta to run the strategy operation.

While a lot of change was underway at Delta, some interesting changes were happening in my personal life as well. In 1995, I was recruited to serve on the board of directors of the Peach Bowl, which at that time was a second-tier bowl. Since Ron Allen had rescued the Peach Bowl and moved it to the Atlanta Chamber of Commerce when he was president of the chamber, he encouraged me to get involved, so I accepted the invitation. In 1996, I

Robert Dale Morgan, managing director of the Peach Bowl, presents me with an award for my work on the Corporate Ticket Sales Campaign.

When Ron Allen was involved with the Atlanta Chamber of Commerce, he got Delta involved with the Chick-fil-A Peach Bowl, and I remain involved today, serving on its executive committee and board of trustees.

Millie and I are shown here with former Atlanta Falcons coach Leeman Bennett and his wife, Pat, as Leeman and I are inducted into the Peach Bowl Volunteer Hall of Fame at the 2015 Chick-fil-A Peach Bowl on December 31.

was elected vice chair, which meant that I would be chairman in 1997 and 1998. Shortly before I assumed the role as chairman of the bowl, Robert Dale Morgan and Albert Tarica, who was the current chairman, negotiated a deal with Chick-fil-A to become the sponsor of the bowl, and the bowl later became the Chick-fil-A Peach Bowl. Shortly after I became chairman, the City of Houston recruited Robert Dale Morgan, who was serving as general manager of the bowl, to move to Houston and manage the upcoming Super Bowl game. As chairman of the Peach Bowl, I became chair of the search committee to find Morgan's replacement. After interviewing a number of candidates, we chose Gary Stokan, who was running his own sports marketing business. We couldn't have made a better decision, as Gary and his staff have taken the Chick-fil-A Peach Bowl from a second-tier bowl to one of the six college football playoff bowls.

I am now on the executive committee and board of trustees of the Bowl, and I also chair the Investment Committee.

Next Challenge: Leadership 7.5

The first Gulf War had a significant negative impact on the global economy, with most of the Western World experiencing one of the worst recessions the US had faced since the Great Depression. This recession caused the US airline industry to experience significant losses during 1994 and 1995, and Delta was no exception, as our losses were extensive.

Ron Allen and the senior management team met in January 1995 to develop an aggressive plan that would return Delta to profitability and achieve a 12 percent operating margin. Achieving this goal would require aggressively reducing Delta's operating costs.

As the result of a great deal of research, led by McKinsey Consulting, we determined that based on our projected revenues, we would have to reduce our average available seat miles (ASM) cost to 7.5 cents to achieve our 12 percent operating margin. The cost- reduction program was officially branded as "Leadership 7.5." This target represented a reduction of about 2 cents per seat mile, which was aggressive. Every division was required to carefully analyze their costs and submit the costs they would focus on reducing. After several meetings, the cost-reduction plan was approved, and each division began working on implementing the plan they had submitted. Based on the cost-savings opportunities that we identified, we expected that when the plan was fully implemented, the areas targeted for cost reductions would produce savings in excess of a billion dollars annually.

While Marketing did target significant savings by reducing our advertising spend, distribution cost, and head count, the most significant cost reductions opportunity involved reducing travel agency commissions. Vince Caminiti and his staff developed a plan to cap travel agency commissions at a flat $25 per transaction. Vince and his team get all the credit for putting this program together and managing our relationships with the travel agents after it was implemented. I don't recall the total savings from the commission cap, but it was in the tens of millions. Needless to say, as head of Sales and Marketing, I was very unpopular and caught a lot of flak from the travel agents and tour operators. While the travel agents initially threatened to divert business from Delta, it didn't happen, primarily because all the other airlines except TWA immediately adopted the commission cap.

The American Society of Travel Agents (ASTA), the travel agent trade group that represents the travel agents, did sue the airlines and claimed that we secretly colluded on the commission cap. They were never able to make the case, but to bring this lawsuit to a close, the airline agreed to provide the travel agents with some nominal compensation without admitting guilt.

In about one year, we reduced our cost per available seat mile from slightly more than 9 cents to about 8.4 cents as a result of all the cost-saving actions taken by the various divisions. During this same period, our revenues per available seat mile (RASM) had increased significantly from where they were when we started Leadership 7.5. As a result, we were already at the 12 percent operating margin. Maurice Worth and I worked hard to convince Ron Allen that it was time to "declare victory" and not do more damage to our product by implementing additional cost reductions. Ron felt that we had made a commitment to Wall Street to reduce our cost to 7.5 cents per mile and wasn't ready to celebrate. We finally convinced him to declare victory and start rebuilding the Delta product.

Another Challenge: Dissolution of TransQuest

In mid-1994, John King, Delta's CIO, and Rex McClelland, senior vice president of administrative services, presented the Delta Executive Council with a recommendation that Delta partner with a leading technology company and create a joint venture that would manage all of Delta's IT activities. There were some concerns about going down this path, but John and Rex made a very compelling case, and we decided to go forward with their recommendation. Following the approval of their request by the executive council, a new company called TransQuest was created. Since IT was one of my areas of responsibility, the overall responsibility for TransQuest landed on my desk. Rex and John took the position that by creating TransQuest, we would have

When my Delta responsibilities in Atlanta were expanded to include the Advertising Department, this congratulatory artwork was prepared by one of my colleagues in Advertising.

many opportunities to generate revenue by reselling the software that had been developed for Delta. Rex and John also saw this as an opportunity for Delta/TransQuest to become the software developer for the travel industry. After the executive council gave approval to go forward with TransQuest, we launched a search for a CEO to manage the new business unit. After considering a number of candidates, we hired Bill Belew.

By the first quarter of 1996, it became obvious for a number of reasons that this concept was very flawed, and in July 1996, we began the process of shutting down TransQuest. For more details of this development, please see Appendix 7, which tells the full TransQuest and Delta IT story.

Terrence Burns, Judy Jordan, and I were among the Delta officials tasked with making sure Delta was prepared for the 1996 Olympics.

The Olympics

Atlanta operation 'humming' through the Olympic Games

Atlanta airport operations are "humming" despite added Olympic pressures, taking advantage of plans first made more than a year ago. The smooth Atlanta airport operation is proving a delight to 60,000-plus daily

and on-time performance was averaging near 70 percent, both as good or better than normal.

Atlanta airport personnel are catching the Olympic spirit, Smith said, and there's an "upbeat, caring, friendly style – even more than ng they do."

volunteers each high levels of on by meeting eased number nta passengers. rs are also on ng passengers. ying the extra mith. Despite y to handle two a month, the)&D passengers rity were cause

ty precautions d we're getting ments on our government d

Delta torchbearers help flame complete Olympic journey

More than 100 Delta people have proudly carried the torch since April 27, when Delta's *Centennial Spirit* touched down in Los Angeles with the Olympic flame onboard.

Delta torchbearers made an early morning detour through the General Offices July 19 past cheering co-workers as the 115,000-mile trek neared an end. Norma Bolds (Dept.913/ATL,left) carried the flame through the gates, handing off to Jim McNiff (Dept 608/ATL).

Among other torchbearers during the flame's run through Georgia were (top right) Vicki Escarra, vice president reservation sales, and Bob Coggin (top left), executive vice president–marketing.

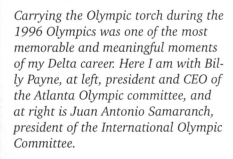

Carrying the Olympic torch during the 1996 Olympics was one of the most memorable and meaningful moments of my Delta career. Here I am with Billy Payne, at left, president and CEO of the Atlanta Olympic committee, and at right is Juan Antonio Samaranch, president of the International Olympic Committee.

CHAPTER TWENTY-TWO

Delta and the 1996 Olympics

In September of 1990, Atlanta was selected to host the 1996 Olympics. When I was promoted to senior vice president of sales and marketing, I assumed a lot of responsibility for Delta's involvement with the Olympics. Director of Advertising and Sales Promotion Judy Jordan was already engaged in some of the early planning, but as the event grew closer and the scope of work increased significantly, Ron Allen and I picked Terrence Burns to be Delta's point person for the Olympics, and he reported directly to me on Olympic issues. Billy Payne, the president and CEO of the Atlanta Olympic Committee, reached out to Ron on many occasions with a request of "Will you do this for us?" and we usually accommodated Billy and the Olympic committee.

We had many exciting activities related to the Olympics, but the one that I treasure most was being part of the Delta team that flew to Athens, Greece, with Atlanta's Olympic Committee to attend the special ceremony launching the 1996 Olympics. The most exciting part of that event was flying the Olympic torch from Athens to Los Angeles. The Olympic torch we were flying to the US was lit, and to maximize safety, Delta's Maintenance Department constructed a special container in which we could safely store the lit torch. Actually, three or four lit torches were stored in the safety container just in case the flame went out on one of them.

Since the run to carry the torch across America prior to the start of the games was beginning in Los Angeles, we flew nonstop from Athens to Los Angeles, where the torch was handed off to representatives of the Olympic committee. I have a great picture of Ron and me standing by the aircraft and handing off the torch. Being part of that event was a very special experience made even more so since Millie was with me in Athens and on the flight back to Los Angeles.

From a personal perspective, the second most exciting aspect of the 1996 Olympics was having Richard Branson and his family as our houseguests for a couple of days. Richard didn't want to have his family stay in a hotel, and when I invited them to be our guests, he didn't hesitate to say yes.

We invited several hundred of our best customers to be Delta's guests at the Olympics, and Governor Zell Miller invited us to host several dinners for them at the Governor's Mansion, which was a big hit with the guests. Millie and I participated in many other special events related to the Olympics and attended many of the games. I also had the pleasure of carrying the torch for about two miles, and the torch I carried hangs on a wall with my other Olympic memorabilia. Millie collected a significant number of the pins that various sponsors were handing out in their suites.

The entire Delta team deserves credit for doing a great job with the Olympics. Hartsfield's ground and customer service personnel really did an outstanding job in every aspect of their responsibilities, and Terrence Burns also did an outstanding job of delivering on his responsibilities.

CHAPTER TWENTY-THREE
Going Forward

In the spring of 1996, with Leadership 7.5 and the Olympics behind us, some members of Delta's board of directors began pushing us to considering changing how we were marketing Delta, including changing advertising agencies. Ron and I both pushed back and worked with BBDO, our agency, to get them to come to the table with some new strategies and creative ideas. Since they didn't come up with anything exciting, we told BBDO that we were putting the Delta account out for bid, and they chose not to compete. Gayle Bock arranged for us to meet with several agencies, and after reviewing all the proposals, we selected Omnicom to become Delta's advertising agency in April 1996.

Omnicom based a lot of their pitch around the new technology that Delta was making available to passengers on board our wide-body aircraft. This new technology was related to improving the in-flight use of laptops, a very big deal at that time. There were mixed reactions about the work of the new agency. Most of the board of directors didn't think the agency's work was very effective, and as head of marketing, I took most of the heat. While I had many great accomplishments during my career at Delta, my handling—or mishandling—of our advertising agency and their creativity really cast a shadow over all the good things I had accomplished over the past twenty-plus years. I will also confess that hiring Gayle Bock for the advertising position was not a good decision, and I take full responsibility for that decision.

The advertising was apparently just one of several issues the board was unhappy about. Some members of the board had been critical of the cost-reduction action we took related to Leadership 7.5, especially the negative impact on the employees. At the April 1997 Delta board meeting, the board advised Ron Allen that they were not going to renew his contract when his current contract ended on June 30, and he would be terminated. This development shocked many of us, especially the senior officers. Neither Maurice Worth, Harry Alger, nor I were aware that the board was going to take this action. I'm sure that someone inside Delta was aware of what was going on. One incredible aspect of this development was the fact that the board let Ron stay on until the end of his contract on June 30. They even allowed him to attend the June board of directors meeting.

On Ron's last afternoon at Delta, hundreds of employees gathered in the parking lot to say goodbye to him. Ron was famous for playing his guitar and singing country songs, and he got his guitar out of his car, sat on the back of the car, and played the guitar and sang about a half dozen songs. Then he said goodbye and got into his car and left. It was a sad day for many of us.

The board's decision to fire Ron was certainly not related to Delta's financial performance, as 1997 was on track to be one of the most profitable years—if not the most profitable year—in the history of the company. The record profitability in 1997 and the record earnings over the next two years can be attributed to Ron Allen's vision and leadership related to implementing Leadership 7.5 and the cost reductions we achieved as a result of implementing Leadership 7.5.

The Delta Board of Directors formed a search committee to recruit a new CEO, and while the search was in progress, Maurice Worth was made acting president. Maurice, Harry Alger, and I ran

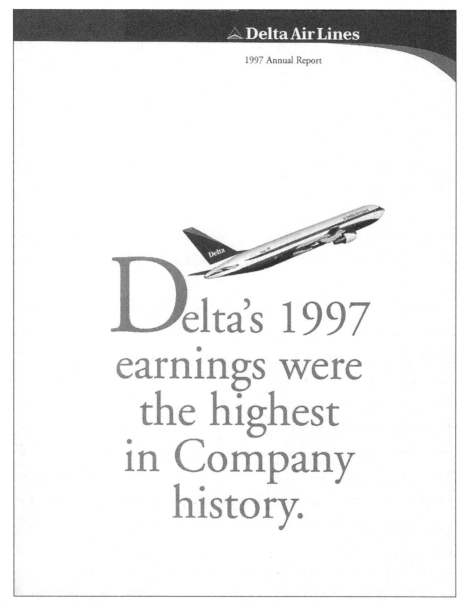

The cover of Delta's 1997 Annual Report notes the company's outstanding earnings that year.

the airline on a day-to-day basis until the board announced they had hired Leo Mullin to be the new CEO. Leo had held executive positions in banking, utility, and other industries but did not have any airline or travel industry experience. Leo came on board as the team that had been running the airline was about to deliver the most profitable year in the company's history. Of course, Leo and his new team took credit for this high level of profitability. One of my colleagues described it this way: "Leo and his guys were born on third base but claimed that they had hit a triple."

Leo was not at all impressed with me, as I didn't have an MBA, and he didn't give me any credit for my accomplishments or the leadership I had provided over the last twenty-plus years. Consequently, after about nine months, Leo and I agreed that it was time for me to retire, and I retired on May 31, 1998. I requested that Leo let me draft the press release announcing my retirement, and he quickly agreed.

I engaged my friend and attorney Dean Booth to draft my separation agreement, which Leo accepted without question. This surprised me, as it was a very "generous" package. About two years after I retired, the other two EVPs, Harry Alger and Maurice Worth, retired, or should I say were "pushed out the door." Both Harry and Maurice liked my retirement agreement so much that they used it as a template for their own separation agreements. Leo also replaced Tom Roeck, the chief financial officer, and Bob Adams, the senior vice president of human resources, with people from outside Delta. The CFO Leo hired turned out to be a complete disaster.

After I retired, I spent a lot of time thinking about what I could have done better. The four things that stood out in my mind were:

- I should have done a better job of picking the person to replace Paul Matsen as director of advertising and sales promotion.
- I should have been much more involved in managing the work of our advertising agency.
- I wish I had housed the Delta Board of Directors in a five-

star hotel during the Olympics versus housing them with our customers.

- While it was not all bad, I might have been too internally focused, and by that I mean I focused on communicating internally and keeping everyone across all divisions informed on what we were doing in Marketing versus spending more time in front of the customers.

While I certainly wasn't perfect and didn't accomplish everything on my agenda, I am very proud of many of my key accomplishments during my forty-two-year career at Delta. Appendix 9 details some of my more significant accomplishments, and I have referred to some of them in the book.

Leo reportedly made the comment to several people that "these old Delta people are dinosaurs." He should have kept some of us "old dinosaurs" around, as lots of costly mistakes were made over the next five-plus years, resulting in Delta's debt exposure increasing significantly.

When Leo became CEO of Delta in September 1997, Delta's long-term debt was approximately $1.4 billion. When Delta filed for bankruptcy in September 2006, the debt was $28.3 billion. Most of this long-term debt occurred while Leo was CEO of Delta.

When the 9/11 disaster occurred, the airline industry was in turmoil due to many factors related to 9/11. Wall Street's outlook for the airline industry was pretty grim, but one Wall Street analyst posted an opinion that Delta would be the most likely airline to survive the damage to the industry caused by 9/11. Delta did survive 9/11, but it was not a pretty picture, and by 2003-2004, Delta was well on its way to Chapter 11 bankruptcy.

When Leo and his team of senior officers realized that Chapter 11 was on the horizon, Delta arranged to have an accrual calculation on the nonqualified pension benefits each senior officer would lose in the event of a Chapter 11 bankruptcy, and he placed that amount of money in a trust to protect their nonqualified pension payments. I don't know all of the details, but I understand that these officers did receive a lump-sum payment equal to the amount they would have received in retirement. All of the officers like me who had already retired lost all of our nonqualified pension benefits. In my case, that equated to about two thirds of my pension annually.

The retired Delta senior officers who had lost their nonqualified pension benefits hired an attorney and tried very hard to prevent Leo and the Delta board from forming and funding the trust. Unfortunately, we were unsuccessful.

Delta After Leo's Departure

Jerry Grinstein became Delta's CEO on January 1, 2004 and managed the bankruptcy filing in 2006. Jerry and the attorneys Delta hired joined forces with a Delta retiree group (DALRC) to protect the benefits of the Delta retirees. Jerry also donated $2 million of his own money to help fund the insurance trust for Delta retirees. The retired officers who lost our unqualified pension benefits received shares of Delta stock to offset some of our pension losses. Jerry contributed significantly to Delta's survival through the bankruptcy and was very involved in implementing a very effective restructuring program. Jerry also assisted in derailing an attempt by US Airways to secure approval of the bankruptcy court to force a US Airways-Delta merger. Jerry strongly supported a successful Delta-employee-driven "fight" to "Keep Delta My Delta." It is my personal opinion that Jerry devoted so much time and attention to restoring Delta to the great airline it had been as payback for his involvement in the management changes that occurred in 1997. Jerry retired as CEO in 2007.

When Jerry retired, the Delta Board of Directors hired Richard

Anderson as the new CEO, and the financial performance of the company reflects that hiring Richard was a great decision. Richard put Delta on the right track to be the great airline it was prior to the management change in 1997. In 2012, Delta's net income was $1.01 billion, as revenue rose 3 percent year-over-year to $37.77 billion. In 2013, Delta reported a net profit of $10.54 billion. These 2012 and 2013 numbers are a significant contrast to the $5.2 billion net loss Delta experienced in 2004. Under Richard's leadership, Delta became the most profitable and best run airline that consistently delivers excellent customer service.

Richard chose to retire in May of 2016 and was replaced as CEO by Ed Bastian, who has continued to make improvements in all aspects of the Delta operation. Ed has been described as a critical part of Delta's success. He is an exceptional leader and has been an invaluable partner in leading the remarkable transformation of Delta over the last decade.

CHAPTER TWENTY-FOUR

A New Career: Alpine Marketing Consulting

Within a couple of days of the announcement of my retirement, I had several job offers that I did not accept, as I had formed Alpine Marketing Consulting a couple of weeks before I retired and had no interest in taking on another full-time job. I initially accepted consulting opportunities with Accenture, Priceline, and the Nassau Paradise Island Promotion Board. The amount of time I needed to spend with each account was such that I could work for all three without neglecting any of them. I spent most of my time with Accenture, as they recruited me to be their "Senior Advisor for Travel and Transportation," which required a good bit of international travel. I worked mostly with Ron Stewart, who was the partner responsible for the travel industry consulting work. I also worked with Marty Salfen, who had worked for me at Delta and left the company to take a much better job with Accenture. His job at Accenture paid significantly more than he had been making at Delta. To the best of my knowledge, Marty was the one who had suggested that Ron reach out to me about working with Accenture.

Priceline was the other consulting project that initially took up a lot of my time. I had known founder Jay Walker for a while, as he had been bugging me about making "distressed inventory" available to Priceline.

Soon after the press release was posted announcing my retirement, Jay called and asked if I would do some work for Priceline. He said, "The first thing I want you to do is tell me what I have to do to secure inventory from Delta and the other airlines." I told him it was simple, just focus on those markets/hubs where airlines have a lot of unsold inventory, not markets like Delta's Atlanta hub, where the flights run very high load factors. He said, "Okay, come work with me and help me identify these markets." During that call, Jay asked if I would fly up to New York and meet with him so he could make a formal proposal.

I agreed to meet with him, and he booked me a flight on Delta and had a limo pick me up at LaGuardia. I arrived at the office about noon and was shocked when I went into the break room for a cup of coffee and saw dozens of people having lunch, with all kinds of great food sitting on the counters. I quickly learned that none of the employees went out to lunch, as it was all brought in and paid for by Priceline. I also soon learned that this was how it worked at most of the internet start-ups.

After I met several members of the staff, Jay and I went to his office to discuss my interest in working for Priceline. The conversation quickly moved to the compensation package Priceline would offer if I would come to work for them as a consultant. We agreed on a package that worked out very well for me, and I soon learned that what Jay offered was the norm for internet start-ups. He also offered me a seat on Priceline's board of directors. I was interested in learning how the online travel business was going to work, and I was especially interested in learning more about Priceline's business model since it was so unique. As it turned out, accepting the stock options versus cash was a brilliant decision on my part, as my options were worth millions a couple of years after Jay took Priceline public in 1999. The value of the shares in the initial public offering reached $12.9 billion by the end of the first trading day. This number set a record, as it was the highest of any IPO that had been launched. While my shares were worth millions in 2000 and 2001, I wish I could have held them until 2017, when they would have been worth much more.

My task with Priceline was challenging, as the airlines didn't think Priceline was real until they heard all the buzz related to the value of the IPO. Even then, the industry was still uncertain about giving Priceline—or any online travel agent—any commissionable inventory. The issue was complicated by Priceline's unique business model.

In another brilliant move by Jay Walker, he hired William Shatner of *Star Trek* fame to be the voice and face of Priceline on TV and in their other advertising. Priceline's message to the consumer was, "Name the airfare you will pay, and we will get you a seat at that fare." Priceline's software would search every possible routing and airline to find the fare the customer had requested, or something close to that number. They also had a program to secure the consumer the lowest price for a hotel room.

The airlines were not sure how all of this was going to work out, and they were also not sure they needed Priceline to sell their "distressed inventory," especially at the low fares the Priceline technology would produce. The airline executives, especially the finance people, were envious of Priceline's market value, which further complicated the company's relationship with the airlines.

During this "get rich with the internet" period, I met with Mark Drusch, Delta's vice president of planning, about giving Priceline access to commissionable inventory, and we discussed how Delta might benefit beyond selling the seats. The Priceline team developed a strategy that we presented to Delta that involved issuing warrants to Delta at one dollar per share. The number of warrants that Delta received would increase as the number of seats sold by Priceline exceeded certain thresholds that Priceline proposed and Delta accepted.

I arranged for the Priceline team and myself to meet with Drusch and Ed West from Delta's Finance Department to finalize the deal. I don't recall the exact number, but when all was said and done, Delta earned about a billion—yes, a billion—dollars off the warrants they received. When the other airlines and hotels understood what had happened at Delta, everyone wanted that kind of deal. Fortunately, the internet and online travel agents were getting so popular with the consumer that Priceline didn't have to do any more deals as rich as the Delta deal.

I continued to remain on the Priceline board and worked with them over the next couple of years, even helping them set up their operation in Europe.

Nassau Paradise Island Promotion Board

In early 1999, I received a call from George Myers, the chairman of the Nassau Paradise Island Promotion Board. He called to tell me that Mr. Sol Kerzner, the chairman of the company that owned Atlantis, was concerned that there wasn't sufficient air service into Nassau and told George that they needed to find someone who could help them with that problem. George was aware that I knew practically every decision maker in the airline industry, and he asked if I would fly to Nassau and talk to Mr. Kerzner.

I flew down and met with George and Mr. Kerzner, and they agreed to retain me to manage the airline relationships. I have continued to do work for the promotion board since that first meeting in 1999. Today I report to Fred Lounsberry, the CEO of the promotion board. In those early days, we went through some interesting times, including the aftermath of 9/11. With the assistance of Doug Blissit, I have successfully maintained and increased the air service to Nassau. One of my best contributions was to convince JetBlue to serve Nassau from JFK, Boston, Orlando, Washington Reagan, and Fort Lauderdale. With the exception of Washington Reagan, those routes have worked well for both JetBlue and the destination.

A lot of the work involved crunching numbers, and since I am not the best number cruncher in the world, I recruited Doug Blissit, who worked for me at Delta, to come on board and do the number crunching. Doug also takes the lead in putting together the presentations we use when meeting with the airlines.

In the last five years, our greatest challenge has been the additional rooms that would become available when the new Baha Mar resort opened in 2017. Fred Lounsberry, Doug, and I have worked very hard to secure additional air service. The opening of Baha Mar created the need for approximately 2,100 additional airline seats per day to match the growth in hotel rooms. As of July 2018, we have secured approximately 2,300 additional seats. Fred, Doug, and I are continuing to aggressively pursue additional service into Nassau, as the demand is continuing to increase.

In early 2000, I received a call from Ed Rudner, who wanted to let me know that he was starting a new cruise line, Renaissance Cruises, using 100-passenger ships. He asked if I would be interested in doing some consulting work for Renaissance. I flew down and met with Ed, we worked out a deal, and I worked for Renaissance until Ed's aggressive expansion put them into bankruptcy. When I worked for Ed, I spent a lot of my time with Frank Del Rio, who was the senior vice president of marketing. Frank and I became very good friends and have stayed in touch.

While I was doing the work for the Promotion Board, Priceline, and Renaissance, I was still doing work for Accenture. After 9/11, consulting work in the airline and travel business just came to a screeching halt. I still had over a year left on my contract with Accenture, but with absolutely no work to do, I could not continue to take their money, so I resigned in December of 2001.

Oceania Cruise Lines

In early 2002, I had been on a consulting project in Turkey and was returning to Atlanta via Paris. While waiting to board my flight to Atlanta, I ran into Frank Del Rio, my friend from Renaissance Cruises. Frank told me he was in France to meet with the company that owned a ship that had been operated by Renaissance. Frank was trying to acquire one of the newer ships that Renaissance Cruises operated. He wanted to acquire the ship to start Oceania, a new cruise line. He told me that he was three to five hundred thousand dollars short of what he needed to secure a contract on the ships. Frank was aware of the money I had made on the Price-line deal, and he asked me if I would consider investing. I told him I was interested but that I needed to discuss the investment with Millie. After Millie and I discussed it, we decided we would invest. I called Frank and told him I was wiring him the money.

Frank was able to close the deal and launched Oceania Cruise Lines. He had a great crew working for him, and it didn't take long for Oceania to gain a great reputation as a five-star cruise line with four-star pricing. Frank appointed me to Oceania's board of directors, and I really enjoyed being part of that great venture. Over the next couple of years, Frank added two more of the Renaissance ships and later ordered two new larger ships. In

2007, the great product and the profitability of Oceania caught the eye of Apollo Private Equity group, which bought a majority interest in Oceania. The original investors enjoyed a significant gain from their initial investment and still retained over 40 percent of their equity. Apollo also bought Regent Seven Seas Cruises and combined Regent with Oceania, changing the name to Prestige Cruise Holdings.

In September 2014, Norwegian Cruises bought Prestige Cruise Holdings, and the original Oceania investors enjoyed another significant return on our original investment. I have been thinking about planning another trip to Paris to see if I can find another Frank Del Rio.

When Norwegian bought Prestige Cruise Holdings, everyone assumed that the Norwegian management team would run the new operation. Much to the surprise of many, including myself, the Norwegian board of directors turned the operation of the cruise line over to Frank and his team. This was a great move, and I am sure the Norwegian shareholders will benefit from that decision.

Between my retirement in May of 1998 and March of 2002, I had been very busy with the consulting and investing activities. In early March of 2002, life got even more exciting.

Cendant/Travelport

Sometime between mid-1998 and late 1999, Cheap Tickets, one of the first online travel agents or OTAs, convinced my friend and colleague Sam Galeotos to leave Worldspan and come to work for them as chief operating officer. In late 2001, Cendant, a very large holding company, acquired Cheap Tickets, and Cendant recruited Sam to stay on board in a senior position in the Cendant Travel Unit. The Cendant Travel Unit owned and operated Apollo, a Global Distribution Service (GDS) company that served airline and travel agents in the Americas, and Galileo, an international GDS.

In March of 2002, I received a call from Sam, who was trying to recruit me to join the Cendant Travel Unit, as they needed someone with my experience and relationships with the senior-level travel industry executives. They needed this kind of person to enhance their share of the Global Distribution System business. Since they were now in the travel agency business, they also needed someone with my airline contacts to help secure content for Cheap Tickets.

While I was not looking for a new career, the compensation package Sam put on the table was sufficiently attractive that I was interested in continuing the conversation, provided Cendant would meet certain conditions that I planned to request. My conditions included that I would not have to move to New Jersey, and they would provide me with housing and transportation. They agreed to these conditions, and I accepted the job as executive vice president of the Cendant Travel Division. I was responsible for managing the people who handled our airline, hotel, and car rental relationships.

The travel unit had offices in Parsippany, New Jersey, and the Parsippany Hilton Hotel became my second home for the five years that I commuted to New Jersey. The hotel was within walking distance of my office.

I reported to Sam Galeotos, and he reported to Sam Katz, president of the travel unit, who reported to Mr. Henry Silverman, chairman of Cendant. Cendant's headquarters was in a beautiful office at Nine West Fifty-Seventh Street in Manhattan. All the business unit presidents had offices in that complex, and all big meetings concerning financial issues, acquisitions, and other corporate matters were held in the Manhattan office.

Shortly after I joined Cendant, Sam Katz and Sam Galeotos tasked me to find a person who could enhance our relationships with the airlines based in Europe and the Middle East. I was also tasked with finding a person who could manage and enhance our relationship with the Asia-Pacific-based airlines.

I flew to London to meet with and interview some of the staff based in London to determine if we already had this talent we needed within the company. After interviewing the candidates, I recommended Bryan Conway for the Europe-Middle East position and Brad Holman to manage our Asia-Pacific airline relationships. I spent a lot of time with both Bryan and Brad, calling on our key European, Middle East, and Asia-Pacific airline clients. One of the highlights of meeting the international airline executives was the opportunity to spend time with many of the key Emirates airline executives, including the chairman, Sheikh Ahmed bin Saeed Al Maktoum, and CEO Maurice Flanagan.

In addition to the time I spent meeting with the international airlines, I also represented Cendant at international trade shows and conferences, which involved a lot of international travel. I visited Dubai, Kuwait, Saudi Arabia, Qatar, India, Hong Kong, Thailand, Australia, New Zealand, Japan, Korea, Brazil, Argentina, Mexico, and almost all of the countries in Europe. In 2005, I was promoted to vice chairman of the travel unit.

Dubai was a fascinating place. When I first started visiting Dubai, so much commercial construction was going on there that more than half the world's construction cranes were on the ground in Dubai. About the time I made my first trip to Dubai, construction had begun on what was to become the world's tallest building. Since Dubai is part of the United Arab Emirates, it is primarily a Muslim city, with many women walking down the street dressed from head to toe in Muslim attire. Contrast that with the beautiful Russian tourists walking around the streets of Dubai while dressed in short shorts and halter tops. The Muslims didn't seem to mind as long as the Russians were spending money.

Dubai has many great restaurants that serve alcoholic beverages, which is contrary to Muslim beliefs, but all religious rules seem to be put on the back shelf where the businesspeople and tourists are concerned. The other observation I made was that very few of the locals worked, as they all received a check from the government.

Conducting Business in India

I also had to make several business trips to India, as we had a very good partner in New Delhi that represented Cendant as our GDS representative. I both enjoyed and dreaded the trips to India. You only have to be in India a short while to see the effects of the caste system. Those who have money have no sympathy for those who do not. It was an experience to walk along the streets and watch the motorized rickshaws coming down the street with a dozen people hanging onto the sides.

While calling on Spice Jet, a local Indian airline, I observed a huge crater in the street and a large pile of gravel a block or so away. Then I saw more than a dozen Indian women with baskets of gravel on top of their heads. As I watched them, they were dumping the gravel in the big crater. While we were talking to the Spice Jet vice president, I asked him, "Why don't they just get a bulldozer and push that gravel into the crater?"

He said, "You fool, filling that pit is how these women feed their families."

So I shut up.

I arranged for Millie to accompany me on several of my international trips, including visits to Dubai, Sidney, Auckland, Hong Kong, and Florence, Italy. She also accompanied me when I traveled to Qatar to represent Cendant at the World Travel Council. Since Millie had never been to Dubai, I arranged for us to stop over for a couple of days on our way to Qatar. The Cendant country manager acted as our tour guide and took Millie to all of the key sites.

My most interesting and rewarding international trip occurred when I flew to the Phuket, Thailand, region with Sam Katz to deliver a check for $500,000 on behalf of the Cendant Cares program. The donation was designated as funds to help replace the Bang Sak School and Orphanage that had been destroyed by the tsunami that struck in 2004.

Sam and I flew into Phuket then traveled by car to the Khao Lak area, where the school and orphanage was located. Traveling to Khao Lak was an incredible experience. Initially we traveled through a lush green Thai countryside dotted with beautiful beaches and resorts. This did not prepare us for the dramatic change as we entered Khao Lak. Suddenly, the space between the road and the sea was a barren brown wasteland with the wreckage of damaged properties. The people were also gone—not just the 40,000 deceased—and the space was eerily empty versus the busy populace we'd passed only a few miles back. We pulled off the road into a clearing, where a flagpole served as the only reminder of the destroyed Bang Sak School. In a gray tree near the flagpole, a chair from a school desk sat wedged in a tree some twenty feet in the air—an odd memorial. You turn and see that the sea is probably two miles in the distance and try to comprehend how the water could have climbed that high. It makes you wonder about all that was swept away on that fateful December 26.

Coweta resident Bob Coggin visits with students of the Bank Sak School in Thailand. His company raised $500,000 to help rebuild the school, which was destroyed by the tsunami.

Newnan's Coggin observes tsunami aftermath firsthand

By SARAH FAY CAMPBELL
sarah@newnan.com

Coweta resident Bob Coggin got to see

orphans.

Coggin and Sam Katz spent time with Thai officials and the school children.

"It was emotional and touching," Coggin said. "I sat at the table with the

when you see pictures, it's really hard to grasp it," he said. "When we went there everything was just wiped clean."

The school was about two miles from the ocean. Approximately 40,000 people

My most rewarding trip on behalf of Cendant was to Phuket, Thailand, where the Cendant Cares program gave $500,000 to help replace a school and orphanage destroyed by the 2004 tsunami. The trip was featured in my local newspaper, the Newnan Times-Herald.

As we drove up the hill, where the new school was being constructed at a safe elevation, a buzz of activity emerged. On the dusty ridge, a team of engineers and laborers manned cranes that were clearing land and laying foundations. Some 120 children and several dozen adults awaited us under an open triangular metal structure. The structure served as classroom, dining room, and today, ceremony room, and with a group of temporary tent and caravan structures, comprised the current Bang Sak School.

The younger students' uniforms were pink and red while the older children were in shades of blue. They eyed the visitors with curiosity while they appreciatively enjoyed the buffet lunch set out for the occasion. They were really cute children and chatted away. We looked for signs that the devastation had affected their lives, and it was hard to see until the headmistress pointed out a girl who had been orphaned. Her sullenness was striking, and it became more so as someone pointed out the site where the dormitory would soon stand for the 120 orphaned children who would also attend the new Bang Sak School.

While we were there to deliver the check, we had lunch with the children, and a couple of them came over and got in my lap and hugged me. It was really a great and emotional experience to be there and know we were helping these children. After delivering the check and having lunch, I had to rush to a local airport and fly to New Delhi, India, as the executive committee meeting of the World Travel Council conference was scheduled to start in a few days.

While I was flying in from Thailand, Millie was making the trip from Atlanta to New Delhi by herself, quite an experience for her. Not only did she have to make the trip to India by herself, but she also had to make the trip from the airport to the hotel by herself. As challenging as it was, she made it okay.

The year the World Travel Council conference was being held in New Delhi, India's minister of tourism invited the council's executive committee to fly down to Agra to visit the Taj Mahal prior to the start of the conference. Several members of the committee and their spouses accepted the minister's invitation. The morning after we arrived in Agra, we toured the Taj Mahal, which was an awesome experience. We also toured the area around Agra. The trip from the Agra airport to our hotel was also an experience, as the streets were full of cows and elephants, with an occasional monkey in the trees. The next day we flew back to New Delhi to attend the conference.

While I was attending the conference, a lot was going on back in the New York home office, as Sam Galeotos had decided that this was the right time to cash out his options and move back to Wyoming.

About five years after I joined Cendant, Mr. Silverman began to focus on the fact that while Cendant owned five travel-related companies, Cendant wasn't seeing much synergy between the travel-related business units.

To explore why that was happening and find ways to create more synergy between the travel units, Mr. Silverman called a two-day meeting that was attended by all management-level people in the three divisions. After two days of intense dialogue, it was determined that the customer base of the three travel units was so different it would be difficult to develop the level of synergy Mr. Silverman was seeking. A few months later, a decision was made to break up the company and sell off the various business units. In 2005, Cendant's travel company was sold to Blackstone Private Equity Group and renamed Travelport.

I retained my vice chair title and my office in Parsippany. I also continued to be the primary contact with the travel industry's C-level executives. In December 2006, Travelport announced that they were acquiring Worldspan, one of our major competitors based in Atlanta. Travelport retained the Worldspan offices in Atlanta. My responsibilities continued to evolve, and I spent most of my time calling on those travel industry C-level executives and representing Travelport at global industry trade shows and conferences. Since the Worldspan offices were in Atlanta, I relocated my office there, which was a good thing since the Parsippany offices were shrinking.

By the time the Worldspan acquisition was completed, Gordon Wilson had been promoted to president of Travelport, based in London. Gordon held regular senior staff meetings in London, which I attended. By January 2010, I had become weary of these London trips and all the global travel and negotiated a deal with Gordon that I would become vice chairman emeritus and still represent Travelport as needed. I remained as vice chairman emeritus until August 31, 2010, when I retired. Gordon graciously hosted a retirement dinner for me at the 2010 Global Business Travel Association annual meeting. Gordon's hosting the dinner for me at GBTA was a real treat because so many of the travel industry people I had called on and worked with were present.

I worked with some really great people at Cendant/Travelport, including Ken Escrow, Sam Galeotos, Flo Lugli, Bryan Conway, and Brad Holman. I also had great administrative assistants in Amy Chang, Terre McGrath, and Susan Hirsch.

While I was tired of traveling around the globe, I didn't let my retirement from Travelport slow me down any, as I increased my Alpine Consulting work and became much more involved in community activities. When I accepted an executive position with Cendant, they agreed to let me continue doing work for the Nassau Paradise Island Promotion Board (NPIPB), and after retirement from Travelport, I increased my involvement with NPIPB as a new $4 billion resort was being planned.

Here at home, I became more involved with a number of organizations after I retired from Travelport.

- I was elected to the Newnan City Council and served until 2015, when I chose not to run for reelection.
- I was appointed to the City of Newnan Planning Commission.
- I chaired the Atlanta Convention and Visitors Bureau International Tourism Task Force.
- I currently serve as senior advisor to the Board of Directors of DALRC (Delta's retiree organization).
- I'm a member of the University of West Georgia Foundation Board of Trustees.
- I chair the local advisory board of the University of West Georgia. UWG was very interested in expanding their presence in Newnan, and when the historic Newnan Hospital facility became available to the university, I chaired a fund-raising committee focused on raising a significant amount of money to help cover the cost of the renovation of the facility. The committee raised approximately $1 million.
- I also serve on the executive committee and board of trustees of the Chick-fil-A Peach Bowl.
- I serve on the board of directors of the Newnan/Coweta Boys & Girls Club.
- I serve as government liaison for the Newnan-Coweta Chamber and represent the Chamber at county commission and city council meetings.
- I'm very active in the Newnan Presbyterian Church.

Because of my involvement in the community, the travel industry, the Chick-fil-A Peach Bowl, and the Newnan Presbyterian Church, I have received several awards and recognitions for my contributions to the awarding organizations.

- In 2009, I received the President's Award from the Atlanta Convention and Visitors Bureau for the leadership role I played in developing the international tourism market.
- In April 2010, I was named Citizen of the Year by the Newnan Presbyterian Church.
- In 2012, I received the "Golden Eagle" Boy Scout award from the Flint River Council of the Boy Scouts of America.
- In December 2012, *Business Travel News* inducted me into their initial Business Travel Hall of Fame along with Bob Crandall, retired CEO of American Airlines, and Gordon Bethune, retired CEO of Continental Airlines.
- In December 2013, I was inducted into the Peach Bowl Volunteer Hall of Fame.
- In February 2016, I was named Newnan-Coweta Citizen of the Year.
- In February 2018, I was named Newnan/Coweta Boys & Girls Club Volunteer of the Year.
- In March 2018, I was named the Newnan-Coweta Chamber's Volunteer of the Year.

As I reflect on my forty-two-year career at Delta, the thing I value most is the unbelievable support I received from the people I worked for and from the people who worked for me. Those people who worked for me always made it a priority to make sure they never disappointed me, and they were always striving to deliver on our commitments to senior management. The culture of "Trust and Honesty" that I experienced at Delta during my career was very unique in the business world. One of the things I enjoyed most was the breakfast meetings I had with small groups of rank-and-file staff, as they were always so appreciative that a person in my position would take the time to share information with them and seek their input.

After retiring from Delta, I had a very strong desire to stay involved in the travel industry, and I accomplished that through my involvement with companies such as Priceline, Oceania Cruises, and Travelport. I had an even stronger desire to enjoy more leisure travel with Millie, and as a result, we visited many international destinations, with Russia, Turkey, and Ireland being our favorites.

My other priority was to be more involved in my church and my community. Through my involvement in community organizations and projects, I have gained an appreciation for the favorable impact a person can have on their community if they will just get involved.

———————————

2012 Coweta County
Golden Eagle Dinner Honoree

Mr. Bob Coggin

Dinner Leadership

Dennis McEntire
Dinner Chair

Andy Sharp	George Alexander	Luke Thompson
Anne Bell	Jay Boren	Mark Pass
Ben Robuck	Jeff Phillips	Mitch Headley
Bill Headley	Joe Crain, Sr	Nathan Crow
Brandon Lovett	Joe Crain, Jr	Patrick McKee
Charles Wyrick	Joe Guerra	Ronnie Jones
Don Chapman	Kip Oldham	Sarah Shirley
Fred Hamlin		Will Conoly

Past Golden Eagle Dinner Honorees

Dennis McEntire	Dr. Joel Richardson	Captain Wendell Whitlock

In 2012, I was honored to receive the Golden Eagle Award from the Flint River Council of the Boy Scouts of America.

My local newspaper, the *Newnan Times-Herald*, has chronicled many of my activities as a councilman and community volunteer.

— BOB COGGIN —

2016 Citizen of the Year

'Charity isn't about the giving of your financial resources, but it's about the giving of your time and everything that you have. I take a great deal of pleasure in being able to do the things I have done.'

Photo by Elizabeth Richardson
Bob Coggin is sworn in as the newest member of the Newnan City Council during the first council meeting of 2008 Tuesday. Coggin's wife, Millie, holds the Bible while City Attorney Brad Sears, not pictured, swears him in.

New councilman sworn in; another says goodbye

By ELIZABETH RICHARDSON
erichardson@newnan.com

The Newnan City Council held two brief meetings Tuesday afternoon, the first of which addressed unfinished business from 2007 and afforded council the opportunity to say a proper goodbye to long-

Bradshaw farewell on behalf of the council, Brady described Bradshaw's service to Newnan as being filled with "distinction" and "honor."

"It has been an honor to serve with professional people," said Bradshaw after being presented with a parting gift and plaque from the mayor.

page 2

Bob Coggin and former Atlanta Falcons coach Leeman Bennett are inducted into the Chick-fil-A Peach Bowl Volunteer Hall of Fame at the 2015 Chick-fil-A Peach Bowl on Dec. 31. From left, Coggin's wife Millie, Coggin, Bennett, and Bennett's wife Pat. The bowl game took place at the Georgia Dome in downtown Atlanta.

A Vote for Responsible Growth.

BOB COGGIN
for city council • District D

Coggin elected to Peach Bowl Hall of Fame

By CELIA SHORTT
celia@newnan.com

Coweta and longtime volunteer Bob Coggin was recently inducted into the Chick-fil-A Peach Bowl Volunteer Hall of Fame, honoring his 29 years of volunteering with the bowl.

The Chick-fil-A Peach Bowl is the ninth-oldest bowl game in the country and one of New Year's six bowls selected to host the College Football Playoff. It is operated by Peach Bowl, Inc. Its volunteer hall of fame was created to honor significant and meaningful contributions to the bowl's success by a number of longtime and dedicated volunteers.

"For the past several years

I have worked down on the field during the game and one of my responsibilities has been to organize and escort people out onto field who were being honored for whatever reason," said Coggin.

"Being escorted out on to the field to be recognized for my contribution was a little weird at first but very gratifying in the end to be recognized for my contribution to the bowl's success. Several members of my family and some friends were at the game, which made it even more special to be out there.

Coggin and former

COGGIN, page 2A

Bob Coggin is surrounded by his family after being honored at Newnan Presbyterian. From left are son Jeff, daughter-in-law Cindy, Coggin, wife Millie and grandson Robby.

NPC honors Bob Coggin as Citizen of the Year

HONORING A 'TITAN'

Photo by Jeffrey Leo

Bob Coggin stands in front of the poster that was given to him at his retirement party. It is signed by members of the management team. Coggin spent 42 years with Delta and retired as executive vice president of marketing.

B&G Club members learn art of public speaking

Newnan's Bob Coggin in Travel Hall of Fame

By SARAH FAY CAMPBELL

sell distressed inventory," Coggin said. But "they were on the rose red as presi ter retir his own One of h as an u Priceline had this at tech lp the a

Coggin had the idea to offer Delta warrants to buy

The Times-Herald

Focus on Education

New Boys & Girls Club scholarship established in honor of youth advocate Loula Davenport

Newnan's Art Arace built this replica of Delta's original plane by this stuff Delta made in 1924, giving Delta its first start in the flight industry. It is hanging in the renovated Delta Flight Museum, which had its grand opening on June 17.

Newnan man helps Delta recreate its history

By BRADLEY HARTSELL
bradley@newnan.com

APPENDIX ONE

Growing Up In Sargent, Georgia

Mr. John Willcoxon, Capt. Harrison Sargent, and the captain's brother George Sargent built a plant in 1886 in the area where the village of Sargent sits today. In 1919, the Arnall family acquired full ownership of the mill. The Arnall family partnered with Mr. Ellis Peniston and began manufacturing blankets in the mill. Both families continued to be involved until Mr. Peniston passed away in 1963. After his death, the mill was acquired by Bibb Manufacturing, which closed the Sargent mill in 1986.

Members of the Coggin family began working at the Sargent mill during the Great Depression. My dad and other family members were very young when they began working there, and some of the Coggins worked there for more than thirty years. I remember hearing my dad and Uncle Raymond talk about the poor working conditions, the twelve-hours shifts, and very low wages.

My dad was working in the mill when he and my mother were married in 1935. They moved into a mill village house located in the "New Town" section of Sargent, and I was born in that house.

Shortly after I finished the first grade, my parents divorced, and my brother, Gary, and I went to live with my Coggin grandparents. While living with the Coggins, I started the second grade at Welcome School. Gary and I were living with our Coggin grandparents when my dad met and married my stepmother, Vera. After I finished the second grade, we moved in with my dad and Vera, and that fall I started the third grade at the Sargent school. Not long after my half brother, Roy Lee, was born, my stepsister,

Darlene, moved to Sargent to live with us and help take care of Roy Lee, as Vera was still working.

I will never forget Ms. Mary Elliot, my third grade teacher at Sargent. I believe she was the meanest teacher I had in all of my school years. My fourth grade teacher was Ms. Grace Davis, and she was probably the sweetest teacher I had in all my school years. My fifth grade teacher was Ms. Katherine Sewell, and she was an excellent teacher. She worked very hard to make sure you were learning math and reading, and like many teachers in those days, she was a single lady.

My sixth grade teacher was Ms. Fanny Baxley, whose husband ran a grocery store in Welcome. She was also a good teacher. My seventh grade teacher was Mrs. Wortham, and she was also a very sweet lady and a great teacher. She lived in Welcome, and her husband, Joe, ran a grocery store.

When I attended school in Sargent, there were no school buses, so everyone in the village walked to school. I remember one day in the winter when it was freezing cold and I had put water on my hair that morning to hold it down, and on the walk to school, my hair felt as if it had frozen. In the sixth grade, I became a crossing guard at the intersection of Main Street and Old Carrollton Highway. It was my job not to let the kids cross the street when cars were coming. I also have great memories of playing baseball on the school ball field down near the Old Carrollton Highway.

I haven't said much about Darlene, my stepsister, but she was always so attentive and helpful with schoolwork and work around the house. I will always have great memories of those days that I spent time with Darlene.

Sargent consisted of two different villages, one referred to as "Old Town," which was located on the north side of Georgia Highway 16. The rest of the Sargent homes were on the south side of Georgia 16 and were newer. Most were smaller shotgun-style houses than the houses in Old Town. Most of the Sargent management staff lived in much nicer houses located on a hill near the Sargent Baptist Church.

The type of house where we lived in "New Town" was a shotgun house with a front porch, a front bedroom, a second bedroom that was also the living room, and the third room that was the kitchen. When Sargent was originally built, there was no running water in the houses, and all the toilets were the old-fashioned outhouses. The water was provided by a hydrant, which was located at about every fourth house. We were very lucky, as the neighborhood hydrant for our four houses was located in our front yard. About the time I was in the sixth grade, the company decided to—or was ordered by the government to—install a sewage system, bathrooms, and running water in every house in the village. The shotgun houses had to build an additional room on the side of the house for the bathroom. What a huge change. We went from bathing in a washtub every Saturday night to bathing whenever we wanted to in the bathtub.

The central gathering point in Sargent was the company store, which was located on the corner of Welcome-Sargent Road (also known as Railroad Road) and Main Street. The company store sold everything from groceries to work clothes, shoes, and small food items. Most of the employees charged their purchases and had the cost deducted from their pay. The company store also had a great old black man named Uncle Brad who drove a one-horse wagon and delivered groceries. He was loved by everyone, and the kids often rode in his wagon. One of the other stores was in "Old Town" and was owned and operated by the Cook family. A lot of people who lived on that side of town traded with the Cooks, who also operated a movie theater. The cost for a ticket was less than twenty-five cents, and my stepsister, Darlene, used to take us to the movies pretty often. The Cooks were also some of the first in the area to own a TV, and people would come in the store and sit there and watch Roy Rogers and other western movies.

There was a train station on Welcome-Sargent Road near the company store. The passenger service operated from Griffin to Chattanooga, with stops along the way including Newnan, Sargent, and Whitesburg. My Richards grandparents lived in Whitesburg, and my brother, Gary, and I would ride the train to Whitesburg to visit them. The fare to Whitesburg was a whopping sixteen cents one way.

The Sargent post office was also on the Welcome-Sargent Road, just about a block down from the company store. Everyone picked up their mail at the post office, and I don't recall any postal service delivery of mail in Sargent.

The Sargent mill office was just down the street from the company store on the left-hand side of Main Street, and that is where you went if you wanted to speak to Mr. Arnall or Mr. Peniston. It was also where everyone went on Friday to pick up their pay. My dad would look closely at the pay envelope to see what had been charged at the company store. If it was a week where I had charged one or more RC Colas, he would raise hell and occasionally take me to the woodshed and whip my butt.

I can't write my Sargent memories without telling about Dr. Elliott, who worked for the mill. The mill deducted a fee each week that allowed a family to see Dr. Elliott at no cost. I know in the early days, that fee was only fifty cents per week. Everyone who worked at Sargent and paid the fee could see Dr. Elliott anytime they had a medical problem or needed any kind of vaccination or other shot. If you were really sick, he would make house calls.

Another of my favorite memories of living in Sargent is of going to the Sargent Baptist Church on Christmas Eve, as they gave all the children a big bag of oranges and other citrus fruit. That might not sound like much today, but in those days, getting a bag of oranges was a big deal, as none of our families had a lot of money to spend on those kinds of goodies.

I also have great memories of roller-skating on Main Street in front of the mill. Sometimes there would be ten or twelve of us skating up and down the street. I also discovered that I could ice down some Cokes, put them in my wagon, park it in front of the main gate, and people would come out to buy a drink. When the mill management found out what I was doing, they made me stop, as it was distracting people from their work. It was great while it lasted. I also tried a paper route for a while, but my daddy started taking most of the money when people paid me, and I eventually found a way to get out of the paper route.

Our house was just across the street from the Sargent baseball park, which was near Wahoo Creek. Sargent had a great baseball team, and I used to really enjoy going to the ball games. There were two Burnham brothers who were very good ball players and hit a lot of home runs. There was also a pitcher named Griffin, who was a little older than the rest of the team, but he was a great pitcher. His best pitch was a knuckleball, and I still remember standing behind home plate and watching that baseball float up to the plate. The ballpark had a grandstand where most of the fans sat and a concession stand where folks could buy soft drinks and snacks. I was able to get a job selling Cokes in the grandstand, and I think I made about a dollar at most ball games.

We had some great neighbors that I spent a lot of time with, especially the Jones, Cash, and Helton families. Melvin Cash and Charles Helton were both in my class at school. My dad's best friend was Mr. Julian Haynes, and they spent a lot of time together hunting and occasionally having a drink. I can't talk about good neighbors without mentioning Mr. Cecil Davis, a supervisor in the mill, who lived almost directly across from its main entrance. He also ran the concession stand at the ball games. Mr. Davis was one of the first people in Sargent to have a television, and on Friday nights, he invited the Coggins, Julian Haynes, and a few others to his house to watch wrestling. In the late 1940s, TV wrestling was a big deal.

There was a group of boys about my age, and we spent a lot of time playing baseball and fishing. We played baseball in the Sargent ballpark and enjoyed fishing in Wahoo Creek. One area of the creek was very rocky with a beautiful waterfall, and that was where we frequently fished, as there were some larger fish there. Mr. Henry Bryant lived nearby, and we occasionally visited with him when fishing in that area. He was a nice older gentleman who would sit on the front porch in his rocking chair and talk with us. He sometimes offered us a glass of iced tea.

My brother, Gary, and I really enjoyed spending time with our Coggin grandparents, and if our dad was too busy working to drive us out to Handy, we walked to Handy. During the watermelon season, my granddaddy Coggin and Uncle Asa would load their wagon with watermelons, take them to Sargent, and ride through the streets of Sargent peddling them. If Gary and I knew they were going to town, we jumped on the wagon and rode around Sargent with them.

APPENDIX TWO

The Coggin Family

My Coggin grandparents were always known as Mama and Papa to all the grandchildren, and we looked forward to visits with them. I recall hearing my dad talk about how he and Uncle Raymond worked twelve-hour shifts six days a week at the Sargent cotton mill even though they were in their early teens. At a relatively young age, Uncle Raymond managed to save enough money to buy a nice tract of land with a house. He and his wife, my aunt Eula, lived on that farm until they both passed away. Their grandson lives there today.

The Coggins were typical "dirt farmers" of that era who worked hard just to survive and put food on the table. Their unpainted wood-frame house reflected this lifestyle. The lumber used to build the house was 1-inch by 10- or 12-inch-wide heart-of-pine boards that ran from roof to ground. A piece of 1x4 pine board was nailed over the cracks between the wider boards. As these old houses aged, it wasn't unusual for the boards to separate, letting a little light and air into the house through the cracks.

When I was growing up, the only room in the house that was actually sealed and finished on the inside was the big room used as a kitchen and bedroom for Mama and Papa. I suspect the only reason it was finished inside and as large as it was could be attributed to Uncle Raymond tearing off the old kitchen and adding the larger room. The room next to the kitchen had a large fireplace and served as both the family room and Uncle Asa's bedroom. I describe it as "a family room," as that room was where they all gathered and sat around the fire in the wintertime. This was a room where you could actually see a few specks of daylight where the outside timbers had cracked. The ceiling in that room consisted of six or eight planks that were laid across the rafters. Rat snakes, as they were called, occasionally worked their way into the house, especially the ceiling, and I heard stories about the rat snakes falling from the ceiling to the floor or on Uncle Asa's bed. The third room of the three-room house was primarily a bedroom with two double beds, and the only closet in the house was there. For many years, my great-grandmother Storey lived with Mama and Papa, and that was her room.

I don't ever recall Papa owning an automobile, as he always depended on his mule-drawn wagon or someone with a car to take him where he needed to go. Based on my memory of those early days, he really didn't need a car, as he rarely left the farm. When he did, it was to go to the cotton gin, church, the doctor (rarely), and the gristmill. The majority of those trips were in his wagon. When he did have to travel by car, Uncle Raymond usually provided the transportation.

The farm was located in the Buckeye area, about twelve to fourteen miles west of Newnan and about five miles from a larger community called Handy. Handy had the distinction of having a large general store, a polling place, and a gristmill.

In those days, Handy was a social center. People gathered to find out what their neighbors and other folks were doing and how the crops were coming along, to talk a little politics, and to talk about their hunting experiences. Handy was also where they shopped for essentials, including clothing. The Lyle family owned the store and other buildings and lived up on the hill just beyond the store. Jack Camp, one of the heirs of the Lyle family, lives in the old family house and owns much of the property once owned by his ancestors.

The old buildings that housed the store, the gristmill, and the polling place were still standing in the early 1950s when my dad moved us to a farm on the Chattahoochee River. I still remember driving by all those old buildings. Unfortunately, they were torn down in the early 1960s.

Like most farms of that era, the Coggin farm had a couple of barns near the house. The barn closest to the house was primarily used as a corncrib and stables for the mules, with a lean-to type of building attached to the rear of the barn and used as milking stalls, where Mama milked the cows. Pigeon houses were attached to the barn just above the milking stalls. The mules were kept in their stalls overnight so they would be fresh, easy to catch, and ready to go the next morning. On the weekends and occasions when Papa knew he wouldn't be using them the next day, he put them out in the pasture to graze.

The second barn was a secondary corncrib used to store bought feed, hay, and fodder. The hay and fodder were stored in the loft. The corn stored in the cribs was used to feed the livestock and to make cornmeal. On a rainy day when Papa and Uncle Asa (who still lived at home) couldn't work in the field, they spent part of the day shucking corn and put it aside to take to the gristmill to be ground into cornmeal.

The area around the two barns was surrounded by a wooden fence and was called "the lot." A small building called a gear house was very near the two barns and was where they kept all the gear used with the mules. The gear consisted of bridles, trace chains, collars, harnesses, and other equipment they needed to put on the mules before they worked in the fields or pulled the farm wagon. Also in the gear house were the brushes that they used to brush the mules down after a long day in the field. When the grandchildren visited, which was often, we used to fight over who was going to brush the mules.

A pigpen was located directly behind the big barn. They kept the hogs they would slaughter that fall and winter in one of these pens. In addition to some other types of feed, the hogs that were going to be slaughtered were also fed what country people called "hog slop," which was primarily kitchen scraps and some dishwater.

They had a fairly large pasture that ran alongside the road in front of the house and all the way down the bank of the creek to where Papa's farm bordered Uncle Bo's farm. The creek separated the pasture and the big cornfield that ran alongside the creek.

There was also a "foot log" that connected the pasture and the cornfield, and it was a big attraction to all the grandkids. We would sit down on the foot log and watch for fish and the occasional snake that swam in the creek. A number of excellent fishing holes were located a mile or so upstream from the pasture. The pasture and creek bottom also served as the neighborhood baseball field.

Like all farmers in that era, the Coggins had a henhouse where the chickens roosted at night, hopefully protected from foxes and other varmints. Attached to the side of the henhouse were hen's nests, where most of the hens laid their eggs. The henhouse was to the left of the big barn and below the smokehouse. A maverick hen would occasionally make her own nest somewhere else around the barn. The hens would also make a nest under the barn, lay eggs, and sit on them until they hatched a bunch of little chickens. When a hen did this, she was called a "setting hen" and was key to replenishing the chicken population. Every now and then when Mama was gathering eggs, she found an old chicken snake coiled up in one of the hen nests. She wasn't the least bit afraid of the snakes and just ran them off.

The smokehouse was located about a hundred feet from the back door of the house, on the left-hand side of the backyard. It wasn't a huge building, and they didn't actually smoke any meat in the smokehouse, but they did store meat in the smokehouse after it was smoked outside. They also had a salt box in the smoke-house, where they stored pork that had been salted down.

Mama kept some "fryers" in a couple of chicken pens out to the side of the smokehouse, and since the chickens attracted insects, Papa put up martin gourds on long poles behind the smokehouse. The gourds attracted the martins, as this was a favorite place for the martins to build their nests. The martins' primary source of food for their baby birds was the insects they caught around the chicken nest and the barn. Martins were the best pest control you would ever want, as they really took care of mosquitoes, gnats, and other insects.

In another building, located on the other side of the house, Papa kept the wagon and stored the cotton before it was taken to the cotton gin. Papa also had a "poor man's" blacksmith shop in a lean-to type shed on the back side of the building. I enjoyed watching Papa and Asa work in the blacksmith shop, where they sharpened the plows and shod the mules.

No farm was complete without hunting dogs, and the Coggins certainly had their share of redbone and bluetick hounds plus a few bird dogs. Hunting was a big part of their life, as hunting not only provided their recreation but it also helped put food on the table and was a small source of income. My uncle Asa was the primary keeper of the hunting dogs, as Papa didn't have the time or patience to fool with them.

The Great Depression occurred during my dad's early years and created many hardships for the Coggins and most of the other folks who farmed for a living. Over the years, my dad shared many stories of how they struggled to put food on the table, pay taxes, and buy a few clothes.

I recall my dad telling me how they would pay their county taxes by hauling wagonloads of rocks to fill in deep ruts on the old dirt roads to make them passable, especially for the rural mailman. They also supplemented their farm income, such as it was, by working in sawmills. The sawdust piles created by the sawmills also had value, and many farmers hauled off the sawdust to put around the barn, chicken pens, and other places on the farm. Foxhunters liked the fact that sawdust attracted foxes, who frequently made dens in the sawdust to raise their puppies.

Out of necessity, farmers like my Coggin grandparents were thrifty people, and one way they saved money was to make sure that any feed, seed, or fertilizer they bought came in cloth bags that could be used for bedsheets, shirts, or underwear. I vividly recall that every bedsheet in the house was made of fertilizer sacks, and most of Asa and Papa's underwear was made from flour sacks. All of the aprons Mama used in the kitchen were also made from flour sacks. I don't think my uncle Asa ever wore a pair of underwear that was made of anything but a feed sack until he was a grown man.

It was more or less a family tradition that everyone make every effort to be at the Coggins' on Sunday to take part in the family dinner. Back in those days, it was a standing rule that the children would eat last, so we got what was left over, but I don't remember any of the kids going hungry.

It was also a tradition in the wintertime for some of the cousins, Uncle Bo's family, or some of the neighbors to visit on Saturday night, sit by the big old battery-powered radio, listen to the *Grand Ole Opry*, pop popcorn in the fireplace, and eat peanuts

Mama roasted in the kitchen stove.

I have heard some great stories about the adventures of the Coggin clan as they were growing up and after they got married. One of the best ones involved my aunt Mary Lou Rainey and her husband, Clem Rainey. Uncle Clem had a reputation for really enjoying a good drink of corn liquor, a source of great frustration to Aunt Mary Lou. She was always on the lookout for where he was keeping the whiskey and usually found it, and when she did, she poured it out.

As time went on, Uncle Clem became very clever at hiding his whiskey. His most inventive scheme was to tie a knot in the bottom of the leg of a pair of overalls hanging in the closet and put the bottle down inside the leg. As the story goes, it took Aunt Mary Lou a long time to figure out where he was hiding his whiskey after he started hiding it in his overalls.

APPENDIX THREE

The Richards Family

My Richards grandparents were known as Mama and Daddy Richards to all of the grandchildren, and the Richards family was really about Daddy Richards. The family was very close and very emotional where the family was concerned. While the entire family didn't get together for Sunday dinner as frequently as the Coggins did, it was a big event when it did happen, and we all looked forward to seeing the rest of the family.

Most of Daddy Richards's ancestors and his generation of the Richards family had their roots in Carroll County, Georgia, and they lived, farmed, or worked in or around Whitesburg during his lifetime.

Much like Papa Coggin, Daddy Richards was a farmer, but there was a big difference in the size of their farms. Papa Coggin had a much smaller farm and was always in the field with a plow or doing other farmwork himself, while Daddy Richards had a very large farm and a large crew of laborers and sharecroppers doing all the work in his fields.

The other big difference was that Papa Coggin struggled to make enough money from farming to put food on the table and clothe the family, while Daddy Richards made significant money on his farm, especially before the Great Depression. While the Depression had a serious financial impact on Daddy Richards, Papa Coggin was already so poor he hardly felt the impact.

Daddy Richards did pretty well financially until he made some bad investments. My cousin Calvin Richards told me that Daddy

Richards, along with Roy Richards, took some of the income they had made off their farms and cotton brokering and invested in Florida property when the Florida real estate market was so hot. These investments apparently occurred just prior to the Depression and disappeared when the bubble burst. Obviously they lost the money they had invested and had to come back to Carroll County to start farming again. Daddy Richards also lost a lot of money as a cotton broker about that same time.

Before the Depression, Daddy Richards farmed a large tract of land called Black Dirt, and there is some speculation that he might have lost the land during the Depression. In any event, leaving Black Dirt was a big emotional issue with the family, as they were apparently very attached to that farm. I still recall the many times that family conversations would ultimately turn to reminiscing about the good old days when they lived at Black Dirt. Regardless of the Depression and the loss of Black Dirt, Daddy Richards was always considered "well off," as people would say back then.

When they had to move from Black Dirt, they moved to a farm on what is now Georgia Route 5 that connects Whitesburg and Douglasville. They didn't live there long, as the main house on the farm was destroyed by fire around 1937-38, just a few years after they moved there, causing the Richards family to move again. This time, they moved to a farm just a few miles away, the Jones place. The main house on the Jones place was a beautiful old Civil War–era structure. The house had a real plantation feeling about it, as the kitchen and dining room were actually separated from the rest of the house and were connected by a long covered porch. The main house was a two-story structure with a sitting room or "den," as we would call it today. This room had a big fireplace where everyone frequently gathered on those cold winter nights. There was also a room where Mama Richards kept her sewing machine and quilting frames. Mama Richards and several of her friends and relatives would sit around the quilting frame and sew quilts.

On the main part of the house was a long front porch where Mama Richards kept several rocking chairs. When some of the other older ladies came to visit on Sunday afternoons, they sat in those rockers. One of Mama Richards's favorite pastimes was to sit and rock in one of those chairs and dip snuff.

When Daddy Richards wasn't involved in the farm, his favorite pastime was to drive to Whitesburg and sit in front of an old grocery store and play checkers and cards with "the boys." I suspect that they might have also enjoyed a drink or two.

Like my Coggin grandparents, the Richards family had the typical chicken pens, smokehouses, blacksmith shop, and barns but on a much larger scale than the Coggins, as Daddy Richards ran a much larger operation.

The one thing the Richards family had that the Coggins didn't was a possum box. The possum boxes were located near the henhouse, and that is where they kept the possums after they caught them. In those days, any good Southern farmer took his hounds out at night and hunted possums. When they caught one, as they frequently did, they brought him back to the farm, kept him in the possum box, and fed him for several weeks before killing and eating the possum.

Since Daddy Richards was a big-time cotton farmer, he had a cotton shed where cotton was stored before it was taken to the cotton gin. The building Daddy Richards used to store cotton had previously been a country store and was laid out more like a store than a barn. The basement was used to store sweet potatoes. When a bunch of us grandkids would visit the Richards family, we always headed to the cotton shed, where we had loads of fun playing in the cotton. I vividly remember being scolded on several occasions for scattering the cotton all around the building.

Even though he had lost much of his wealth during the Depression, Daddy Richards continued to have a fairly large farming operation while he lived at the Jones place. He had a large number of people working for him, including several sharecroppers. My aunt Ruby and her husband, Ralph Jennings, lived on the farm for several years and helped Daddy Richards run and manage the farm. My mother's youngest brother, Tom, also lived at home, along with Aunt Gloria and Aunt Betty, and they all worked in the fields. I'm sure Gloria and Betty also did a lot of work in the house.

Around 1940-41, my uncle Ralph Jennings had an opportunity to buy a farm in Oak Mountain near Carrollton. After he moved, Daddy Richards struggled with the farm. He decided to quit farming and moved to Whitesburg, where he lived until he passed away. Mama Richards continued to live in that house for several years afterward. Every time I drive by it, I have great memories of "the good old days."

A chronological list of positions I held during my forty-two-year career at Delta Air Lines

- Hired in April 1956 as ramp service agent in Atlanta.
- Promoted to station agent in Montgomery, Alabama, in September 1956.
- About a year after I reported to Montgomery, Delta reduced staffing there due to schedule reductions, and being the only single person there, I volunteered to transfer to Hot Springs, Arkansas, as station agent.
- After spending a year and a half in Hot Springs, I took advantage of an opportunity to move nearer to my family and accepted a transfer to St. Simons Island (Brunswick, Georgia) as station agent.
- About a year into my St. Simons assignment, R. J. Reynolds, the famous tobacco tycoon, started Golden Isles Airlines and recruited me to become the Golden Isles sales manager. We had been operating about four months when Mr. Reynolds married a "trophy wife" and decided to shut the airline down and move to Italy. He called Mr. Woolman and arranged for me to be rehired by Delta without any interruption in my seniority.
- A station agent position was open in Montgomery, and I was reassigned there in October 1960.
- About fifteen months later, I was promoted to sales representative in Washington, DC.

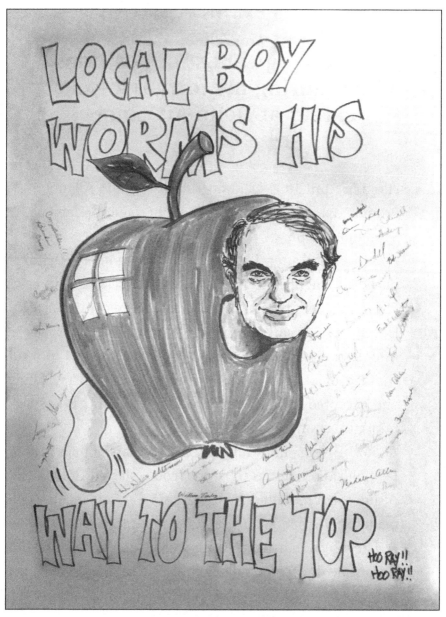

When I was promoted to senior vice president of sales and marketing, some colleagues said that I had "wormed my way to the top" and gave me this artwork as a joke.

- About two and a half years into the DC job, I was promoted to district sales manager in Jackson, Mississippi.
- After a little less than two years in Jackson, I was promoted to district sales manager in Philadelphia.
- About eighteen months into the Philadelphia position, I was promoted to district director in New York. My New York tour of duty lasted eleven-plus years, which was much longer than I'd expected, but finding a successor within Delta's sales and marketing organization was very difficult. I brought a couple of people to New York in the number two slot with the anticipation that they would succeed me, but that didn't work out, and there was no one else in the Sales and Marketing Division outside of my New York staff who wanted any part of being in New York. I finally decided

Following Delta's merger with Northeast, we used one of the party boats in New York to promote these new "Yellowbird" flights.

that I would have to develop some local talent, and that is when I moved Al Kolakowski into the number two slot, and he did succeed me.

- In May of 1979, I was promoted to regional sales manager, based in Delta's Atlanta General Office.
- In a little less than a year, I was promoted to system manager of planning, which included scheduling, route development, and pricing. Later, revenue management was added to this list of responsibilities.
- Two years later, I was promoted to assistant vice president of planning (scheduling, market analysis/route development, pricing, and revenue management, later to become known as "yield management").
- In about eighteen months, I was promoted to vice president of planning, which included all of the above plus a significant role in choosing and working with Delta's alliance partners and evaluating new aircraft for the Delta fleet.
- In 1990, I was promoted to senior vice president of planning and advertising, a role that included all of the above plus responsibility for advertising and sales promotion.
- In 1992, I was promoted to senior vice president of marketing, which included all of the above plus responsibility for reservations sales, Datas II (Delta's computer reservations system), and the entire sales organization, including both staff and field.
- In 1995, I was promoted to executive vice president of marketing and was one of four members of the Delta Executive Council.
- In 1996, my responsibilities as executive vice president of marketing were expanded to include IT.
- In May of 1998, I retired from Delta Air Lines.

Atlanta Municipal Airport in April 1956

When I joined Delta, the passenger terminal in use at that time had been built in 1948 using material originally designed for World War II Quonset huts. In 1956, the airport was called the Atlanta Municipal Airport, and it was reported to be the busiest airport in the world in terms of total passengers and connecting flights.

In 1956, to reach the passenger terminal or Delta's offices, you exited Virginia Avenue, and if you continued south on that street after turning off of Virginia Avenue, you would pass the Southern Airways hangar/headquarters, the Delta General Office, and all of Delta's maintenance facilities. The street ended at the building that was Atlanta's original passenger terminal, and that building was still standing at the time I joined Delta.

To reach the passenger terminal, you turned right shortly after exiting Virginia Avenue. This street was about three quarters of a mile long and dead-ended at the passenger terminal. The building that housed the Southern Airways headquarters, maintenance hangar, and some of the Delta facilities was torn down over time. The building that housed Mr. Woolman's original offices is still standing and has been used by all of Mr. Woolman's successors. The two original Delta hangars are also still standing and now house the Delta museum.

When you traveled to the passenger terminal, you passed the building that housed Delta's employment offices, where I was interviewed and hired. This building was on the right-hand side of the street. Eastern's cargo building was on the left-hand side, just before you reached the terminal.

Delta's ticket counter and gates were on the west end of the terminal, with Eastern on the east end. Southern and Capital ticket counters were on the extreme east end of the terminal, and their gates were east of the Eastern gates. After a passenger checked in and left the ticket counter area, they went left to go to an Eastern gate and right to reach their Delta gate. Delta and Eastern had some aircraft parking positions near the terminal, and both airlines had built long wooden fingers along the east and west ends of the terminal to handle the balance of their flights. When passengers were boarding their Delta flight, an agent stood at the boarding gate and took the tickets, as boarding passes had not yet been invented.

There were no security checkpoints in those days, and passengers just wandered out to the ramp area to board their flights.

Eastern's maintenance and cargo facilities were located just east of the passenger terminal. Those buildings survived for many years after Eastern shut down, until space was needed to build a new cabin service facility for Delta in the early 1990s.

The restaurant in the terminal was famous due to the old black gentleman who sat out front and opened and closed the door as people entered and exited the restaurant. I can still see him today just as clearly as if he were standing there. He was relatively short, probably in his sixties, had a white beard, and was surrounded by bales of cotton. He used a rope to pull the door open and closed. Everyone talked about their experience with him. Of course, few if any of the Delta staff could afford to eat in that restaurant.

I have great memories of the Virginia Avenue area, such as the "tin pin" bowling alley and the Hangar Hotel located right at the intersection of Virginia Avenue and the street to the airport terminal and the Delta General Office.

About a half mile west of the terminal entrance on Virginia Avenue was a popular drive-in restaurant that overlooked the airport. This restaurant was a favorite place to go park and watch airplanes take off and land. Across the street from the drive-in was a famous barbecue restaurant patronized by many of the people who worked at the airport.

College Park, Hapeville, and East Point were popular cities in those days, and sections of College Park were upper middle-class neighborhoods. A number of Delta's officers and management personnel lived in those sections of College Park. Many of the rank-and-file personnel lived in one of these three cities, as all three had affordable housing, and there were also many apartment complexes, especially in College Park. Many of the College Park apartment complexes were built on land now occupied by I-85 and the airport's third runway.

When I began my Delta career, Atlanta was served by four airlines: Delta, Eastern, Capital, and Southern Airways. Delta operated a very mixed fleet of aircraft, which included DC-3s, CV340/440s, DC-6s, and DC-7s. Lockheed Constellations and Martin 404s made up a large part of the Eastern fleet. Southern Airways was flying only DC-3s in 1956. Capital had very limited service into Atlanta, and most of the service was flown with Vickers Viscount aircraft.

Eastern was the largest of the four airlines then, but about the time I was hired, Delta was closing that gap, as the Civil Aeronautics Board had recently awarded Delta some critical new routes from Atlanta to the Northeast.

About the time I started to work at Delta, they were beginning to drop the Delta-C&S logo that had been in place on Delta's fleet and other places since Delta and C&S had merged in 1953. This logo was replaced with the pre-merger Delta logo.

In early 1956, Delta began participating in a unique scheduling agreement with American and National Airlines called an interchange agreement. This was a strategy to provide single plane service beyond the markets an airline had the authority to serve. An example of this strategy involved using a Delta aircraft to fly from Atlanta to Los Angeles via Dallas. In this example, a Delta crew flew the flight from Atlanta to Dallas as a Delta flight, and the aircraft was flown from Dallas to Los Angeles by an American crew as an American Airlines flight. A passenger flying from Atlanta to Los Angeles just considered it a one-stop flight to Los Angeles. Very few airlines entered into this type of arrangement.

APPENDIX SIX

Evolution of the Airline Industry

- The introduction of the jet aircraft was the first phase of the modern commercial airline industry evolution, which began in December of 1958 when Pan American Airways took delivery of its first Boeing 707. In late 1959, Delta and United Airlines took delivery of their first DC-8s. Delta took delivery of its first CV-880 in 1960.

- The second major step occurred in the early 1960s when the Civil Aeronautics Board granted a significant amount of new route authority to Delta, Eastern, and National airlines, which greatly expanded their route networks and included new markets west of the Mississippi.

- The third big event in this evolution also occurred in the early 1960s, when IBM introduced the first fully computerized reservations system. This phase of the evolution ranks right up there with the introduction of the commercial jet aircraft. The technology used to operate the computerized reservations systems resulted in the industry focusing on the development of technology in a number of other areas, with one of the most significant being new technology that allowed the airlines to improve the efficiency and dependability of aircraft maintenance and repair processes.

- The next event in this evolution occurred in 1978, when Congress deregulated the US airline industry. Deregulation dramatically changed the airline industry and significantly increased competition in many markets.

- The next element of the evolution occurred in the early eighties, when the major airlines introduced a computer reservations system, or CRS, which allowed travel agents to book airline, hotel, and other products directly with the supplier. This was a significant development for all parties in the travel chain, including travel agency customers. This development greatly altered the relationship between the travel agencies and their suppliers and gave the supplier, especially the airline, new tools to track travel agency bookings and leverage their relationship with a specific agency. It also increased the power of the agencies, allowing them to gain significantly more control over the corporate or business travel accounts. In the early stages of these systems and for many years to come, the airlines owned these systems, but over time they decided to monetize these assets and sold them to third parties. If you want to see a frown come onto the face of an airline marketing or distribution executive, just mention the term Global Distribution System (GDS).

- The creation of the Frequent Flyer programs in the early 1980s provided the airlines the tools needed to track travel volume of their frequent business travelers. Trans Texas was the first airline to launch a mileage-based Frequent Flyer program. American followed Trans Texas and was quickly followed by the other major airlines, including Delta.

- Airline alliances, which included codesharing, were the next major step in this evolution, with the first significant alliance occurring when KLM Airlines and Northwest created their alliance. This was quickly followed by the Delta/Swiss Air/Singapore Airlines alliance, which was branded as the Global Excellence alliance. Today, strong alliances are a significant element of the global airlines' strategies.

- One of the saddest elements of this evolution occurred in the early 1990s with the disappearance of Eastern Air Lines and Pan American Airways when Delta acquired PAA's European routes, with United Airlines acquiring the Latin American operation a few months later.

- The next phase of evolution occurred in 1994, when the airline industry, led by Delta, capped domestic travel agency commissions at twenty-five dollars. This action was part of a major cost cutting being implemented by most airlines as a result of the recession in the early 1990s. Wall Street analysts calculated that in the 1991-93 time frame, the airline industry lost more money than it had made during its entire existence.

- The next phase occurred in 1996-1997, when all major airlines used the evolving reservations booking technology and social media to launch their websites, which made it possible for a customer to book directly with the airline and bypass travel agents in an effort to reduce their cost.

- Mergers by some of the major carriers were the most recent phase of this evolution. It is possible that the mergers of four major carriers that took place in 2013 and 2014 may represent the last step in this phase of the industry's evolution.

APPENDIX SEVEN

Delta's Information Technology

To understand the changing role of Information Technology at Delta, it's important to consider where the airline industry was at this stage of its evolution. With the introduction of the jet aircraft, technology began to emerge as a major issue for the airline industry in the late 1950s and early 1960s. The introduction of the jet aircraft created a significant increase in the volume of bookings and other passenger-related activities. This increased volume of activity necessitated the development and implementation of a high-speed computerized reservations system that could manage inventory and passenger name records.

A few carriers, including TWA and Eastern, initially acquired a simple technology-driven inventory system that tracked the number of seats available and the seats sold on any flight. This was an inventory system only and didn't create any type of computerized passenger name record.

In 1957, American and IBM signed a comprehensive development agreement to develop a state-of-the-art reservations system for American Airlines. The other airlines, including Delta, elected to forego this interim phase of development. After several years of development, American's first experimental system went online in 1960, and the system began handling all booking functions in 1964. The development cost for this initial phase of Sabre was an astonishing $40 million—about $350 million in the year 2000.

Based on information obtained from a variety of sources, I've learned that Delta did not have an official technology organization in place when IBM and American began their initial development of Sabre. As IBM and Sabre made progress with their development strategy, Delta realized that they must develop or acquire an automated reservations system similar to Sabre. Delta's senior management recognized that the development and implementation of this new system would be expensive and would require some special skills not possessed by many existing Delta employees.

Bob Parsons, whom I believe was working in Engineering at the time, was identified as a person with the skills to manage this project. Bob was a highly respected individual who possessed many great qualities. Unfortunately, Eastern Air Lines lured Bob away from Delta sometime in the mid to early stages of this project. Those close to the situation at the time have indicated that Bob's frustrations with management's less-than-enthusiastic commitment to technology contributed to his decision to accept the Eastern offer. In any event, Bob's departure negatively impacted the development of technology at Delta throughout the 1960s and early 1970s. Senior management did cobble together a group that completed the creation and implementation of Deltamatic, Delta's automated reservations system. Delta phased in Deltamatic, with the final use of the old manual system and the switch to Deltamatic occurring in Dallas in September 1964.

Since it was obvious that technology projects were going to be an expensive undertaking, a decision was made to have Technology report to Finance. The responsibility for Technology remained in the finance division until the late 1980s or early 1990s.

To understand why technology was assigned to the finance division, you would have to understand the frugal financial environment Mr. Woolman had created. I have heard stories about Delta employees not being able to get a new pencil until they turned in the stub of the old one. Mr. Woolman trained his successors and

Delta's finance leaders to continue that same "thrifty" approach toward investing. I don't have any data that I could use for comparison, but it would be interesting to compare Delta's technology spend as a percentage of revenue with that of the other major airlines in the 1960s, '70s, and '80s.

Another factor that I believe made Delta management reluctant to spend money on technology was that Delta was one of the most profitable airlines—if not the most profitable—leading up to deregulation, and senior management apparently didn't see how technology would improve Delta's profitability. With deregulation on the horizon, that was very short-term thinking.

While the finance department held the purse strings, they can't be entirely blamed for Delta's lack of technology spend, as each of the division heads, including Marketing, should have understood their technology needs and made a case to show the financial payback for any technology that was developed to support their area of responsibility. Unfortunately, senior management's narrow view of technology was present in almost every facet of Delta's operation in the fifties, sixties, and seventies. If it didn't involve flying and maintaining aircraft or taking care of the Delta people, they simply didn't spend any money.

Leadership

After Bob Parsons left, Lamar Durrett was the only person to hold the top technology position who really possessed the right set of skills and attitude to maximize the benefits of technology for Delta. Lamar left Delta after about a year in the technology position to accept a job at Continental. My view of Lamar's contribution is generally shared by most of Delta's management team who were impacted by technology—or lack of technology.

From the time the IT group was formed until about 1995, the IT department exercised virtual control over the projects they worked on and the funding of all technology projects. This "total control" environment caused a few of us to (secretly) set up our own "mini" IT shops within our business units. When I ran the Planning Department, if I had an opportunity to expand my staff or replace someone in Pricing, Scheduling, or Route Development, I hired only those individuals who were capable of writing computer programs or who had Operations Research backgrounds. In less than two years, I built an effective IT group within my area of responsibility, as that was the only way I could get the technology to do the job the way it had to be done.

In every area of marketing that required technology support, Delta was far behind all of our competitors. Some examples:

- Delta's failure to automate any of our scheduling and pricing decision-making tools in preparation for deregulation was an expensive mistake.
- I have already shared in my book a lot of information about our deficiency related to the computer reservations system (CRS) product, but this is another example of how far behind the industry we were in another critical area.
- The Frequent Flyer program is another good example of where we were far behind many of our competitors.

A Bad Situation Gets Worse

In mid-1994, John King, the Delta CIO, and Rex McClelland, the senior vice president of administrative services, presented the Delta Executive Council with a concept and recommendation that Delta partner with a leading technology company to create a joint venture that would manage all of Delta's IT activities. Delta and the technology partner would each own 50 percent of the new joint venture. Rex and John's justification for creating the joint venture involved partnering with a major technology firm that would assist Delta in addressing many of our technology short-comings, sell existing Delta software to third parties, and become a major provider of technology products to others in the travel industry in competition with Sabre. From a financial perspective, the business case was compelling, with a significant portion of the financial benefit flowing from the resale of existing software and the joint venture's ability to do third-party work in the travel industry.

Why Create a Joint Venture?
(Presented by Rex McClelland and John King)

The shortcomings Rex and John described related to the state of Delta's technology platform in mid-1994 validate all the issues I have written about related to Delta's failure to develop broad IT strategy as early as the late 1970s. I want to commend Rex and John for having the courage to acknowledge the deficiencies in Delta's IT strategy, which are listed below. If the people who were responsible for Delta's IT strategy ten-plus years earlier had come forth with this analysis of Delta's IT shortcomings, we might not have even been having this discussion concerning the need to create a joint venture.

- Both Rex and John acknowledged that the existing Delta IT organization could not deliver the technology the company needed in a cost-effective and timely manner.
- They also acknowledged that this poor track record of delivery was influenced by the limited skills possessed by many of the people working in Delta IT, who had previ-

ously worked in reservations, on the ramp, or at the ticket counter. The IT workforce included very few professional programmers or other technology experts who had been hired "off the street."

- The absence of an active training program to improve the skills of the incumbent staff simply added to the problem.

- In addition, Delta didn't have the time or financial luxury to make the necessary investments in technology or people to improve the situation.

- Delta's reputation as a poor workplace for IT experts made it difficult to recruit good people.

Selecting the Joint Venture Partner

A team was appointed to embark on a thorough due-diligence process to select a joint venture partner. We focused on four potential partners, including AT&T-Global Inbound Service (the NCR Division,) EDS, CSC, and the ISSC division of IBM.

AT&T-GIS was chosen based on several key Delta-oriented attributes. In addition to their willingness to make a significant financial investment, they agreed to supplement the existing Delta IT staff with state-of-the-art technologies, to provide training to the incumbent Delta staff, and to offer attractive pricing on PCs, servers, and other technology produced through their NCR (GIS) business unit. In addition, the AT&T-GIS group had an established travel and transportation practice that originated at NCR.

The AT&T-GIS group also appeared to be committed to building a company that could compete with Sabre and other prominent vendors in the travel and transportation services market.

Shortly before the joint venture was formed, it was branded "TransQuest," and that was how we referred to it going forward.

Changing Landscape

Unfortunately, even before the contract details were finalized, many aspects of the relationship with AT&T started to unravel. The AT&T senior executive who had made the commitments to Delta resigned his position at AT&T and accepted a senior position with Microsoft. AT&T broke up into four or five smaller business units, with the GIS group spun off to become part of NCR. Consequently, our deal became an NCR deal and not an AT&T deal.

NCR quickly announced they were returning to their core business and would discontinue selling technology equipment, including PCs and servers. They also announced they would shut down their travel practice, which really negatively impacted the deal.

Even in the face of these setbacks, Delta's senior management decided in early January 1995 to go forward with the launching of the joint venture with NCR based on strong recommendations from John King and Rex McClelland. Jimmy McCullough was responsible for managing the relationship between Delta and Trans-Quest.

By July 1995, it had become obvious that creating the joint venture was a mistake. The process of dismantling the joint venture began in the fall of 1995 and was completed in the spring of 1996. When the dismantling process began, my responsibilities were expanded to include the management of Delta IT and the subsequent dismantling of the joint venture. John King elected to retire, and while Rex McClelland elected to remain for a while, he retired later in 1995.

After we dismantled the joint venture, it quickly became apparent that TransQuest was not meeting our IT requirements and couldn't compete with Sabre as a software solutions provider for the travel industry. They had also failed in their efforts to resell the software that had been developed for Delta. In the face of this reality, I was given the task of shutting down TransQuest and bringing IT back to Delta. I completed this task in the summer of 1996. Part of that task included the termination of Bill Belew, the CEO, and several other executives who had been hired to manage TransQuest.

In the early stages of the joint venture planning process, it was envisioned that Delta's reservations platform, Deltamatic, would be folded into the PARS reservations platform being operated by Worldspan for TWA and Northwest Airlines. This decision was reversed after Delta's management learned that PARS lacked a lot of functionality available in Deltamatic, and the cost to add this functionality would be approximately $90 million. However, a decision was made to outsource the operations, applications development, and maintenance of Deltamatic to Worldspan in order to eliminate these positions at Delta and gain some economies of scale. This outsource arrangement was executed in early 1995.

Delta IT after TransQuest

All of the issues surrounding the formation and breakup of the joint venture with AT&T/NCR resulted in the Delta IT users receiving the lowest level of IT support that they had experienced in the recent past. The breakup of TransQuest began in September 1995 and was completed in June 1996.

The technology challenges at Delta didn't really begin to improve until the Y2K issue provided a platform to take a fresh look at Delta's IT. As part of this IT assessment, Ron Allen and I met with Charles Field, at the recommendation of Jerry Grinstein, to review our position on Y2K and IT in general. Following that meeting with Charlie, I requested and received permission from Ron to reach out to Charlie and ask if he would come on board as an IT consultant. We wanted him to give us some recommendations on how we could improve the Delta IT situation and make sure we were in compliance with Y2K requirements. He agreed, and after two or three months on the job, he met with Ron and me and advised us that only 25 percent of our IT expenditures were being used to develop new and current software. He said 75 percent of our IT funds were being used to support programs that were either outdated or that no one was using. He also gave us recommendations on how to correct the situation plus a recommended budget to address the issues. I don't recall the exact number, but it was huge, like a couple of hundred million dollars.

Charlie later became Delta's CIO and brought in some excellent talent and implemented many new programs that really improved the Delta IT situation. Some of the programs developed under Charlie's guidance are still being used today.

With the exception of the expectation of generating revenue by reselling software developed specifically for Delta, I think that the plan that Rex and John presented to the executive council would have really benefited Delta in many ways, as we were desperately in need of many of the benefits the joint venture would have produced. We just chose the wrong partner.

APPENDIX EIGHT

Delta's Alliances and Codeshares

The first phase of our alliance strategy began in 1989, when Delta's international network expansion combined with Delta's great customer service reputation caught the attention of Swiss Air, which requested a meeting with Delta. We agreed to a meeting, which was led by Whit Hawkins and me from the Delta side and Paul Maximilian Müller for the Swiss Air team. After some in-depth discussions related to Swiss Air's vision for an alliance, I realized that a codeshare with Swiss Air would allow Delta to significantly expand our international presence. After several meetings, we struck a deal that resulted in the two airlines flying codeshare flights between Zurich and JFK and Zurich and Atlanta. We also agreed to have flight attendants from both airlines on the codeshare flights, which I believe was an industry first. As I expected, the Swiss Air alliance increased my responsibilities.

I realize that many non-airline individuals might not understand what "codeshare" means. Quite simply, when two airlines agree to a codeshare alliance, either airline can put their "booking code" on the other airline's flights. For example, Swiss Air could show Delta's Atlanta-to-Zurich flight in their schedules as a Swiss Air flight. This allows a Swiss Air customer to book the flight as a Swiss Air flight, even though the flight will be operated by Delta. In most codeshare agreements, the operating airline receives all of the revenue. This same example would apply to all of the airlines in a multi-airline alliance.

In 1990, Singapore Airlines initiated alliance discussions with

Swiss Air, and when Singapore became aware that Swiss Air had recently created an alliance with Delta, they began discussions with Delta and Swiss Air about a thee-airline codeshare involving Delta, Swiss Air, and Singapore. Delta and Swiss Air agreed to the three-airline alliance, and we named it "Global Excellence," as the name really communicated the value of the alliance.

Once again, Whit Hawkins and I were leading the Delta team, which resulted in several trips to Singapore. Whit and I took advantage of a couple of weekends in Singapore to see the World War II Museum, which was very interesting. We also visited the famous Raffles Hotel, where we enjoyed Singapore Slings.

After some negotiations, the three airlines agreed on the terms for this codeshare alliance, and the three airlines began to very aggressively market Global Excellence. The Global Excellence alliance received a great deal of favorable coverage in the travel industry trade press.

While we were satisfied with many aspects of the alliance, in order to achieve their revenue requirements, Singapore's field sales management had begun to abuse the interline pricing we had all agreed to. This action was costly to both Delta and Swiss Air, resulting in our canceling the alliance agreement in November 1997 since Singapore senior management wouldn't take any action to address this violation of our agreement.

While we were participating in Atlantic Excellence, we had begun discussions with Virgin Atlantic to create a codeshare between New York and London, which would give Delta more access to the London market through Heathrow. Ron Allen, Ivan Dezelic, and I were leading these negotiations, which were basically conducted directly with Virgin CEO Richard Branson. We actually held a couple of these negotiations in Branson's home, followed by a good dinner at a nearby restaurant. The day we finalized the negotiations, Richard hosted a dinner for many of the personnel on both sides who had been involved in the negotiations. Richard hosted the dinner at a pretty fancy London restaurant. Unfortunately, the alliance hit a few bumps in the road in early 1997 and was canceled.

Delta partnered with Swiss Air in 1995 to create another alliance that included Austrian Airlines, Maley, and in March of 1995, Sabena was added to the alliance, and Finnair was added a few months later. In early 1997, the alliance was branded "Atlantic Excellence." The Atlantic Excellence airlines were able to obtain antitrust immunity, which added a lot of value to the alliance. With the formation of Atlantic Excellence, Delta worked out an arrangement with the New York-New Jersey Port Authority to allow all of our Atlantic Excellence partners to operate out of Delta's JFK terminal. When your flight taxied into the Delta ramp area during the afternoon peak, it looked like the United Nations with all the international livery parked at the Delta gates.

As in the past, Whit Hawkins and I were leading the effort for Delta, and due to the growth of Delta's alliance program, we created a special group to manage the alliances on a day-to-day basis. This group reported directly to me. Ivan Dezelic headed up this group and was assisted by Susie Snider. A few months after this group was formed, Ivan took on some new responsibilities, and Susie Snider was promoted to director of alliances.

The new Atlantic Excellence alliance worked extremely well, and I made several trips to Switzerland to meet with the senior management team. Ron Allen and Marty Braham also attended some of the meetings when the senior management-level people were involved. These meetings could best be described as "strategic retreats." After Atlantic Excellence was created in 1995, Swiss Air began making some bad investments in other airlines. Unfortunately, in 1996-97, Swissair began to encounter some financial issues, which resulted in Swiss Air shutting down in 2002.

When Swiss Air began to struggle financially, Delta began having alliance discussions with Air France. An alliance agreement with Air France was signed in late 1997. The alliance with Air France has been a good strategy for Delta, as Air France subsequently acquired KLM, which gave Delta access to KLM's Amsterdam hub. The alliance with Air France and KLM resulted in the creation of Sky Team.

While an alliance with Air France was being finalized, Delta was in the early stages of negotiations with several Asian and Latin-based airlines concerning the possibility of creating alliances. As in all of the other alliance negotiations, I was the point person for most if not all of these negotiations.

I had personally been very involved in discussions with Aeromexico concerning an alliance and had made several trips to Mexico City to meet with the CEO and other senior executives. We reached an alliance agreement, and part of that agreement required Delta to invest in Aeromexico. This agreement gave Delta a lot of access to the Mexico market and a significant amount of feed through our Atlanta hub.

As part of Delta's strategy to expand our Asian presence, we began codeshare discussions with China Southern in 1997-98. I made several trips to China to meet with China Southern in an effort to secure the codeshare agreement.

About the same time we were developing the relationship with China Southern, we also began having codeshare discussions with Korean Airlines and All Nippon. Making the deals happen required several trips to Seoul and Tokyo. Ron Allen and later Leo Mullin accompanied me on a couple of these trips. With the exception of Korean Airlines, the alliances with the Asian carriers began to unwind just prior to my retirement in May of 1998.

From a personal perspective, on a couple of occasions I took advantage of the Asian trips to stop off in Hong Kong and buy some tailor-made suits and shirts. I would schedule my trip to Seoul or China so that I had a stopover in Hong Kong on the way to my final destination and get measured for my suits and shirts, then schedule my return through Hong Kong to pick up the clothing. I also took advantage of these Hong Kong stopovers to meet with the Cathay Pacific CEO and other Cathay Pacific executives to develop a closer relationship with Cathay and hopefully develop some additional connecting traffic at our Los Angeles hub.

The "partner airline" event that I referred to in my book came about as a result of Delta's acquisition of PAA's European routes, which included routes to Moscow from JFK and Berlin. Doing business in Russia back in the Cold War era was a challenging experience. In order to have the best possible experience, PAA had formed a partnership with Aeroflot, which was then called SPATE, and after Delta assumed the PAA routes, we changed the name to DATE. Initially the objective was related to operations, but later Delta's priority became the establishment of a joint Western-style first-class lounge at the Moscow airport. After the PAA European acquisition, I became involved in the DATE relationship and made a couple of trips to Moscow to meet with the Aeroflot representative in the joint venture.

Since my retirement, Delta's alliance strategy has continued to be a major element of their international growth strategy, including making investments in alliance partners such as Virgin America and Aeromexico.

APPENDIX NINE

Major Accomplishments

The following is a list of some of my key accomplishments during my Delta career:

- Securing a job with Delta was my greatest accomplishment and the foundation for all of my other accomplishments there.
- Securing a position as a Delta sales representative was another key foundation builder.
- Successfully restructuring and rebuilding the New York sales team was a significant accomplishment, as the sales organization/team I built in New York was the envy of my Delta peers and most of our New York competitors.
- My team successfully implemented Delta's first nonstop service from New York to Houston and our first service at LaGuardia. In both instances, we took market share from Eastern.
- The Delta-Northeast merger presented many challenges and opportunities to the New York sales team, as prior to the Northeast merger, we did not fly nonstop service from New York to any Florida market, the Bahamas, New England, or Montreal. Northeast's weak position in the New York market made our efforts to secure a larger share of the market more challenging, but we were very creative in our marketing and sales strategies and succeeded in increasing our market share. I address the highlights in my book, but in the end, we accomplished great success with

limited resources.

- When I was promoted to system manager of planning in the fall of 1979, the airline industry was in the initial phases of deregulation. I inherited an organization that was totally unprepared for the challenges we would face as a result of deregulation. In approximately twelve to eighteen months, we built a very effective Planning organization, including building a great technology platform that allowed Planning to significantly improve our decision-making process where pricing and scheduling were concerned. I address this issue in more detail in my book.

Other accomplishments:

- Led the team that successfully guided Delta through the PATCO strike and took advantage of every opportunity to capture more slots in key airports.
- With the assistance of Bob Cross, implemented Delta's initial revenue management system.
- Played a key role in negotiating the Delta-Swiss Air code-share alliance, which later became the foundation for much larger alliances.
- Was the primary advocate for growing Delta's international network.
- Led the team that successfully negotiated an agreement to name Delta the official airline of Walt Disney World and later Disneyland.
- Played a key role in improving and enhancing Delta's Frequent Flyer program.
- Worked closely with the team that enhanced Delta's computer reservations system (CRS) product and improved our competitive position. I also played a major role in the cre-

ation of Worldspan.

- Led the team that negotiated the Delta-American Express Sky Miles credit card agreement, which is reported to be worth billions of dollars to Delta.
- Played a key role in acquiring Pan American's European routes and the New York shuttle.
- Achieved most of the cost-reductions initiatives Marketing had committed to delivering in connection with the Leadership 7.5 cost-reductions strategy. The single most important achievement was capping travel agency commissions at twenty-five dollars. This initiative produced savings in the tens of millions of dollars.
- Participated in almost every aspect of Delta's involvement/ sponsorship of the 1996 Olympic Games, including flying the lit torches from Athens to Los Angeles. I carried the Olympic Torch almost two miles as part of the program to run the torch from Los Angeles to Atlanta.

Made in the USA
Columbia, SC
22 December 2018